D0945241

SELF-DISCOVERY
THROUGH
SELF-EXPRESSION

Foreword by

Bernard I. Levy, Ph.D.

Professor of Psychology
The George Washington University
Washington, D.C.

SELF-DISCOVERY THROUGH SELF-EXPRESSION

Use of Art in Psychotherapy
With Children and Adolescents

By

MALA BETENSKY, M.S.Sc., Ph.D.

Psychologist in Private Practice

CHARLES C THOMAS · PUBLISHER
Springfield · Illinois · U.S.A.

Published and Distributed Throughout the World by
CHARLES C THOMAS • PUBLISHER
Bannerstone House
301-327 East Lawrence Avenue, Springfield, Illinois, U.S.A.

© *1973, by* CHARLES C THOMAS • PUBLISHER
ISBN 0-398-02574-6
Library of Congress Catalog Card Number: 72-81685

With THOMAS BOOKS *careful attention is given to all details of*
manufacturing and design. It is the Publisher's desire to present books
that are satisfactory as to their physical qualities and artistic possibilities
and appropriate for their particular use. THOMAS BOOKS *will be true*
to those laws of quality that assure a good name and good will.

213301

Printed in the United States of America
I-1

To
Aya

Foreword

In this book about the use of art in psychotherapy with children and adolescents you will find a way of helping which, although old in concept, is not yet popular in clinical practice. But as contemporary group-training practitioners experiment with every verbal and nonverbal means of communication, psychotherapeutic procedures are also moving toward experiments with expression. Enthusiasm is warranted. In the alternation between verbal and nonverbal methods of helping people, the patient will profit by having a broader palette available for communicating his experiences and his memories of them. Patients will talk to us in movements, graphics, solid forms, and patterned sounds as well as in words, and we will listen with greater sensitivity.

Creating art can also bring pleasure, a sense of fulfillment, and feelings of accomplishment. The increase in the number of amateur painters, potters, and sculptors provides evidence for this. It does not stretch our imagination to note that the creative process might also be useful in the amelioration of psychological distress, perhaps by the same mechanism which grants a sense of well-being to the Sunday painter.

Notions like the foregoing are at the base of the rapid development of a set of expressive therapies during this generation. Dance, music, dramatics, and poetry are all being used as therapy.

Alongside this development from the artistic side, there are also psychotherapists who have made a more incidental use of the arts. Analysts, Freudian and Jungian in particular, have noted the interplay of painting and treatment, have gauged therapeutic progress and relied upon the analysand's graphic symbols to clarify personality structure and to plot aspects of the unconscious.

Although art therapy has recently received considerably more attention and a spurt in development, its practitioners, with few exceptions, do not publish their ideas and descriptions of technique too readily. Nor would one expect many publications from active therapists building knowledge at the frontiers of clinical practice. However, Dr. Betensky is a generous colleague to have taken time to share with us her therapeutic style and some of the underpinnings of her approach. Colleagues are always willing to share their knowledge and experience, but few of them are able to organize their thoughts for the difficult job of presenting them in print. As you read this book, you will note the clinician, artist, and psychologist behind the therapeutic decisions being made from page to page.

The graphic arts figure most prominently in the cases Dr. Betensky has presented. She uses drawing and painting (occasionally clay modeling) to facilitate communication with very young children and to help the blocked adolescent move forward. She also uses their art to help her patients recognize recurring themes in their lives and, thus, to bring into focus the problems with which they are struggling. Indeed, Dr. Betensky makes clear her emphasis on the use of art as communication rather than on the creative use of art, by identifying her work as art psychotherapy.

A case study can be a ponderous and overly detailed bore. Dr. Betensky has not fallen into that trap. Her cases are succinct, yet rich with human detail and complete enough to give one a sense of firm knowledge about an individual and about the manner of treatment. Indeed, she makes her patients and herself as a therapist come alive. Her selection of illustrations is noteworthy and they carry the case forward. The cases are a much-needed contribution to the literature about the practice of art therapy.

A small group of essays which closes the book elaborates upon the author's viewpoints by also elaborating upon the material in the preceding cases. She looks at some of the basic problems in psychotherapeutic practice with the young and gives us her attempts to resolve them. They reveal Dr. Betensky's eclecticism and her deep knowledge of the classic works in social science and aesthetics.

BERNARD I. LEVY

Preface

CHILDREN AND ADOLESCENTS with emotional disturbances can sometimes gain a handle on their problems by expressing their feelings through art media and then attending to the results of such expression under the guidance of a therapist.

The young people whose cases are recounted and studied in this book were seen individually in a private setting, twice a week at the beginning of therapy, and once a week as soon as a reduction in the frequency of sessions became possible. The parents of each patient were also seen, together for initial conferences, and separately in alternating visits. Some of the parents were also in group art therapy.

The approach and system of psychotherapy presented in this book, with emphasis on spontaneous art expression, grew slowly in my thinking and probing over fifteen years of learning and experience. I benefited richly from many schools of thought in psychology and psychotherapy, from findings of sociology and anthropology, from a consideration of art and its relevance to psychology and life, and also from trying my own hand at art.

My approach is humanistic in finding a role for opposites in the human psyche, establishing a basis for an individual's acceptance of the dark corners of his past, reaffirming life as livable and suffering, sufferable when it is genuine and a part of life; and still believing that the individual is a unique, responsible-for-his-actions *Socius faber* who needs values and meanings, and who cannot only adjust, respond, and react to environment, but who can also make some changes in it.

The more I worked with young people who confront an impasse, the less I leaned on the medical model of mental illness. I found that all too often the patient tried to fit into his label or live up to its requirements. The problem was not so much finding a name or category for the illness, but rather developing a road to awareness. In the present-day world, the individual, whether he possesses equilibrium or is upset, more than ever before must live in keen self-awareness.

Art expression, put to systematic use in psychotherapy, was instrumental in the development of awareness in the patients who are discussed in the present work. The use of art media afforded these patients authentic experiential sources of awareness and thereby enabled them to find understandable and viable patterns and meanings in their lives.

I, too, found in their communicated art expression new and more direct ways of experiential and intimate understanding of the young expressionists. Together with clinical findings and other psychotherapeutic measures, the art expression was carefully built into a system of therapy.

Part One of the present work consists of ten studies in art psychotherapy with children and adolescents, including photographs of many of their original productions.

This is an assortment of cases in the course of which I observed a growing use of art expression. The order of the cases bears little significance other than an attempt at an even distribution of boys and girls. Titles given by children to their productions became the legends for the photographs inserted in the text. For untitled productions, suitable descriptions were found in the subsequent informal communications of the children who made them.

Part Two comprises seven papers discussing elements or factors at work in the process of art therapy.

M. B.

Introduction

Sᴇʟꜰ-ᴇxᴘʀᴇssɪᴏɴ through art media is the focal point around which the psychotherapeutic process revolves throughout the case studies in Part One.

I combined the art therapy technique with clinical findings, psychological insights, and social considerations to help the individual in therapy discover his authentic self. One of the characteristics of a disturbed person is that he is not always conscious of his own behavior. When an individual expresses himself through art, he sometimes manages to restore his stream of awareness. This is an act of self-discovery.

To make such acts possible, patients were first given art materials and encouraged to use them spontaneously. When they were finished, they were asked to look at their productions. They were then helped to detect personal patterns of behavior and to communicate their findings verbally to the therapist.

The technique of grouping was used to elicit this sequence of expression, discovery, and communication. The patient put together two or more of his art works which seemed to be somehow connected. Self-discovery occurred in the process of comparing them. I often initiated the idea of grouping, and patients quickly picked it up and adopted it as their own routine.

This therapy was present oriented. As soon as the patient came in for his visit, he busied himself with the art materials. Past history was used only where it pertained to the present. Thus, no exhaustive case histories were compiled. Rather, bits of forgotten material had a way of emerging vividly at certain moments in the ongoing therapy. This occurred most often in the very act of self-expression.

The therapy was also change oriented. Therapeutic change for children and adolescents is naturally embedded in developmental change from childhood to adulthood. Since environmental situations are crucial for therapeutic and developmental changes in children and adolescents, most of the parents were also in therapy. And, in order to activate and relate the three facets of change — therapeutic, developmental, and environmental — the young patients and their parents were seen by the same therapist.

In Part Two the reader is introduced to ideas which form the intellectual background for this psychotherapeutic method. These ideas affirm the ties between philosophy and science. In an age of increasing technicianship and technology in mental health, philosophy can preserve the humanity of the human beings whom the technology is to serve.

M. B.

Acknowledgments

IT IS A PLEASURE to express my gratitude to those persons whose generous gift of time and effort, knowledge and professional judgment, enriched this book.

To Elinor Ulman, Editor of the *American Journal of Art Therapy* and Associate Professorial Lecturer in Art Therapy at The George Washington University, for her expert and sensitive editing of the case studies.

To Dr. William Gerber, Lecturer in Philosophy at the University of Maryland, for valuable editorial suggestions which I adopted for Part Two.

To Dr. Bernard Levy, Professor of Psychology at The George Washington University, for his evaluation of the manuscript and for writing the Foreword.

To Dr. Helen Peixotto, Professor of Clinical Psychology at The Catholic University of America, for her careful reading of the manuscript and for pinpointing those areas which needed clarification.

To Dr. Julian Jurand, Psychiatrist and Clinical Director at St. Elizabeths Hospital, for reading a sampling of the case studies and for his professional judgment.

To Dr. Morris J. Chalick, Associate Professorial Lecturer in Psychiatry at The George Washington University Medical School, for helpful comments and suggestions.

To Dr. Robert Kraut, Assistant Professor, Department of Sociology, University of Pennsylvania, for contributing to my better understanding of perspectives in the social psychology of deviance; and for photographing most of the art productions.

To Mrs. Thelma Baker, M. Ed., for devotedly and expertly preparing the manuscript throughout all its stages.

M. B.

CONTENTS

SELF-DISCOVERY
THROUGH
SELF-EXPRESSION

PART ONE
A SHEAF OF CASES

I
Sally

ART THERAPY WAS PERHAPS the only psychotherapeutic technique acceptable to twelve-year-old, fear-stricken, enraged, and extremely resistant Sally.

When she was almost carried into my office, she was in a state of fierce emotional turmoil, breathing heavily from the effort she had made minutes before to fight off her father's firm grip. She declared at once that while her parents could make her come, they could not make her talk; and she was quite surprised to hear me agree with her. When given the choices of staying for the hour and talking things over or of leaving immediately, she chose to stay on the condition that I would not put her back into school, which she had stopped attending.

Thus, she introduced her immediate problem of school phobia, which she and her parents viewed as the only problem at hand. It was typical of her dealings with people that she had attached a condition to bind me.

As soon as I speculated aloud that there must have been reasons which made her unable to attend school and that both she and I might not even know the real reasons, her agitation subsided considerably. But her regained calm only helped her to settle down to being a prim, controlled, neat-looking, well-groomed little lady.

Her hair had been carefully set, not a hair was out of place. The new camel's hair slacks fitted tightly her small, prim figure, and despite the hassle, they remained perfectly pressed. As she reiterated, "But I won't talk," she reminded me of her mother who had occupied the same chair the day before.

Mother was also prim and perfectly groomed and wore tight-fitting slacks, same color, same style. She insisted that Sally had always been stubborn and that she was being stubborn this time, only a little more so. She expected the psychologist to break the spell of stubbornness and put the child back in school, and inquired how soon that would be done.

A young, aggressive woman who had barely made it through high school, her aim now was to make it in the social world of suburbia. As soon as her husband, a former science student, took over his late father's firm, she began to take definite steps toward the realization of her aim. At the time of her first therapeutic contact, she was in the process of successfully replacing her old set of friends with a new one of higher status.

Sally's father was plainly annoyed with the demands made on his time in behalf of Sally. He played down the child's disturbance and considered it a minor outburst, a result of his wife's lack of firmness with the children and her preoccupation with her social ambitions.

Among the significant adults in Sally's life were also her two grandmothers, who were in a state of open warfare. One protected her only son from his demanding wife; the other supported her daughter and supplied her with ever-new objectives for new demands, the latest being the building of a house. The four significant adults in Sally's life acted as a closely knit group, but were separated by many lines of conflict and hostility. Both parents were seen separately. They regarded their visits as part of Sally's treatment and frequently asked when they could terminate.

Sally's strong resistance and controlled unhappiness made it necessary to postpone psychological testing and offer her some art media as a means of immediate release and expression of feelings.

Paint seemed threatening to her as she shook her head at the jars and walked away to another table. Clay she pronounced messy. The chalks she ignored, and she rejected crayons on the ground that she had them at home. This was her way of letting me know that there was nothing I could do for her. At last she noticed, with some relief, the Lowenfeld Mosaic Box with its variety of flat plastic triangles, diamonds, and squares in shiny colors.

Here was a colorful material in definite shapes, not messy, and not threatening. Sally spent the whole of six hour-long appointments in three weeks making designs on the mosaic tray. She kept her silence, except for the frequent, hostile "Hmmm," or "I don't want to," and "See, I told you that you were not helping me."

Despite her seeming sophistication and poise, which she carefully maintained by means of a ladylike manner and precise speech, Sally produced feeble, often unfinished, piecemeal objects on the mosaic tray, mostly unfinished stars and arrows. She used colors indiscriminately, but carefully searched for and chose black pieces. Once she started on the pieces in one storage section of the box, she had to finish that whole section. In the first three hours, she made many fractions of the arrows and sections of the stars on one sheet of paper, but the small productions remained incomplete and separated from each other never forming a whole.

In the second half of the mosaic period, her constructions became a little richer in representational content and in structure. She began to use a variety of shapes while working on one design; she also began to choose more colors; and she even began to put together parts into more meaningful wholes. The first of such productions was "A Garden" with four trees and some grass. The next was "A Sky and Houses Below." None of these was preserved, however, because Sally angrily pulled the paper lining from under each design as soon as she finished and sometimes even before, despite a request to leave her designs on the tray.

The most interesting picture of this series was also the first one left untouched. Sally titled it "Fairy Godfather Looking for Shelter Under a Tree During the Rain" (Fig. I-1). On the right is a black tree trunk, standing like a large foot and topped by a star in green and yellow triangles for foliage; in the middle is the Fairy Godfather in red, blue and yellow with green arms and a white head topped with blue triangle hat. One of his arms is touching the tree, while the other arm touches a smaller figure on the left, which Sally did not care to name — it might have been a person in the guise of a flower. The body of this second figure

Figure I-1.   Mosaic tiles; Fairy Godfather

was in green diamonds and triangles (Sally liked to wear green accessories), and the head in the shape of a whirling star was made of white and red triangles. This unnamed figure seems to be helping the Fairy Godfather into the shelter of the tree. Above are clouds in large black triangles put together into diamonds, and there are small black triangles for rain. Sally was agitated about her production. "I don't like this," she declared, but this time stopped her hand from pulling the paper lining off the tray as soon as I motioned her not to. She watched me trace her design and, quickly picking up the method of marking the traced shapes with letters to indicate colors, she began to dictate the proper letters to me and agreeably waited when I was not ready.

This was Sally's first voluntary participation. She was able to take the role of the leader, and there were other sources of gratification for her: I considered her work important; she had produced a large, unified scene; and she had communicated to me something that was important to her. The design was a meaningful projection of feelings about the inner dynamics of the family. She felt that mother was too demanding and too hard on father. Sally spoke of this, but angrily stopped when confronted with her own increasing demands in the recent past. "Daddy and me" or "Me and daddy" had often been Sally's typical opening of a sentence relating to family situations. Such sentences were usually completed with, "But she [mother] . . . ." This style of speech carried a message to the listener that Sally and father were a duo against mother. The two younger sisters were excluded as though they did not exist. Such had been the emotional background for Sally's spontaneous production. While it had most probably not been Sally's clear intention to repeat her message in the picture, it is safe to say that preexisting attitudes guided her spontaneous art work. Thus, the idea of being her father's special helper through her very understanding of his chagrin about mother was expressed in the picture, but there was no attempt at comments about it on my part. It seemed to me that when Sally viewed her mosaic Godfather picture as a finished product, she had a sudden notion that she had given herself away a little too much to a person whom she did not quite trust yet. That was quite scary for Sally.

To defend herself from overwhelming feelings of her own power and guilt, she wanted to destroy this communication immediately. But I accepted it; I considered it important enough to trace it and keep it. Moreover, she was not blamed for it. Therefore, she could now afford to relax about it somewhat.

In the next two sessions, Sally produced a number of clownlike figures with large, spinning heads. Figure I-2, "Jumping Clown," is typical. "Here he is jumping," Sally explained this time, "and he thinks that he is funny, sort of special." She also volunteered to trace her design and to color it, and did a slow but nearly perfect job. She was overly concerned and apologetic whenever a piece moved even slightly out of place. When the clown was all traced and colored, Sally commented that "a clown is a sort of person; he should have eyes and a nose and a mouth

Figure I-2.　Mosaic tiles; Jumping Clown

that everybody can see, so they don't think that he is like a machine. But this clown's head is always spinning so fast that you can't see his face, and that's what makes him a clown." That was very much, indeed, for Sally to offer. Perhaps it sounded a little vague, yet it was not such a vague statement about herself. Perhaps it was the only way she could say, "See, I really am a girl like other girls my age, but I cannot act like one because I am so overwhelmed by my worries." And perhaps she was saying, "I cannot be myself, so I have to act unnaturally, like a clown. Maybe I am a clown." It is interesting that the clown's head closely resembled the head of the unnamed person in Figure I-1.

Yet, when I ventured a small comment about the clown having a hard time, Sally angrily retorted, "This is only a toy clown, so there!" Of course, she sensed that she was being understood. But Sally was not yet ready to be understood or to be helped to deal with her problems. My remark was too threatening and it came too soon. She needed to be given much time and freedom to express only the presence of her problems.

For some time now, Sally had been on a home instruction program, taking tests in all the subjects and being graded at school. She knew that this program was limited to three months only, and she was most anxious about the future. She felt much relieved when I told her, according to an agreement with her parents, that a new school, small and pleasant, would be found for her next semester. Since an IQ measurement and other tests were needed for her enrollment in the new school, and since she had always been anxious about her intelligence, Sally readily agreed to take some psychological tests. She was told that the ink-blot test and the storytelling test were both tests of imagination, another form of intelligence. At ease about that, Sally showed some eagerness to be tested. She asked bright questions about brightness and finally came around to the question which worried her most: can a person's intelligence deteriorate? In our long and serious conversation about tests, Sally expressed her great fear that perhaps lack of the intelligence needed to comprehend the seventh-grade scholastic program or worse, deteriorating intelligence might have been the real reason for her failure to stay in school. The date was set. She arrived a little tense and somewhat pale, but willing.

On the Wechsler Intelligence Scale for Children (WISC), Sally scored at the top of the Superior group in general intelligence, with a number of indications that she might move on to Very Superior when her emotional stress was eased. She was alert and interested but not relaxed and certainly not spontaneous. She never allowed herself to enjoy a moment, not even on some funny Verbal Absurdities of the Stanford-Binet, which I gave her in addition to the WISC. When given praise for her performance, she would answer angrily, "This was easy, anyway."

Thus, she made it hard for herself to gain gratification even when she well deserved it.

She showed good mental control and an ability to organize her work and plan it, but only with effort could she maintain her use of these capacities. She also showed some obsessive traits, and her reasoning ability was not quite up to the general level of performance. Also, in addition to her conspicuously precise speech, her vocabulary was not quite at the twelfth-year level, but rather at year ten.

On the House-Tree-Person (H-T-P) Drawing Test, she drew a rather large, complicated house and did much erasing on the windows and on the chimney. The house was toppling over. She said that somebody had just bought this house and had not moved in yet.

The tree was small and delicate, done in sketchy lines. She could not make up her mind about the season of the year for that tree, and finally decided that it was fall or early spring.

For a person, she drew a man. It was a good, detailed drawing, but it lacked vigor. The lines were faint and the man seemed to be toppling over, like the house.

Sally's good organization and intellectual control seemed not to carry over to the projection of her personality. About her Rorschach I wrote at the time, among other comments: "she was exact, but her exactness does not serve her well. She does not really succeed in using intellectuality or obsessiveness as a defense. The exactness breaks down often enough and she confines her responses to descriptions and inadequate reactions, only pretending self-control and cool collectedness. Some of the cards disturbed her or moved her more than she was able to express in a controlled response. Some of her responses were "A scarecrow ready to go at you,' 'A snake ready to attack,' 'An eagle setting his claws ready,' and 'A tiger climbing up to cross the river to get you,' or 'An erupted volcano,' and 'A bursting fire.' But there were also responses like 'A cloud with sunset and a hole in it,' or 'A cloud getting the light from the sun behind. It will show up. You can't see it now." She mentioned in a soft tone of voice, "A bird opening its mouth for food."

Other personality tests (TAT, Exciting Scene*) delineated Sally as a very unhappy girl. She felt weighted down and oppressed and tied to her mother in a most unproductive way. She was not a spontaneous child and the normal exuberance of a child her age was alien to her whole being. Her angers were deep and came through only in small, picky, fault-finding. Sally's feelings were so repressed and she so rarely found ways to express them that they, too, weighed her down. For example, one of the things she was doing with people on her test responses was turning them into statues. This helped her evade the difficult problem of responding to people in a spontaneous, casual way.

Sally had tried to pretend for a long time, long before the school crisis breakdown, to control her feelings. She had pretended that everything was fine, while inside she was very unhappy and very hostile. But her controls were beginning to give way and the school crisis was the most alarming sign. She needed intensive help, and all the healthy aspects of her personality needed to be mobilized. Happily, Sally had strengths. Of these, the most important were a capacity to interact with others, an ability to try to look at herself and to understand herself even though she resisted, and an ability to shift her point of view despite some obsessive traits.

After the testing, Sally began to use crayons as though continuing the drawing tests. Indeed, she continued to draw the themes of those tests, but with a sequence of her own: a girl, a tree, and a house.

The girl (Fig. I-3), really a mature young lady, looked dressed up to go out. In conspicuous contrast to the many details, such as gloves, purse, buttons, shoulder-length hairdo, and hat, was the blank face with no eyes or nose, only the tight line for a mouth.

The tree (Fig. I-4) was drawn in brown crayon and was heavily shaded. It had many branches, but, as Sally herself mentioned, no leaves. Outstanding was the bizarre human face on the upper right among the branches of the tree. There it was,

*For the "Exciting Scene" Play Technique by Kessler and Taboroff, see Bibliography.

Figure I-3. Crayons; Lady

staring. Sally studied the face, perhaps a self-portrait, but would not comment.

The house (Fig. I-5), a heavier structure than that on the test, was first drawn with pencil, then with brown crayon over the pencil lines. There was shading along many lines, particularly around the front windows. In place of a door, Sally drew "a large gate to keep the house locked and safe, because nobody lives there right now." There were no trees or flowers around the house; but at the upper left, Sally had placed a spot with yellow crayon for the sun. She then used heavy black crayon to work the sun into an oblong eye and, as she was drawing the eyelashes, she

Figure I-4.   Crayons; Face in Tree

announced, "Now the eyelashes are the rain." This sun-eye with its yellow and black spots curiously resembled Sally's Rorschach response about the cloud and the sun with a hole in it. While she drew the eyelashes for rain, she was fighting tears in her eyes, but when I remarked that it was all right to cry, she gave me an angry look and soon was dry-eyed again. Being seen tearful was to Sally being caught in a despised act of weakness. She was very angry with me for seeing too much and suddenly said that she might come to see me "just one more time." But she listened intensely when I talked of anger and of the need to cry as a sign of human feelings.

At home, in the meantime, Sally's behavior was rapidly

Figure I-5. Crayon over pencil; House With Large Gate

changing in two directions. One was retrogressive, toward modes of behavior of earlier childhood. The other was leading toward adulthood: she was adopting mother's style of life in most of the daily routines. Thus, on the one hand, Sally would whine, play with her little sister's toys, or spill food; and on the other hand, like her mother, she slept late, insisted on going with her mother on the rounds of department stores and beauty shops, and advised the maid about housekeeping. This intensified the conflicts at home and made mother most impatient to see Sally back in school.

At about that time, Sally stopped working with crayons, having discovered the dolls in the playroom, and opened a period of four or five weeks of intense play with dolls. She dressed and undressed them, sewed for them, and talked to them, all in a hostile and openly aggressive way. At first there was angry but perfect management of the dolls' routine. Gradually, however, as the angry feelings came into the open, tender feelings also began to emerge. There were occasional hugs and caresses and even soft, pleasant talk. One day Sally came in radiant with a walking and talking doll, half her own size. In recent meetings mother had said much about Sally's demands for this doll. The family was impatient with the retrogressive traits of their eldest child, and mother felt that the purchase of this doll was an investment that might help her to behave in a more grown-up manner.

With her grown-up beauty-shop hairdo, prim as always in her slack suit exactly like mother's, with a stern, unsmiling face and with the large doll in her arms, Sally was a strange combination of premature old age and regressive childishness. Clearly, she was trying to skip adolescence for fear of it. At the same time, she seemed to be satisfying, in her preoccupation with dolls, a need to reexperience childhood, a child's need to be cared for, and perhaps also a need to care for others.

It was at the end of the period of playing with dolls and of caring for her large doll that Sally suddenly returned to art expression and painting Figure I-6. This is an aggressive-looking figure of a woman in profile, outlined with black crayon. She has a blond hairdo, facial details, brown-shaded skirt, blue, tight-fitting sweater, and a black belt. Standing with legs tightly closed, the figure is toppling forward and holding a purple vase of flowers, which she seems about to drop. Sally left the painting on the table without comment. When she found it the next time in the same place, she said angrily, "If you think it's me, you're wrong. It's my mother. This is another antique piece of junk she just bought to show off. She always has to get new things. Now she nags Dad to build her a house, and I know that he doesn't want to. Some day she will kill him; that's what Grandma says." When I added a word about Sally's wish to help father, she nodded vigorously. This was followed by an outburst of crying and shouting that "she [mother] doesn't understand a thing." I hung up Figure I-6 and opened Sally's folder, wondering aloud if she had not painted, in the past, a picture about helping father. Sally immediately recalled that it was the mosaic design about the Fairy Godfather seeking shelter from the rain (Fig. I-1), and pulled it out of the folder. We began to discuss Figure I-1 again. She was able to talk with me about the person with the whirling head on the left who was father's helper. I wondered whether father really needed help. Sally's reaction was an astonished look, but she uttered no sound. When I wondered about the sizes of

Figure I-6. Crayons; Lady With Vase

the three persons, Sally noticed that the helper was only slightly smaller than the father. She volunteered that mother was almost as tall as father and that she, Sally, was quite short, "a shrimp."

In the following hours, I often scribbled with Sally on large sheets of paper. At first, it was hard for her to be spontaneous, but she soon discovered that scribbling could be a time for fun and enjoyment. A laughing, sometimes hilarious Sally was something entirely new.

At one of these scribbling times, Sally introduced her "private scribble" and related that whenever she was scribbling for herself, she invariably produced that one. She added that it was not a fun scribble, and that if it was funny, it was not so in a laughing way. For three hour-long visits Sally drew, seriously and obsessively, various versions of two drawings, in some ways related to one another: one was a full figure of a girl, the other a large face. Sally used crayons, chalks, and felt pens. She reverted to her old tense, touchy mood.

Figure I-7 was the largest and clearest of the series of nine private scribbles.

The girl had red heels, a blue, tight-fitting skirt, a red and blue striped sweater, and a wide black belt. She had brown hair down to her shoulders. Her face had slanted eyes and

Figure I-7. Crayons, chalk, and felt pen; The Private Scribble

brows, all in blue crayon, and a red mouth. As soon as Sally finished the face, she wrote "Me" on the right. But then she quickly crossed out the face with a few angry motions and also crossed out the "Me." Next, she drew the large female face, almost horizontally placed, at the lower right.

This time the face was unusually large, particularly the eyes. Sally stared at the posterlike painting and picked up the pen again to add a bizarre detail: an arm in the form of a fork reaches out of the left corner of the female face and moves along the girl's leg up to her skirt.

We studied her painting. There was a certain softness about the girl, a softness absent in previous paintings of female figures. The eyes on the girl's face behind the crisscross lines resembled another face in one of Sally's earlier productions. When I shared this impression with Sally, she nodded, searched in the folder and brought out Figure I-4, Face in a Tree. I then took out Figure I-3, also, Girl with Blank Face, and placed it with the other two. "Tell me more about it," I said as I motioned to Face in a Tree. Sally quietly told me that Face in a Tree had really been a recurrent, scary dream she used to have long ago, when she was still going to school. The face would appear in the tree, high up, while Sally was playing. It would whisper, "Sally, Sally." When Sally would look up to answer the call, she would see her

own face "like in a mirror." Yet, at the same time, it was also the face of someone else, she did not know who. I recalled aloud the painting of the girl with the blank face. Sally nodded and said, "I know." No more was said or done about the faces. I thought that Sally now realized through feeling that the face that had become detached had returned to its natural owner.

There remained the bizarre detail of the arm, so very puzzling. Sally described it, saying, "She is going to tear off my nylons because she says that I am too young to wear nylons

every day." Sally said these words in a rather detached way; but the anger must have been acute, for she picked up a crayon and quickly scribbled on the left side of the female's forehead in confused writing, "Murder that mom." Such was the rage behind the quiet answer.

In the sixth month of her therapy, Sally began to use poster paints. Very cautious at first, she soon declared her preference for paints. She maintained that there were great advantages to the use of paint: large areas could be painted more quickly than with crayons, and paints could be mixed together to make new colors. This was a welcome change from the restricted linear crayon drawings to the more emotionally charged expansive areas of free-flowing paint. It was also a new freedom to experiment. She showed some joy in this activity, but occasionally this was too much for her to bear or perhaps only to admit. She would then suddenly throw the brush at the painting, noisily move the chair away from the table, and have a confused outburst of anger. When this happened, she would be encouraged to return to painting and to choose something specific to paint. She readily responded. As the disruptive moods occurred less frequently and became shorter Sally talked more willingly. But in talking she was still careful to focus on what she had projected on the paper.

She turned to the painting of trees. One of them (Fig. I-8) takes on particular significance in relation to the way it was painted. Sally first painted the large, richly green tree with many branches and with a sturdy, reddish-brown trunk. Next, she painted a blue sky, in short strokes. She described the tree as "spreading against the sky." She added daubs of brown and red to accentuate parts of roots, visible above ground. She then stopped, but had not finished. She stared at the painting a long while and, with some determination, added the last feature. It was the low fence in black around the tree (see Color Plate I).

Sally examined the finished painting. Her face showed a quick transition from satisfaction to perturbation. She complained that "it [the tree] came out much older than the tree in front of our house that I was going to paint. We don't even have a tree like this." As her eyes moved from the foliage downward to the

Figure I-8.   Poster paints; Fenced Tree

trunk, she became upset about "this funny fence" and repeated that the whole painting was "crazy" and that "something is wrong with it, definitely." There followed confused statements about liking and disliking the painting and about taking it home or leaving it with me. A small-scale tantrum followed. It consisted mostly of shouting, "I hate it," six or seven times in crescendo, the last cry sounding high, but pitiful rather than angry. She did not try to destroy the painting and did not throw brushes at it.

When some of the contrasting feelings which Sally had expressed about the painting were repeated to her in her own words but in more orderly fashion; when she was told that hatred was not the only feeling she had; and when she was asked to try to remember what else she felt or thought during her work on this painting, strong emotional expressions were seen on Sally's face as she began to talk. She said that there were "different things about different parts, and everything is mixed up." She agreed to say as much as she remembered about each part and to choose which part to speak about first.

She had really wanted to paint the small tree which is the only tree in front of their house. She always considered it her own tree. She wanted more trees, Sally sniffed and cried, but mother refused to plant more trees or shrubs because she wanted dad to build her a new house with a garden "like for a queen" and she, Sally, liked this house, except for the carpeting.

She told what the sky was about. While she was painting the blue sky and saying that the tree was spreading against it, she had really had in mind the blue carpeting that mother had just installed throughout the whole house in order to sell it more profitably. As she painted the sky, Sally visualized mother rolling about and spreading over the carpet. It must have been a frightening fantasy. There was much crying and more nodding when she was reminded, at this point, of the large female face scribbled on Figure I-7, which seemed to spread over Sally and reach with the arm to grab her or to rob her of her nylons.

Sally did not know why she put "that awful fence" around the tree; perhaps, she thought, to show "that nothing fits in this painting." Referring to her many feelings and thoughts that "were mixed up" in the parts of the painting, it was not difficult now to talk with Sally about the small tree that was never painted because it had become mixed up in the painter's imagination with a big mother tree. When the small tree thought that the best thing would be to pretend that it was old and to act like the old tree, life became terribly lonely, even impossible. "You mean me and mom," Sally said, summing it up simply. As Sally's time was up, all I could say was that without her painting and without her readiness to say what she felt and thought during the painting, we could not have known any of this and could not have helped her. On her way out, Sally planned for the next session.

Regrettably, however, that was the last time I saw Sally. She was abruptly withdrawn from therapy.

SUMMARY

Presented was a brief span of six months of art psychotherapy with a twelve-year-old girl who experienced an acutely schizoid episode. Caught in an unproductive relationship with her mother, she was blocked by anger and was fearful and uncommunicative. Unable to compete with mother or to find room for herself, she was afraid to grow up and reached out for the unproductive solution of trying to be mother. The focus of her disturbance became school phobia. Generally suspicious and resistant, the young girl responded to art therapy and communicated her tangled emotional problems to the psychologist through art expression. At the time of the unplanned termination, she was beginning to trust the psychologist and to untangle some of her conflicts.

FOLLOW-UP

In the last two months of therapy, Sally made rapid progress in her school work. When her final exams brought in A's and B's, her parents hastened to place her in the new school which had accepted Sally and had agreed to wait for her. Despite renewed resistance at a later time, Sally stayed in school. The family considered this a success and saw no need for further psychotherapy.

II

Ricky

A CASE IN WHICH art therapy proved most useful is that of Ricky. His expressive use of pastels, finger paints, clay, and other media helped me guide his slow, uneven progress toward self-acceptance and normal maturation.

Ricky was adopted when he was four days old by bright, well-educated, prosperous parents of New England background. From a somewhat turbulent but, on the whole, normal adolescence, Ricky's mother emerged as a sophisticated, imaginative, active woman of liberal orientation. She gave the impression of a highly self-sufficient, controlled, rational person who would not ever be helpless in a crisis. But there she was, in a deep crisis, feeling hopeless about her marriage, worried about her child, and confused about herself. A first marriage for her, it was the second for her husband, who had left two children with his former wife. Ricky was their only child, whom they happily adopted when it became clear that there would be no child of their own.

At nine, Ricky was uncommunicative, he masturbated and wet his bed, could be violent and destructive, tortured his pets whom he also loved, had outbursts of rage, and made trouble in school. He did not respond to questions or instructions, acting as though he had not heard them.

When neurological examinations showed no evidence of organic deficiency or damage, I administered to Ricky the following psychological tests: the Weschler Intelligence Scale for Children (WISC), Rorschach Technique, the Bender-Gestalt Test, Thematic Apperception Test (TAT), House-Tree-Person (H-T-P) Drawing Test, Color-Form Sorting Test, and an Exciting

A condensed version of this case appeared in the *American Journal of Art Therapy*, Vol. 9, No. 2, Copyright 1970. Reprinted by permission.

Scene assignment. The results of these indicated Very Superior intelligence, strong aggressive drives, tenuous controls, and a pressing need to gain approval in an environment which Ricky viewed as hostile. His greatest fear was of his own impulses. Outstanding in his defensive system were rigidity and denial. Spasmodic eruptions appeared to be his only mode of release.

The psychological findings, together with Ricky's developmental history and current behavior, suggested, in sum, emotional disturbance of a schizoid nature, overwhelming fears, and a tendency toward depression. All this seriously interfered with Ricky's use of his high intellectual ability. Life for him was threatening and dangerous, full of monsters without and within.

He spent the first few therapy hours in evasive, destructive behavior which paralleled his destructive behavior outside the hours with me. Clear-cut aggression occurred only at home during his occasional spasmodic eruptions when he would break objects of importance to mother, such as his framed photograph on her dresser. Otherwise, his aggression was highly manipulative. It took the form of teasing or playing, but ultimately it led to destruction if it was directed toward an object or to harm if it was directed toward an animal or a person. A whining "It wasn't my fault" immediately followed such acts.

Eventually, Ricky began to use finger paint, crayons, poster paints, and clay to produce monsters, a recurrent preoccupation dating from earlier childhood. This stage lasted about four months. The faces of the monsters were multicolored and the backgrounds were black (see Figs. II-1 and II-2). At the height of this phase, Ricky had brief hallucinations of monsters; they appeared to him on a towel or on the wall of the bathroom when he was there alone.

Later in the same period, Ricky worked with great intensity, using clay almost exclusively. All his productions were monster heads, which showed skill and had a good deal of artistic quality but were marked by bizarre, often asymmetrical, anatomical features. The eyes might appear on two different levels (Fig. II-3); or there might be a third eye placed on the forehead (Fig. II-4). Ricky destroyed most of the clay heads before they

Figure II-1.   Crayons; Monster

were finished, talking about how these monsters frightened him and about his inability to understand why they had "chosen" him. Only the three shown here were saved. In color, some of them were scary, with a lot of blood on their faces (see, for example, Fig. II-5).

After this group, the monsters changed: they began to be clearly divided into "good" and "bad." Each single head had its inhuman side and its human one. Ricky would turn these sculptures, none of which was preserved, back and forth, saying, "From this side nobody would know how bad he is, nobody would even think he is a monster. Would you?" Then he switched

Figure II-2.   Poster paints and crayons; Monster

to painting and to drawing with crayons so as to show both of these aspects at a single glance. Figure II-6 is a picture of a head only, and Figure II-7 shows the full body of the divided monster (see Color Plate II). Ricky studied this monster as if it were an independent object, and observed, "On this side [the left], he is a real monster and I kind of like him; on this side [the right], he is sort of weak, but he is human." At this point, Ricky stopped hallucinating monsters.

During the next two months, he produced monsters in a less excited manner. He was willing to talk about the coexistence of

Figure II-3.   Clay; Monster

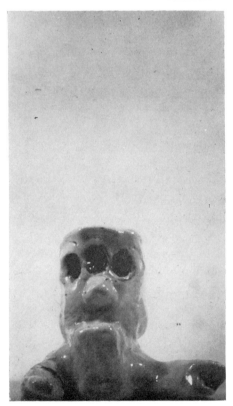

Figure II-4.   Clay; Three-eyed Monster

Figure II-5.   Clay; Bloody Monster

Figure II-6.   Crayons; Head of Divided Monster

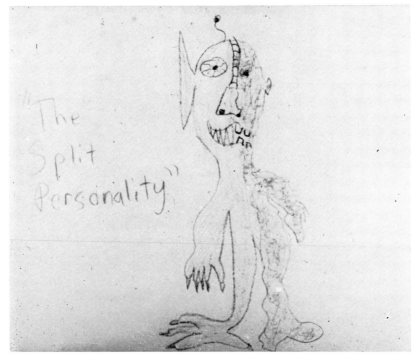

Figure II-7. Crayons; Divided Monster

"good" and "bad" in them as well as in some people. He also began to make finger paintings which appeared to be landscapes, with sharp red and black forms that suggested fires and explosions.

Toward the end of this time, Ricky began to mix paint and use milder color combinations. He enjoyed actually making something new, but there was no end to his demands for praise. He not only stopped destroying his paintings, but he also began giving them to his mother as presents. When he was angry with her, he took them away from her and gave them to the maid instead, thus using the pictures to manipulate both women.

Ricky's relationship with his mother rested on many contradictory feelings, and since his father was traveling most of the time, he was involved with mother much more than is a boy whose father is around every day. For a while, Ricky used to hurt her with "You are not my real mother anyway." That disappeared in the early stages of therapy. Yet, at the some time, he feared that she might walk out on him one day. His angry dependence upon her, his need to be cared for by her, his alliance with father against her, his manipulation of her along with his constantly disappointed desire to be stopped by her once and for all, all these were mixed together in Ricky's tumultuous inner life. And all these made up the very close but very confused relationship with mother.

The monsters seemed to have been done with. For about four of five weeks now, Ricky drew many faces of an angry-looking man. He worked with felt pens or with large soft pencils. He produced over twenty such portraits, all alike with only slight variations. All had the same square shape, black or red hair, sharp blue eyes set in black frames, and large mouths showing a set of black or red teeth, open or closed. Most of these heads were set on necks only or on feeble bodies out of which grew little arrowlike arms or hands. Some of the faces had a scar or bruise on one of the cheekbones, black or red, in this respect resembling the monsters. He was very careful not to speak about them and was also careful to tear them into shreds.

In time, after about a dozen of them, he crumpled each finished portrait into a ball and tossed it at the waste basket. Toward the end of this period, he began to leave his portraits on the table. One time, perhaps puzzled by my interested but silent watching of his work, he said, "I bet you think I am back at the monsters. Well, these are not monsters, I'll have you know." He then began to add some color in chalk — a deep orange or bright red, spreading the powdery substance with his fingers over an area on the right side of the portrait. This is shown in Figure II-8, which was to be the last of the series. This time the colored area on the right was orange mixed with red. When Ricky finished coloring that area, he said, "This is his madness. Why don't you have him mess with clay to get the madness out?" There was stress on "him."

No, this was not a return to monsters. It was a post-monster period, but neither Ricky nor I identified verbally the model for

Figure II-8.   Chalk; A Man's Portrait

the portraits. There was no need for that. In his own way, Ricky was now expressing another problem, I thought, and in due time, he would let me know more about it.

That time arrived when, a few appointments later, Ricky commented on a small sculptured bust which he had often seen. Made by another boy long ago, it was of a solemn and stern-looking man. "Is this his father?" exclaimed Ricky, "He must be mad. If I had such a father, I would die!" Thus, the time came when Ricky could speak a little bit about his father, a theme about which he had been completely blocked. In the past, at the mention of his father, he used to take himself bodily away from the spot in the room where it had been made.

When at home, father gave in to all Ricky's whims, much to mother's chagrin. Underlying this indulgent attitude was father's deep admiration for Ricky's brightness. Father felt a great satisfaction in having, at long last, a brilliant child. In that sense, he considered this adopted child more his own and more appropriate to him, the very bright man with a serious interest in art, than the older children of his first marriage. As the man was loud and clear about these feelings, Ricky knew them rather well. In fact, he was quite scared of father's angry cursing about his own children and about other matters, and obtained mother's permission to have dinner alone in his room. So he sat with his plate in front of the television, scared of the violence on the screen and scared of what "they" might do to each other during their dinnertime quarrels downstairs, and scared that it was all his fault.

He was now cautiously talking about his father, at least readily giving information about father's travels. For the first time, he noticed some paintings in my waiting room which had been there all the time, and was able to talk at some length about his father's interest in art and about the paintings he bought.

There were a few other people at home who were also somewhat confusing to Ricky even though he liked them.

The maid was young, and playfully flirted with Ricky, teasing him about marrying her. Half sister Pam, who spent much time at Ricky's house during college vacations, had a very warm relationship with him, but confided in the little brother as one would in a mature contemporary, mixing fantasy with her meager supply of actual romance. Ricky often worried about the danger of her stormy, imaginary love affairs.

During Pam's visits, Ricky would produce many confused paintings about her being beaten up or running away and getting caught by her cruel man. Those paintings would start with a rather realistic, gruesome scene of a man beating a crouching girl. But the painting would soon be so covered up with red and blue lines and blobs in all colors expressing the man's violence and the girl's pain, that the original scene could not be discerned anymore.

There was also the half brother, a year younger than Pam, but, unlike her, rather hostile toward father and an infrequent visitor to the house. While Pam was afraid of father and begged for his attention, this brother was interested in father's financial help.

Certainly, Ricky was caught in a complex network of loyalties, hostilities, and maneuvers. He either had to outsmart others in the game of manipulation or seek relief from his deep-seated anger by detaching himself from it. Ricky was weary of both manipulation and detachment.

Some of these difficulties were gradually lessened or eliminated. The maid was persuaded to stop the teasing. Pam's confidences became more realistic when Rick's mother, guided in her own therapy hours, helped the young girl.

Ricky entered a new phase which lasted seven weeks and was marked by the characteristic persistence he had shown in his production of monsters. This time, dramatic action took the place of art media. He apparently felt the need to express his emotions in a way that demanded my immediate response. He worked with small flexible dolls and toy soldiers. Time and again, he would come in and immediately set up, on a table or on the floor, the same scene: a dense group of soldiers surrounds and aims guns at one unarmed man who has no way out, since all roads leading past the soldiers are hopelessly blocked. While constructing this scene, Ricky would talk earnestly: the victim must die; he was born bad; the soldiers are right. It is the unarmed man's last moment of life. Ricky would urge the soldiers to "finish him," at the same time anxiously asking me, "Do you think there is any hope for him?" (see Fig. II-9).

At this point, I took to bringing my hand down with an airplane and lifting the man to safety. At each session, now twice a week, Ricky eagerly awaited my assurance that I would always rescue the man "no matter how bad he is." Long after this pattern had been abandoned, Ricky would sometimes recall the scene and ask, "Remember how you would save the man? How did you do it so fast?"

It is appropriate to say here a word about the relationship between Ricky and me. Suspicion and anger, aggression and manipulation, all these had been directed toward me. But there was a growing trust. At the same time, there was a continual testing of my acceptance of him. Once, at the peak of a long period of aggressive and destructive behavior during which I had to be quite firm a few times, he said, when his session was over, "I bet each time I go, you hope that I never come back." What he was really saying was stated right there at the door.

Figure II-9.   Blocks and flexible figures; Soldiers' Scene

I assured him that I wanted to see him next time, and after that there was no more aggression toward me or open destruction in the playroom.

In the ensuing three months, Ricky repeatedly drew pictures of children from his classroom — a few boys, but mostly girls. This was something new. Although his portrayals were caricatures, he showed a new interest in facial detail and expression of individuality. Though his portraits of them were distorted, at least he showed an interest in his classmates. He noticed them and stated through the paintings his recognition of their importance. In the portraits of the girls, he emphasized the characteristics he particularly disliked, and labeled them accordingly: "Big mouth," "Head full of Books," or "Mammoth Mouth" (see Fig. II-10). Figure II-10 also seemed to reflect Ricky's feelings about father.

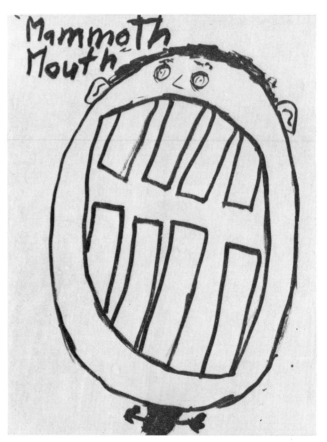

Figure II-10.   Felt pen; Mammoth Mouth

When I suggested that he draw himself, he refused, but did agree to draw his family (Fig. II-11). Here the smaller of the two main figures is father; next to him is the larger figure of mother (in reality, she is noticeably smaller than father). She holds Ricky's half sister Pam in her hand. Ricky himself is the dot

Figure II-11. Crayon; Family Portrait

labeled "Me" behind the father's back. The dot alone is black, the other figures having been drawn with pastels in red and blue.

When I asked to see "Me" a little closer up, Ricky drew Figure II-12: a map of the city, his house in it, and "Me" inside the house, practically invisible. But he conceded that perhaps next time, "Me" would come out of hiding. In Figure II-13, "Me" was permitted to come to the window so as to show his face alone, suggesting his negative feelings about his body. But before he could do so, I had to be warned about his awful freckles, buck-teeth, unruly red hair, and big ears. Some sessions later, "Me" came out into the open "for a minute" in Figure II-14, but Ricky immediately scribbled over the large head and face and the dwarfed body, explaining the scribbles as a stomachache and other aches, and marking the aches in writing, of which only traces were caught by the camera (see Color Plate III).

Of course, the distorted drawing of the body and the scribbled "aches" indicated Ricky's feelings about his own body. His painful belief in his own bodily distortion was evident in his guarded, stiff-legged walk when he was with me or with

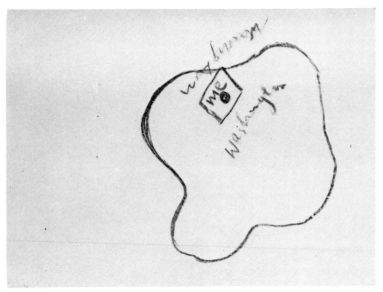

Figure II-12.   Crayon; "Me"

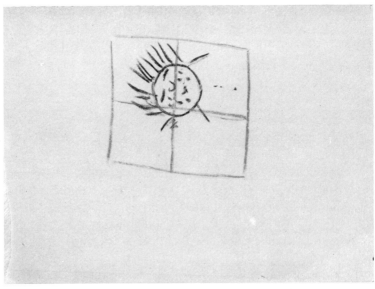

Figure II-13.   Crayon; "Me" in the Window

Figure II-14. Crayons; Dwarfed "Me"

other people, particularly marked in his early psychotherapeutic visits and in all moments of weariness or self-consciousness. At such times, he would take himself out of the chair opposite me, lower his head, turn his shoulders inward, slightly cross his arms as though to protect himself, and move around the room or into the other room, aimlessly wandering about.

Both physical and emotional factors contributed to Ricky's body image. He was small, the smallest or close to the smallest in each successive class throughout the elementary grades; he was not very good at the sports so highly valued in school and was afraid of being hit by a ball; he had protruding teeth, but resisted correctional treatment; he had a fear of heights which mother dated back to his training in skiing early in childhood when instructors found him crawling down the hill in tears; and deep inside, he had a notion that somehow he was "made bad" and that sooner or later people, particularly significant people, would recognize it. His own aggressive behavior, then, was highly defensive for he felt that he must strike before the blow came down on him, that he must plunge into making himself unlikeable before the significant others let him know that they disliked him.

The sessions immediately after the scribbled-over self portrait were marked by much aggressive and some regressive behavior. In the third and last of these hours, Ricky found "that man," the doll whom I used to rescue. He played with it aggressively, but he did not need to stage the old drama again. He was also able to listen thoughtfully to my speculation that "that man" and "Me" were, perhaps, a little alike.

Figure II-15 marks a brief and most illuminating phase of Ricky's therapy. It was the outcome of the following events: Ricky made a stormy entrance into my office and told the story of a fight with his mother. She, meantime, had applied some insights gained in her art therapy group for mothers. She had learned to respond in a constructive way to Ricky's manipulative maneuvers, which previously had often succeeded in causing conflict between her and her husband. As Ricky stormed about mother's firm way with him, I put up the picture shown in Figure II-11 and asked what the dot called "Me" was really doing in the family. Hastily, and with mounting excitement, Ricky drew with pastels five different versions of the picture shown in Figure II-15. In Figure II-15, "Me" is sitting in the center, above the

Figure II-15.   Crayons; Superintending a Fight

small father and the big mother, superintending a fight between them. The father is stabbing mother in her breasts. Some of the five versions included cartoon-style exclamations of violence (bam! zap! ugh!). Other balloons were more specific. In one· version (Fig. II-16), the child is shown as saying, "Give it to him" and "Give it to her," while the father says, "Let me at her," and the mother, "I'll kill him when I get my hands on him."

When they were all done, Ricky's relief showed on his face. This was not a sudden confrontation with a truth previously unknown; rather, it was an unburdening of something too heavy to have been borne so long.

At about that time, mother began to do some very expressive and illuminating work in the art therapy group. The calm, proper, and perfectly controlled lady found the situation sufficiently free from threat so that she could begin to open up and allow her stored-up angers to pour out on paper. "Anger" (Fig. II-17) was immediately succeeded by "Cyclone" (Fig.

Figure II-16.   Crayons; Superintending a Fight

II-18). "Anger" is linear, in black with a somewhat stronger massive base in black and red. The anger seems to ascend but is contained, and does not actually culminate anywhere, as though it went right back the way it came. Not so "Cyclone." Made with crayons and chalks in strong reds and blacks, "Cyclone" had green and yellow objects flying into clouds of smokelike sand. Tables, beds, ornaments, and curtains were all drawn into the wild whirl, and soon the person herself became just another object (lower right) swept up in the all-consuming storm.

This series of paintings was followed by another, a series of dreams which were puzzling to the dreamer and somewhat upsetting. "A Glimpse of Beauty" (Fig. II-19) is one of them. This

Figure II-17.   Crayons; Anger

painting, in glowing oranges and reds with some strong blues, greens and blacks, shows (on the right) a sunset coming through the dark foliage of many trees. The picture is divided by a wide semicircular path turning left and leading to a steep staircase. To the left of the path is a rather empty hill, with some thorns or weeds at the extreme left. The dreamer was pushing a wheelchair up the steep path. It was heavy and grew ever heavier. She dreaded the hardship of getting the chair up the staircase and when she leaned over to see what made it so heavy, she noticed that it was empty. Puzzled and upset, she continued and found herself at the turn of the path. There she noticed the beautiful sunset. She parked the empty wheelchair on the left and turned to watch the sunset through a window which was suddenly there. In a green dress, with her back to viewers, she stood at the window watching and crying.

Figure II-18.   Crayons; Cyclone

This painting indicated the integrative value of the dream. Having aired the long-borne angers and the preoccupation with sorrow for herself, this mother was able to "park" that sorrow which she had nurtured too long. Suddenly, there was a window, there was a new perspective of life, of the family, and of its members. Unconsciously on the painter's part, the dreamer at the window also looks like a painter at the easel.

Ricky sensed some of the changes in mother and commented on them. He sensed that she could now be softer yet firmer, and that she now knew what to do when he was trying to maneuver. For some time his own behavior, his whole mode of functioning,

Figure II-19. Crayons; A Dream

had been showing improvement. He no longer wet the bed; torturing the pets was long past; he was more cooperative at school and more attentive to homework; there were no more explosive outbursts at home or destructive acts outside the house; he stopped instigating fights between the parents; and even managed to discuss this aspect of his past behavior with his mother.

Soon after he produced the cartoonlike paintings, summer vacation began and Ricky went to camp by his own choice. He enjoyed it and even made friends, though he still antagonized some of the boys and provoked them into fighting with him.

In the first hours of the new school year, Ricky made new but abortive attempts to behave in a destructive manner. Once, while he was pounding nails into small building blocks, he kept saying to me, "See, I am destructive." As he would never have done in the past, he willingly accepted an old piece of board as a substitute for the blocks, and pounded the nails into it with enjoyment rather than as a purely aggressive act. He settled down for the rest of the hour and worked seriously with the nails and board, asking me not to look and promising to show me the finished product. This was Figure II-20, a "painting in nails." It really is a portrait of Ricky himself, with freckles, buckteeth, big ears, and unruly hair, boldly titled "ME." He presented it to me and eagerly awaited my reaction.

SUMMARY

Successive phases have been presented to demonstrate the four-year development of art therapy in the treatment of a boy who was at the outset nine years old, schizoid, and uncommunicative. As with all children, his artistic productions abstracted the essential character of his subjective experiences. At first, his own inner world was emotionally distorted, as was his self-concept. His art products show corresponding distortion. The changes that followed demonstrate that spontaneous art expression in psychotherapy develops according to a logical pattern of its own. Each

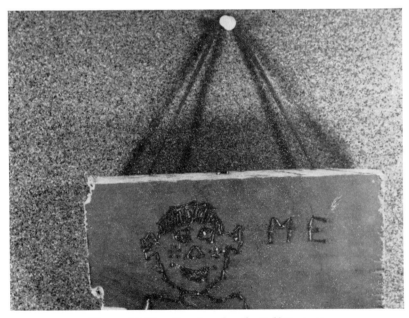

Figure II-20.   Board and nails; Self-Portrait

portrayal of an aspect of Ricky's inner reality was made possible by the preceding one, and, in turn, made the next one possible. Thus, there was a sequence of steps toward awareness, change, and the possibility of recovery. Psychotherapy through artistic expression succeeded in reaching this child.

FOLLOW-UP

Ricky was given a long summer vacation from psychotherapy and spent the time resting, reading, raising his pigeons, and not making any trouble. It was a summer of quiet growing.

When I saw him again in September, he had grown taller and rather handsome. He had just started high school and liked it. More cooperative than in the past, he was willing to talk about specific problems that were not previously given a chance to be worked through.

III

Barbie

THROUGHOUT HER LATE CHILDHOOD and early and middle adolescence, Barbie came at three different times for some psychological help. The first and longest period of psychotherapy, about two years, is the theme of this chapter.

At the age of eight and a half, Barbie was stealing at home and in school; she set fires, was intensely involved in sex play, had screaming spells, disappeared from home for many hours, and was generally uncommunicative and hard to control. It was surprising that her third-grade school work was passing and often good without special effort on her part.

Barbie had been tested in a child guidance clinic, but was not accepted for treatment. Staff felt that with the magnitude of her problems, which suggested an early stage of psychopathic personality, the child should be placed in residential treatment. This the parents could not afford.

Tests administered to Barbie in the clinic and forwarded to me were Revised Stanford-Binet Intelligence Scale, Drawing Test, Mosaic Test, and Rorschach. The main parts of the interpretation read as follows: "This is a child of superior general intelligence . . . . She had a basal year at eight and a range through year XI . . . . She is a highly self-centered youngster who reveals considerable perseverated impulsivity and tempestuousness on the Rorschach. Hers is quite a strange Rorschach and her thinking is not in accord with what one generally finds in a child of her age. She perseverates in seeing blood and anatomical answers which have very little relationship to what actually is in reality. She certainly does not try and this may be the reason that she gives this very strange Rorschach in an effort to get it out of the way."

" . . . The things that come to mind as possibilities are organic involvement and impulsivity arising from that or, possibly, the beginning of a psychopathic kind of personality."

When the parents approached me about psychotherapy for Barbie, we agreed to try six months, twice a week, and that they, too, would be seen. They were seen separately.

Barbie was a sturdy, tough-looking little girl with a rather cute round face. She was solemn, spoke very little, and never looked directly at me, turning her head away when she was saying what little she was ready to say. But soon enough she showed that she could smile and talk about things she enjoyed — such safe things, for example, as the hamburgers and cheeseburgers in the nearby Hot Shoppe, where mother treated her to lunch on appointment days. Other than that, she was quick to say, "I don't know" in response to anything that sounded to her like an attempt to probe or to threaten her with being "found out." That might have been the reason for her strange Rorschach. My impression was that Barbie was careful not to come close to anybody for fear of being rejected. Hence, her coldness and detached mode of acting, which, I thought, might be Barbie's defensive solution rather than her authentic mode of being. Whatever the reason, this child was uncommunicative. Art therapy seemed to be the only technique that might work.

Barbie immediately responded to finger painting. For eighteen one-hour visits in nine weeks she worked solemnly and intensely with both hands, making circular and oval motions, mostly using red and brown paint. Figure III-1 is representative of over sixty finger paintings of that type.

She would come in and eagerly get to work, standing all the time and not talking at all, but visibly appreciating the large sheets of paper and the fresh jars of finger paint which she found ready. She used enormous quantities of paint, dabbling with much pleasure in puddles of the various colors she eventually began to mix. She would start with a bright yellow and gradually darken it to a muddy greenish-brown mess. There was no pattern or design, representational or abstract, and there was no center or focal area in these paintings. What Barbie needed at the time was the continuous circular motion with all her fingers in the

Figure III-1. Finger paint; Circular Motions

wet paint. It was an output of emotional energy charged with long stored-up infantile rage. Now Barbie derived gratifying bodily sensations from contact with the paint.

  After a while she discovered the poster paints which had been there, unnoticed, all the time. She announced one day that she was going to paint something for her father "because he is good to me." This was Barbie's first spoken communication of a feeling about somebody outside herself. But the painted expression of it revealed that this feeling was rather ambivalent. Interestingly enough, Barbie left the picture on the table and never gave it to her father. It was Figure III-2, "A Tree, Two Colors." The color was divided along a vertical split from top to bottom of the tree, bright blue on the left and bright red on the right. Of course, the tree might be regarded as a phallic symbol. The divided color might indicate Barbie's conflict about her sexual identity, or the disparity between her intellectual and emotional development.

  Two weeks later, Barbie painted what she described as "a happy man; he is up in the air" (Fig. III-3). The air was in-

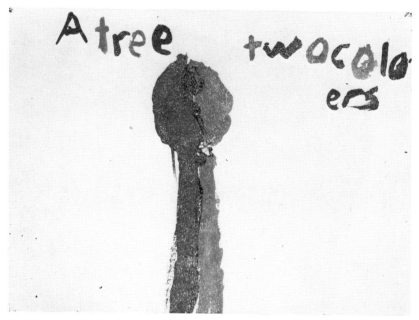

Figure III-2.   Poster paints; Bicolored Tree

dicated by the light brush strokes in blue. In the center of the sheet, floating upward, was the man in orange jacket and black pants. His facial features painted in blue were eyes, nose, a smiling mouth, and a beard; and his long head was topped with a high black hat. Of special interest was the infantile oval body of the man. While Barbie was unable to offer any spoken associations with her painting, it was reminiscent of her mother's complaint about her husband's remoteness. In addition, this painting also expressed Barbie's ambivalent feelings about father. She was offering the tree to him, but he is "up in the air."

At about that time, Barbie became interested in the snap blocks and also in the miniature building bricks. There followed a period of about six weeks of intense activity, building houses and also putting snap blocks together into objects. Painting and clay work continued, but Barbie seemed more involved in the two newer activities.

The brick houses were outstanding for their complex design

Figure III-3.   Poster paints; A Happy Man

which she invented herself or elaborated from the printed samples. These buildings had fine proportions, strong foundations, and decorative details. Her first two structures had no windows or doors. The second of these was kept for Barbie's next hour and, as soon as she noticed it, she commented, "Did I make it? It looks like a prison." She shot it down with some darts and settled down to build more sophisticated houses with a variety of windows and doors.

In dealing with the snap blocks, which she combined into objects following linear outlines in print, she showed a fine grasp of perspective and a quick understanding of three-dimensional representation. When she discovered that a human figure could be snapped together, Barbie was quite excited and made a

number of seated and standing figures, calling them her "robots."
On one occasion, Barbie decided to paint a portrait of her most
recent "robot" (Fig. III-4). She painted the body red, the
shoulders and arms white, and the head and feet black. She then
painted around the portrait the same blue wavy lines that surrounded the "'Happy Man" of Figure III-3. I asked whether this
person was as happy as "Happy Man," and Barbie took a black
crayon and, using round scribbly motions, added a penis. She
then said, "He was just born and he is a boy and he is also happy
and up in the air." The painting and comment were both important expressions about Barbie's sexual identity problems. At
that time, Barbie played only with boys. In games, sports, and
climbing trees, she was their equal, but in sex play she certainly

Figure III-4.   Snap blocks and paint; Baby Boy

was the girl. She was hostile toward her brother but envied him his role of the boy. Because of her sex play, she felt guilty and unworthy as a girl, but she liked, nevertheless, to be Daddy's little girl. Mother, who herself felt too tall and too thin and not feminine enough, tried to dress Barbie in very feminine clothes, often pushing the issue too hard. Barbie resisted mother's efforts and probably was depressed by the ambivalence in her feelings about herself.

One day toward the end of the third month of therapy, Barbie came in as she often did, wiping her tears and sniffling. Such moods were usually the aftermath of a scene with mother or with some neighborhood children about one of Barbie's thefts or some act of aggression she had committed. The mood was usually one of self-pity. This time she sat down and declared, "Everybody hates me and you, too, don't want me." The question, "What else do you feel?" remained unanswered, but Barbie went to the painting table. She splashed much paint on the paper, coated her hands with green and yellow paint, carefully painted her fingernails green, and settled down to produce Figure III-5. "This is a terrible creature," she said, "who will come to cut off your and mommy's hair and head."

The disheveled and defiant-looking "creature" was first painted in yellow, then overlaid with light and dark greens. It had no arms or legs. There was a frame around the page. That frame, painted in strong blue arches with yellow vertical lines in them, resembled a fence rather than a picture frame (see Color Plate IV).

Barbie nodded at my comment that the creature must be very scary. She also nodded when I wondered aloud what mommy and I might be doing that makes the creature want to punish us. But she remained silent. I did get an answer, though, when I observed that not having arms or legs must be rather tough on the creature. When I wondered whether people knew how tough it was, Barbie's first reaction was to meet my eyes — for the first time in almost four months of psychotherapy — with a long and tearful look. Next came another "first," a verbal explanation about the creature: "See, something makes her go to

Figure III-5.   Poster paints; A Terrible Creature

these places and do these things." The legless and armless wild creature surrounded by a fence expressed Barbie's dawning awareness of her inability to control her behavior and of her wish to be stopped.

Barbie's words and the painting itself opened a very slow-moving but meaningful verbal exchange. There she was, almost stuttering, shyly asking and wondering, believing and not believing, embarrassed and searching for words, but talking to another person about the "creature," really about herself. "Going to these places" came to mean disappearing from the house to hide from her parents. "Doing these things" was not translated at all. Barbie told me that twice she had packed a suitcase to run away, but was "caught" by mother. She "didn't think of it that way," but agreed that each hours-long disappearance was actually a runaway act. She then told that she was often hiding in a closet at a friend's home while her mother was calling to inquire about her whereabouts, and exclaimed, "I wish she would stop looking for me all over the place." She then said that if I wanted to help her, I should stop mother from this practice. When I wondered why mother would look for her "all over the place," Barbie's first answer was, " ' cause she's after me"; her second was, " 'cause she likes to pester me"; her third, an impatient, "Oh, I don't know." Her last answer came in pianissimo and was charged with doubt and disbelief, " 'cause she cares?"

I associated this answer with another answer Barbie had given on the tests administered to her some six or seven months before. On the Stanford-Binet Intelligence Scale, where the appropriate answer to the question on Year XI as to why the parents burned the boy's clothes is "Skunk," Barbie's answer was "They didn't want him." These two answers, "They didn't want him" and "Because she cares?" both anxiously concerned with the need to be accepted and cared for, cast some light on the inner climate of the child's life at the time.

The technique used to help Barbie express herself verbally had been to have her repeat and finish the sentence "Mother keeps looking for me all over the place because . . . " until a really important answer that "fit" came out of her own lips. It could be seen by the expression on Barbie's face that her last answer was the important and fitting one. That answer expressed a felt experience.

At the end of this series of answers Barbie suddenly asked if mother was also "made to finish these sentences," thus begging for some information about mother and me. Barbie listened with a pensive look in her eyes while I told her that I was helping mother to understand some of her own problems as well as to understand Barbie and the rest of her family a little bit better. Thus, I was not just another mommy. I was, rather, a person who studied many years how to help people understand themselves and their kin.

There was a warmer feeling between Barbie and me after that talk. She began to meet my eyes more often and she also began to mention "my mother," "my father," "my brother," and "my dog." But there was also a change in her art expression which indicated some inner turmoil.

Barbie returned to her muddy finger painting for a few visits. These were no longer the old circular movements in puddles of paint shown in Figure III-1. This time the paintings developed some odd shapes resembling rocks and hills. They were first painted yellow and then overlaid with heaps of brown and black. Soon, other shapes were hanging over or rolling over the "rocks." Figure III-6 was the last of these, and the first to bear a title, "A House."

And a strange house it was. I read the title aloud and thoughtfully regarded the painting. Barbie watched me intently and asked, "What does it look like?" She was telling me something and expecting something of me, no doubt, and I said I would tell her what I saw if she would correct me in case I did not guess right. If it was a house, it was falling off a thin and steep rock. There was only one little window on the right, and a strange door on the left, while the peaks on the top right might be a chimney;

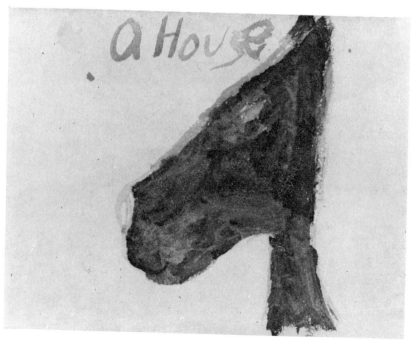

Figure III-6.   Poster paints; A House-Dog

but the whole painting also looked like the head and neck of a dog. I wondered if it could be the portrait of Barbie's dog.

Barbie became quite agitated. "You passed! You passed!" she exclaimed and gave me a big A on the blackboard. I had just been tested. Now I could ask her to tell me about her painting, herself.

Seriously and almost in a whisper, Barbie explained. The has-been house is now just a big chunk of charcoal with a hole for a window and just the metal bars for the upstairs porch on the left; the house has been badly burned; long ago it was standing on a "good" rock, but the rock is getting ever thinner, and now "one push could hurl the house all the way down there"; and whether or not the house will be hurled down depends on her dog, who is inside the house waiting for her. It all depends on which side of the house he will be at, just as in a Charlie Chaplin movie she once saw on television. Barbie added that the dog must soon be given away to a farm, since the neighbors find him threatening and she, loving and always defending the dog because he is her only real friend, finds herself in conflict with the neighborhood children and with her own family; but the minute he is given away, she will run away, this time "for real."

If I had passed a test, Barbie richly rewarded me as she trustingly told what the painting meant to her. She was not entirely aware, of course, that the double story of "The House" and the very way she used the paints and perceived the empty space "down there," implied highly complex and conflicting feelings. These feelings included violence and fear of it, loneliness and a dread of it, and a need to punish and to be punished. At times, all these feelings were swept by a deep-seated rage, expressed in her outbursts of crying. That rage blocked the growth of Barbie's capable, normal self.

The six months of my limited trial engagement with this family were almost up, and it was time for reassessment. The "House" painting was followed by a new battery of tests which I administered to Barbie. The material accumulated during the experimental six months, the findings of the newly administered tests, and the work done with the parents during the trial months were the three sources for the reassessment. The previous findings of the psychologist in the clinic were carefully kept in mind.

A brief review of the new test findings and an even briefer summary of the work done with the parents will now be given.

The tests were the Goldstein Color-Form Sorting Test, the Weschler Intelligence Scale for Children (WISC), parts of the Revised Stanford-Binet Intelligence Scale, a selection from the Thematic Apperception Test (TAT), the Rorschach Technique, the Exciting Scene, and the Bender-Gestalt Drawing Test.

The Color-Form Sorting Test revealed that Barbie was able to shift her way of looking at a problem. She did this, however, with much hesitation.

The WISC placed Barbie in the upper part of the Superior group. She did well on the verbal part of the test, but very much better on the Performance part. The considerable difference between the Verbal and the Performance IQs was most probably due to Barbie's emotional problems, particularly those related to social situations. She was at her best in all subtests representing abstract thinking. Having kept in mind the poor ability to note picture absurdities she had shown on the Stanford-Binet in the clinic, I repeated that subtest and added the Verbal Absurdity subtests to it. Barbie seemed not to remember the pictures. She was quick to note both the pictorial and verbal absurdities, sometimes smiling and giggling — an important indication of humor. Even though Barbie scored Superior in general intelligence on both this and the earlier measurement, the difference was that she was now better able to look and to listen and to focus attention.

On the Rorschach there were no blood responses and no violence, but there were open anger and an indication of depression. Much sadness was suggested by two of Barbie's three human responses: sad faces, tears, "big tears." Even though there were still too many anatomic responses, they were not entirely unrelated to the areas on the blots. Her other answers were generally more emotional than on the earlier testing. The two angels were there, but were now "mad at each other"; and there was one good and normal human response of "two girls kissing the pole because it was from the boyfriend; he just climbed it."

On other personality tests, TAT and Exciting Scene, Barbie appeared as the emotionally starved child who tortured her helpless mother because mother's exasperation was better than no reaction at all; she was the child whose closeness to father was unproductive, as it rested on a tacit alliance with him against mother and brother, on maneuvering, and on her feeling that father had no backbone, anyway. In some stories, she was the child who gets lost; and yet, on the blank card story, the person who had been lost comes back and, to everyone's surprise, has been happily changed by a "secret miracle."

To eliminate any question of organicity, which was not suggested on any of these tests, the Bender-Gestalt Test was given to Barbie. She did well and copied the designs with a sure hand, except for Design 8, which is suggestive of mother and child. While even here Barbie's drawing was quite correct and the handling of the rather complicated angles good, her lines were sketchy and unsure.

The relationships within the family presented a grim picture, even though there was love and care for the children. Mother had given up hope for a closer relationship with her husband. She envied him his college education but despised him for his insensitiveness, and turned to her son, three years older than Barbie, for spiritual closeness. Her high expectations of the boy were frustrated by his low scholastic performance and his emotional problems which, though very unlike Barbie's, posed serious difficulties.

A pattern of family attitudes formed itself around Barbie's thefts. She stole mainly from mother and brother, who became the investigators, while father pitied and defended her.

Mother had been in psychiatric treatment over many years and had grown to depend on it for her very existence, but both parents were ready to work for a change in the family. Arrangements were made for Barbie to continue her twice-weekly hours, for her brother to start treatment in the near future, and for the parents to be seen alternately. We shall now return to Barbie.

The first six months showed that she could communicate through art expression. In fact, she introduced most of her prob-

lems in her drawings and paintings during that time. The next
year and a half of therapeutic work consisted of Barbie's successful effort to express her feelings about herself within the family.
Her hours were filled with spontaneous expression in art, in play,
and in games, and were accompanied by steadily though slowly
increasing verbal expression.

In games, she expressed at first the attitude "People are out
to hurt me, so I'd better fix them before they hurt me."

Later, she expressed the more relaxed feeling "Well, they are
not that mean to me, so maybe I can now afford to play fair."
She then began to enjoy games.

In play, she found release for her rage and suppressed ag-
gressiveness by hitting the punching bag and by shooting down
tall, populated structures built of blocks and cartons.

Art expression was predominant, however. She occupied
herself with drawing and painting, especially finger painting,
which she used in a new way. Gone were the old confused circular movements in muddy puddles of paint, about which she said,
when she found an early sheet, "You don't even know where it
starts and where it ends; it's all so mixed up, like a madness!"
She was now more and more able to specify what she felt, and
she expressed this by painting in clear color. Only color repro-
ductions would show effectively these stripes and circular shapes,
clearly defined by color alone with no overlay. There were over
40 such finger paintings. Eventually Barbie declared them boring
and moved on to representational work.

These productions deal with three general themes: houses,
trees, and portraits, which can be interpreted as self-portraits.
Through these themes Barbie was able to express her problems
about herself and about her relationship with her parents.

It will be remembered that Barbie introduced the theme of
houses in Figure III-6, the house that was also her dog. Figure
III-7 was drawn in black crayon, not long after the house-dog
painting. It is an austere and stern-looking linear drawing with
no attempt at suggesting depth. It represented Barbie's withdrawal to her old detachment, expressed also by the sign, "For
Sale."

This mood continued in a number of similar drawings. Then

Figure III-7.   Crayon; House for Sale

came expressions of aggressive feelings in some paintings of broken-up houses. Finally, the house theme climaxed in a long series of paintings all named "House on Fire." There were well over a dozen of these.

In one of them (Fig. III-8), the frame of the house is painted in bright red (which shows dark in the illustration); between the reds is a glaring green. The fire seems to be spreading; the window on the right is falling out, the wall on the left is folding in, and fire is seen in the doorway (see Color Plate V).

In Figure III-9, Barbie painted the roof black "because it's all burned up now," and she actually tore pieces out of it with the handle of the brush while the painting was wet, saying, "Now the roof will be falling in. Anybody who sticks around better move away if you want to stay alive." On the house wall, red and blue fire is spreading (see Color Plate VI).

Figure III-10 was named "A House on Fire and Children Dancing." Barbie started this painting with a carefully executed Rorschach-style blot in muddy rose poster paint. At first the blot suggested only flames, and there were no outlines of a house or of trees; the faded rose did not suggest a very fiery fire, though.

Figure III-8.   Poster paints; House on Fire

Figure III-9.   Poster paints; House on Fire

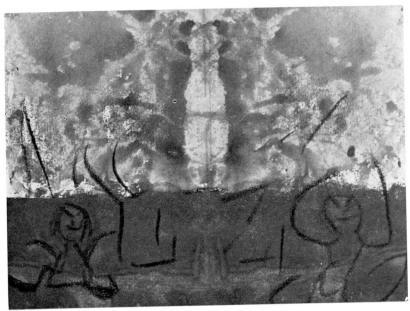

Figure III-10.   Poster paints and crayon; House on Fire

When Barbie was satisfied with the symmetry of the blot, she painted the lower part of the paper brown "for ground"; when this was fairly dry, she outlined with dark blue crayon on both sides of the center trunks of trees and two children dancing in the foreground; there was actually no house. She then explained that the whole center, vertically, was a picture of "Guess who? The Creature," referring in this way to the violent forces still acting inside her. She also explained that there were two cloud-like areas in darker rose on the upper left and upper right, and discovered just then that there was a profile in lighter color in the middle of each of the clouds looking down. When we tried in half-play to guess who the profiles might be, Barbie shyly and seriously whispered, "My parents?" This was an indication, how-ever small, of a dawning feeling that her parents were beginning to see her and perhaps to accept her.

Barbie stopped painting fires and the parents reported that actual fire-setting had long been abandoned. Figure III-11, the last house, painted after a long interval, was a conventional

Figure III-11.   Crayon; A House

crayon drawing for a little girl her age. It shows a house with a chimney and some smoke, a flower pot of red flowers in the front window and the face of a girl with red bow and red dress in the side window. The curtains are pink and there are two trees. Asked about this house, Barbie said, "Yes, a family lives in it. They're cooking dinner now." What an interesting sequence of houses from Figure III-6 through Figure III-11!

Throughout the months of the fire paintings, at times even within one hour, Barbie was also building out of the plastic bricks her houses with balconies and columns and ornate entrances. The difference between these complex, sophisticated structures and the rather simple, often infantile paintings of houses was striking. While she enjoyed her skill and a sense of accomplishment in construction with a pre-formed material, she expressed basic and more authentic feelings in her use of amorphous material, paint. Both modes of producing houses were used at the same time and they probably complemented each other as they also contrasted with each other.

The second theme, the tree, had also been introduced by Barbie during the first six months when she painted the only tree during that time, "A Tree, Two Colors." In her everyday life, many of Barbie's activities centered around trees: she climbed trees with the boys in the neighborhood; she had practiced her sex play, which had now subsided, under trees; sometimes she buried her stolen goods under trees; and there was a tree house to hide in.

Soon after the first six months, Barbie made a pencil drawing of a tree (Fig. III-12), about which she explained, "There is nothing on it, so it's winter." Three months later she made another pencil drawing of a tree (Fig. III-13) and said, "With all these leaves, it's summer."

A few weeks later, Barbie painted Figure III-14, a brown, tall trunk topped by light green foliage. While she was shading the trunk, she was asked how she liked this tree. Her answer was, "It's kind of a happy tree, green and all, but you can't climb it."

Figure III-12.   Pencil; A Tree

Figure III-13.   Pencil; A Tree

Somehow, this answer was reminiscent of Barbie's early painting of the first six months, "Happy Man, Up in the Air" (Fig. III-3). Perhaps she was trying to say that father could not be reached or that he was not quite there. At about that time, father himself and even mother began in their own individual hours to work through the problem of remoteness and its impact on the members of the family. Father realized that he had been leading a detached existence, and mother was able to take a new look at Barbie's attempts at alienating her husband from her.

In Figure III-15, three themes overlap. First theme: the girl in a red dress and with red eyes tries to approach the tree or to reach out for it, but, as she said about Figure III-14, "You can't climb it." The absence of hands and legs underlines the inability of reaching the tree. Second theme: the girl's dark hair suggests in both color and line the movement of the flying birds. Perhaps that was Barbie's unconscious way of saying that those who can be "up in the air," the detached ones such as father and

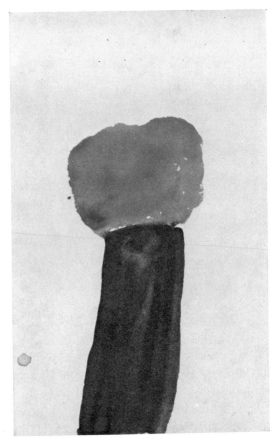

Figure III-14.   Poster paints; A Tree

brother, can be happy, and that she is not included among them. Third theme: the tree as a phallic symbol. The split on the trunk and the heavy shading on the tree and on the girl's hair strongly suggest Barbie's inner conflicts about sexual identity, and about being good or bad and hated or loved.

The girl in Figure III-15 also represents the third theme in Barbie's paintings, the self-image. This had also been introduced in the first six months, in the painting of the green "terrible creature" (Fig. III-5). It was the only representation of the self-image at that time. That creature symbolized a person driven from within to violent and uncontrolled actions.

Figure III-15.   Poster paints; Girl and Tree

In Figure III-15, painted a short time after the six months' period was over, the legless and armless girl in the red dress is no longer disheveled and violent; rather, she seems to be reaching out. Her hair suggests a new need to fly up, but her body is still immobilized by fear of her own anger and confusion.

Figure III-16 is one of many paintings that Barbie made at home and in school on scraps of paper. The girl has legs, thin and unstable; the whole body seems to be moving forward. The head and neck are outlined in blue, the dress in red, and the legs and feet are thin red lines and dots.

Four months later, at the end of the first year of therapy, when Barbie's stealing became worse and she was even less ready to talk about it, she drew with pencil some pictures, of which Figure III-17 is typical. This is a scared-looking girl. She has stronger legs, but her arms are rigidly close to her body; and she seems to be lost on the lower part of the large paper. This painting was done at the time of Barbie's most intense stealing from mother and brother. Only then did she begin to realize that she

Figure III-16.   Poster paints; A Girl

Figure III-17.   Pencil; A Girl

wanted mother more than anything else, and that she was really competing with her brother.

At the same time, however, many changes occurred in Barbie's behavior. She was more openly emotional now, and her ways of showing such emotions as anger, sorrow, or joy were specific and authentic. The screaming spells were replaced by quiet sobbing when she felt hurt; and while she was sobbing, Barbie could be approached and talked to. She began to mention mother in positive ways. School gained new importance in her thoughts. She looked prettier, was bright-eyed, and smiled frequently.

Figure III-18 was the first of her many paintings about school and home. She used a new technique, scratching lines into wet paint. She covered the large sheet of paper with a coat of lively rose poster paint which she had mixed out of red and white and drew her picture with the pointed end of a thin wooden brush handle. There was a new freedom about her scribbly way of drawing and at the same time a concentrated attention to all the

Figure III-18.   Poster paints; My House and My School

things she wanted to include. At the same time, she was describing in words what she drew on the rose-colored surface.

At the upper left, she sketched a house and wrote on it "My house"; at the far left edge of the paper, she drew a tree, and between the house and the tree, she placed "Mom, to see us off." It was the first time mother appeared in any of Barbie's paintings. A path leads from the house to the avenue labeled by name at the bottom of the paper, and "My school" is on the right, filling a considerable part of the painting. The round scribbles are trees and shrubs. Barbie and her brother had just turned from the path to the avenue on their way to school with lunch in their hands, the first time her brother appears in a painting.

This was a new kind of painting. There was the freedom of scribbling, yet the space was well used, with important elements of the painting placed in important positions on the paper. There was movement, direction, and intent as well as contact and belonging; the children both had all their limbs and they knew where they were going. The two items that were rather sketchy were mother and home, especially when compared with the clarity of the children, the school, the path, and the avenue. The most important thing about this production was its wholeness. Barbie's mode of describing her work was correspondingly coherent.

Shortly after "My School," Barbie one day scrawled some sketchy figures of girls and suddenly asked, "Hey, can I make a Japanese or something?" She produced Figure III-19, looked at it, and announced, "I didn't make a Japanese. It's a girl, just a regular girl with a ponytail. She is busy going somewhere." To be sure, the girl is not quite as "regular" as one would like her to be. She is leaning toward the back and her arms and hands are quite weak. But she is on her way.

SUMMARY

A study of two years of psychotherapy through art expression with a bright eight-and-a-half-year-old girl was presented. Violent and depressed at the start, the child could not function normally and was threatened by verbal communication. She could not

Figure III-19.   Pencil; A Regular Girl

control herself and was hard for others to control. She responded
to art media which offered her release and a way to state her
emotional problems.

FOLLOW-UP

When she was ten and a half, Barbie stopped therapy for a
while. She came back a year later and stayed another year to
work specifically on the problem of stealing as it tied in with her
relationship to mother and brother. At age fifteen, Barbie came
back for the last time. For a few months she worked to understand what had happened in her childhood, and to clarify her

attitudes toward boys, her brightness, and her future. She had done well in school, particularly in the sciences and in physical education.

In Barbie's senior year, mother called to report the parents' happiness about Barbie's interest in physical education and the leadership of church youth groups and her winning of a college scholarship in physical education.

Four years later, I received an invitation to Barbie's graduation from college. She is now a physical education teacher, active with church youth groups, and recently married.

IV

Julie

Each of these drawings was made on the bottom of an eight-and-a-half by eleven sheet of paper in response to a standardized drawing test. Because of Julie's compulsive need to cover the rest of the drawing sheets with her signatures, the drawings had to be cut out so as not to show her name. Reproduced here in the original size, they were carefully placed in their original locations on identical sheets of paper. Patients asked to draw a house, a tree, and a person usually do just that. But Julie, who was seven years and four months, did much more than that. She volunteered about Figure IV-1 that "this is a palace and also a house,"

Figure IV-1. Pencil; A House

described Figure IV-2 as "one little tree on a big, big mountain," and introduced Figure IV-3 as "a person, it's me." She then proceeded to sign her full name and insisted on doing this as many times as she could on each of the pages, aggressively and with pride.

Born in a Far Eastern city and reared in a foundling home there, Julie was sent, at the age of two, to the United States for adoption by a very intelligent family consisting of young parents with two sons, aged three and seven. She was an unusually beautiful and outgoing baby, the parents said, and had originally been selected by the nurses of the foundling home for this adoption because of her self-assertiveness and her obvious brightness. At that time, the child understood her native language very well and spoke a number of words. Over five years later, despite her early adoption by a well-educated family rich in verbal communication, Julie spoke with a strong Chinese accent, had a limited vocabulary and had trouble pronouncing such sounds as

Figure IV-2.   Pencil; A Tree

Figure IV-3.   Pencil; A Person

g, th, and r. She had no understanding of clock time or of calendar
time, and did not even know the days of the week, let alone the
months and the seasons. She also did many things that seemed
rather bizarre. For example, on most unpleasant dreary days,
Julie would come in with a strange, detached smile and say,
"Isn't it nice outside today?" It was evident that she was not in-
tending this as humorous. Her name was the only thing she could
write at the time of my first contact with her. She was repeating
her second year in kindergarten and posed a serious problem of
placement for the next year. She had not responded to reading
or writing instruction beyond mastering her own name. Some
remedial reading instructors insisted on placing Julie in a class
for retarded children. In addition, she had a bad stutter and,
being of foreign origin, her pronounciation was poor. During her
first meeting with me, Julie kept pushing herself into my chair,
aggressively clinging to me.

On the basis of early observations and of the first three

drawings, even before I tested her further, I did not think that Julie was retarded. It seemed to me that she thought of herself as an infant; that she felt different, perhaps special, and was very lonely and afraid; and finally, that she lived in a world of concealed fantasy and was really overwhelmed with confusion. But, I thought, she was ambitious and aggressively self-assertive.

Julie was quite willing to be tested, and tried her best to cooperate and to succeed. Her good performance on the Bender-Gestalt Test eliminated the possibility of organicity. She did have some trouble drawing Figure 8, a generally complex figure which also suggests the idea of mother and child.

Julie scored a Full Scale IQ of 120 on the WISC. This placed her in the superior group in general intelligence, and there were also indications of a higher potential. The analysis of the IQ was of special interest because of the significant difference between the Performance (128) and the Verbal (110) IQs. This difference was an indication of two problems: the verbal handicap and the emotional disturbance.

The test also brought out Julie's good comprehension but limited information, and there were indications of sound, practical thinking in problematic social situations.

Personality tests, such as the Rorschach or the TAT story-telling procedures revealed that Julie clung to infancy and that her inner world was overwhelmingly tumultuous and chaotic. The resistance to growing up found its expression in a resistance to and a fear of learning. Yet at the same time, she was eager to learn how to read and write; however, blocked by something deep inside, this eagerness was translated into an obsessive need to sign her name wherever she could and to cling to her picture-reading atlas, which she carried everywhere.

There were indications of fantasy life, but the verbal expressions of it were most inadequate. The performance that most expressively stated what emotional forces might have dominated Julie's inner life at the time was her response to the Exciting Scene assignment. That task calls for making with toys and blocks a scene so exciting that it might be seen on the motion picture screen. With no hesitation, Julie put together a room with

four people seated in it. She spread white cotton loops (designated for making potholders) over an area outside the room and
threw a doll baby on it. With much stuttering she explained that
the baby had been thrown out in the snow "because she was
bad." Julie used much ingenuity and acted quite independently
in search of a way to imitate snow. She used the material to the
best advantage and showed rhythmic grace of movement while
she was arranging the white loops. The same theme of a child
left out in the cold appeared, earlier in the battery of tests, in
one of Julie's stories. While the verbal presentation was impoverished and lifeless, the performed scene was filled with
dramatic feeling.

Julie's parents accepted a program that was worked out for
her. She was placed in the first grade with special instruction in
speech, and an individual summer course in reading readiness
was planned. At home she was to be helped to feel and behave
like a seven-year-old girl going on eight. She was to be introduced slowly and patiently to the everyday aspects of reality,
such as telling time, the meaning of money, names of local streets,
the days of the week, small shopping tasks, and other chores. It
was through her persistent rejection of such aspects of life that
Julie's infantilism was nurtured and her feeling of being a stranger
in a new land maintained.

Julie's understanding and willing parents immediately started
for her a program of psychotherapy three times a week and made
separate weekly appointments for each.

Julie turned to art media quite naturally, in the beginning
mostly to finger painting. She produced a vast collection of
paintings, but none of these could be effectively photographed.
With much anxiety or eagerness, and with sparks of anger or
delight in her long narrow eyes, Julie tirelessly fingered bright
and dark paint, invariably mixing it into a muddy, sticky mess.
There was a correspondence between the motions of her hands
and the expressions of her face, really a drama of movement.
Julie's fingers punched, poked, and scratched through finger
paint and paper. Her fists whirled through the slosh and climaxed
in a splash. "I love to make a mess," she used to exclaim.

In time, however, I noticed that these exclamations were her way of controlling her powerful impulses, for the exclamations had the function of summing up what had been and were usually followed by a change toward moderation. She would then clean up and agreeably accept a suggestion to make one more painting with less than a sea of paint, and to see if she could allow it to dry so we could have a painting to mount during her next visit and then to keep in her folder.

Eventually, Julie began to experience and express warm feelings in the form of concern for small objects drowned in her puddles of finger paint. If a pencil, a toy saucer, and a paper towel were to be rescued, Julie rushed to the hardest hit of the lot, giving to it all the gentle care she could muster, while I earnestly helped her. It seemed to me that the child was acting out a long-forgotten yet deep-seated emotional experience which had overwhelmed her before she was capable of knowing what was happening.

The muddy finger painting as well as the flood-and-rescue game slowly played itself out by the end of five months. That whole period had been marked by little talk and by intense facial expressions. At first, Julie's play in the muddy paint was probably also a way of venting her very threatening impulses. She was able to do this because I was there, always allowing it up to a point, occasionally participating in it, checking it. When the flood-and-rescue routine developed, I thought perhaps it indicated an increase of rational thinking, perhaps only prelexical thinking.

When she reached out, in the second half of the year, for brush and poster paints, she seemed to need them as a means of self-control. Figure IV-4 was produced with poster paints in the style of finger painting. The pool is still there, occupying the center. It is black and gives the impression of depth. Around this center are many blobs of bright colors, darkened with some black. Julie imprinted these with a paper towel dipped in paint. She did not title or describe this depressing painting nor was she asked to do so. But her mood was serious, if not depressed. When I asked her how the painting made her feel, she said that she did not know what I meant. One year later, when she came across the

Figure IV-4.   Poster paints; The Pool

painting in her folder, Julie discerned at the upper left the image of a lady in a long dress, worried "because the girl went swimming in this lake and she didn't come up yet." These words were spoken with apprehension and I wondered what anxieties the child had felt but had not been able to express verbally when she painted the picture a year earlier.

Julie's reaction to bad weather had grown more bizarre and it was time to discuss it with her. She repeated her comments about the nice weather in a succession of visits over a particularly rainy period early in the spring. The last time, however, she interrupted herself abruptly to give me a long, sheepish look and to smile with embarrassment.

She informed me that the same comment had turned the whole family against her the night before and that she had decided not to repeat it for me this time lest I, too, turn away from her. But she recalled her decision too late. So Julie sat snugly with me in my chair, the way she liked to sit when we talked seriously, and was helped to put into a pattern the strange things she was doing, probably out of fear.

I brought out a few of the picture cards about which Julie had composed stories of her storytelling test. Most of her heroes had faced grave danger or death, but in the end, Julie always pronounced them saved or cured, almost magically. In her stories, just as on the stormy days, Julie was turning threat into safety by the magic of a word. This was happening, however, at the cost of pretense. Thus, she was alienating herself from her real feelings and also alienating people, for in this way she encouraged them to form negative judgments about her. "They think I'm some kind of nut," Julie said.

Since Julie's vocabulary was so very limited, she had to be taught certain words essential in the therapeutic work. The first was "pretend." She understood immediately. Yes, she said, she had been pretending a lot, but she would only talk about the example at hand, the "Isn't it a nice day?" since the other things were her secrets. She was really saying that she was not yet ready to tell me about her fantasies. That day, Julie understood that in addition to her need to turn danger into safety (as she put it, "an awful thing that will happen into a happy thing that better happen") she was also trying to test significant people to see whether they still accepted her. It was possible that she even forced rejection in order to feel sorry for herself. After this, she stopped pretending about the weather for good and all.

Figure IV-5, made with poster paints, was Julie's dream about a monster. On the left he stands, tall, his body in dark green and his head blue with black features. At bottom center, teen-agers are shown throwing a bomb at him. The monster is not hit, but the teen-agers die in the explosion, indicated by a smoky green, blue, and black blot in the upper center. On the viewer's far right, behind a black rock, are two small stooping figures, a boy and Julie, in blue and red. Out of this hiding place, they are shooting into the explosion while pieces are being torn away from the rock; their shots are suggested by green staccato lines (see Color Plate VII).

Julie stuttered badly while she was describing the painting.

Figure IV-5.   Poster paints; The Monster Dream

Her speech was agitated, excited, and confused, and she cried when she talked about her own part in the dream: she had hid, then found the boy and exclaimed, "He will be a helper," and finally, there was the shooting. She then looked at her painting in long silence and angrily said, "I must have been so mixed up." Her hiding from the teen-agers, yet shooting on her own, did not make sense to her.

Slowly, Julie was beginning to understand something about her own conflicts and about her great anger that sat deep inside her and, she said, "grabbed a chance to come out." She also became aware of her frequent preoccupation with the threat for which teen-agers stood. With a sense of relief she accepted a general classification of age groups which I offered her and promptly placed herself and the little boy in that of late childhood, still securely removed from adolescence.

The outstanding by-product of Figure IV-5 was a first conversation about Julie's stutter. She herself noticed that her stutter was at its worst when she was describing her own shooting into the explosion. She was fascinated to hear that she could now watch her own stutter and see it get better when she was calm inside, or worsen whenever she experienced confusion or a struggle between two different feelings. This was illustrated by Julie with many examples, particularly about reading, which was smooth or rough according to how she felt at the time. As usual, through dramatic movement rather than words, she communicated the conflicts of two feelings with her arms and fingers, acting out the clash "when one [feeling] wants to do one thing and the other, another."

Figure IV-6, "Grasshopper in the Grass, Really Outside," was done in the same period of bad stuttering. A yellow sun shines with blue rays on the grass, which is the main part of the painting, a jumble of green and brown brush strokes. At the bottom of the sheet stands a large, green grasshopper, more like an animal than an insect. "The grasshopper had just come out of the grass, there is a storm in the grass, that's why the grasses go every which way, and that's what my mother says about my hair," said Julie. I commented that the grasshopper looked thoughtful and wondered what he might be saying to himself.

Figure IV-6.   Poster paints; The Grasshopper

Julie replied, "He says, 'Should I go back in the storm or should I quietly wait here?'"

This interesting answer implied conflict, not only in Julie, but also in her surroundings. To be sure, there were overtones in this painting of actual turmoil in the family beneath the surface. Besides Julie's own tensions, expressed in this particular painting in the jumbled grass going "every which way," there was the tension between mother and father perhaps represented by the grasshopper outside the grass. Father himself was in conflict about whether to become more deeply involved in the family affairs or to maintain his relative detachment. On the other hand, Julie herself could be the grasshopper, in conflict between becoming truly one of the family and staying on the outskirts, remaining different.

As soon as I mentioned something about the latter possibility, speaking only in terms of the grasshopper and not directly of Julie, she picked up the theme with great excitement. She proceeded to abandon herself totally to the role of the grasshopper coming home from school to meet the family.

In ways reminiscent of the early finger painting, she used bodily movement and facial mimicry instead of words. Her playacting epitomized her way of acting in real life: she hopped over to the toy shelves to sniff them and proceeded to toss aggressively across the room those of the toys which she, as grasshopper, disliked. When I stopped her from doing this, she quietly returned to the role of the insect coming home. She rejected my suggestion that she use the doll house with the flexible dolls, instead assigning to me the job of acting "all the persons in our house," each time another member of the family.

There was, however, no need for me to act at all, for Julie promptly took over. She started hugging me as mother so hard that I was soon almost pulled down to the floor; she greeted father by winding her wiry body around my leg, pushing me into the chair, and riding on my lap, pressing down hard; when I played her ten-year-old brother, she poked me slightly and removed herself from me; and when I was her fourteen-year-old brother, she pulled at me angrily and spoke in baby talk.

Julie's abandonment to her fantasy and her use of it as a way of demonstrating her aggression illustrated vividly the parents' descriptions of events at home. There was something very powerful about her behavior which I would not have grasped if I had not experienced it.

Figure IV-7 was produced with chalks two weeks later at a time when Julie had again lost ground in her school work. She had to start at the beginning of a reader which she had just successfully finished, not only being quite unable to proceed to the next reader, but also hardly able to remember letters and the sounds they stood for.

The painting consists of black lines and spots overlaid with blue and green and framed with shaded bands of green and violet. Outside the frame at the upper left corner, Julie painted in blue and green a small girl with raised arms. The painting disturbed her and she wondered, stuttering, why she "put the girl up there."

I hung Figure IV-6, The Grasshopper, next to Figure IV-7. Julie was startled by the similarities between these two produc-

Figure IV-7.   Chalks; Jumbled Lines with Girl

tions and pointed to the most important ones: the confusion of the lines which filled both sheets of paper, and the placement of the figure "outside the picture." She also said laughingly, "I was a grasshopper already; now I have to be me." She was happier about the grasshopper painting than she was about the painting with the girl, but did not know why.

To be sure, Julie had good reasons to be happier with Figure IV-6, even though she was not conscious of them. While we see in it a few realistic references such as grass, sun, and storm, such features are absent from Figure IV-7. There, pure color almost took over. This was reminiscent of two of Julie's Rorschach responses, the first indication of the child's powerful impulses which she found so hard to control.

Julie, in producing Figure IV-7, overlaid her base of black in a most disorganized way. Even her attempt at painting a frame got out of hand and broke down into fragmentary strokes.

Covering black with cold colors contrasted with Julie's early finger painting when she would overlay hot colors with black. Both procedures — covering bright color with black, and the opposite — suggest a struggle to check powerful, pressing impulses.

The overlay of blue and green on black might also suggest Julie's effort to pretend that all was well. When I asked her what the girl might be saying, she answered, " 'It's a mess,' she says, 'it's all smeared up, but Dr. B doesn't mind and I kind of like it.' "

There was a message for me in these words. They told me that my intuitive acceptance of Julie and her art expression must be supplemented by conscious understanding. Her fantasies and acting-up served as vital defenses which she must be allowed to maintain until she could develop enough inner strength to do without them.

After a few more pictures similar to Figure IV-7, Julie began to work with clay, first at the very primitive level of pleasure in just squeezing chunks of it. Sometimes aggression seemed predominant, sometimes pure enjoyment; most of the time there was a mixture of the two. She would eagerly pound the clay on a board or on a cement floor, shouting with anger or joy. When she eventually settled down to making objects, they could be grouped into two categories: (1) containers or receptacles and (2) scenes with some social and personal significance. One showed three cars going in different directions, while a tiny human figure, caught between them, was trying to cross the street. Another showed a revolving door with "too many people and dogs" caught in one of its compartments, "so now they won't be able to move until the people who made the door come and help." A third scene was "The Igloo Man and His House." Julie gave this production much attention and took it to school for display.

The production of the igloo man was associated with two experiences currently converging in Julie's life, one real and the other imaginary. The realistic aspect was represented by the unit on Eskimo life in social studies at school, which had brought out Julie's concealed abilities and her new studiousness and alertness. All of this astounded her teacher. On the other hand, the appeal which the Eskimo unit held for Julie was animated by a fantasy she had been acting out at home and in her visits with me over the preceding month.

During this period, Julie would build an igloo-type dwelling out of cartons, wrappings, cushions, and any odd materials she could find. She would crawl into it for a while and talk to herself aloud but not clearly enough for me to understand her. She did not call it an igloo, she was just "building a house," but as she crawled into it, she did speak of "how good the Eskimo feels when he comes from the cold outside into his warm little igloo."

For some time now, a few positive changes had become apparent. Julie's behavior was generally less bizarre, she was calmer and better put together. She met my eyes with a clear look, clung to me less often, and almost always knew the time of day and the day of the week. Also, the periods of scholastic retrogression were somewhat shorter now and Julie was beginning to be aware of being backward for her age in school. Her parents also felt that Julie was "more here and now" and that she knew better what was going on.

These changes coincided with the end of Julie's first-grade

school year. Now, of course, she posed a new placement problem.

At this time, Julie was diagnosed as being at the beginning of the first-grade level in oral reading, within the first-grade range in silent reading, satisfactory in writing and numbers, low in rhyming common words, and "unable to sustain her attention for the completion of the last three of the ten tests on the Keystone Visual Survey."

In answer to the school's request for a psychological report and recommendations, I wrote, among other things: "At eight and a half, Julie has high-average intelligence, but her verbal development is still seriously lagging behind her ability to perform. That ability, however, is used by Julie imaginatively and effectively. She is now only beginning to come out of the fairy-tale world in which she was engrossed, and she still has a long way to go. In that world, words and numbers were unnecessary. Coming to reality will make them important. Julie is essentially an ambitious child who will do well when she is ready to set her mind to it. The prospect of promotion to a higher grade may now become a powerful incentive for her. Even though this child is still overstimulated by her own impulses, she is on the whole much calmer now and therefore more receptive to tutoring. Emphasis on the expressive aspects or oral language will help her deal more effectively with reading and writing."

Julie was placed in a combination second-third grade class.

This was also the end of her first year of psychotherapy. Her behavior was still often inappropriate even though her general, diffuse confusion had been checked. In fact, in view of her improved orientation to reality, the lapses were even more conspicuous now.

Sometimes she would suddenly forget her age and even her name. She might lose her ability to read, or mutilate certain words and pretend that she did not know what she was doing. She made constant demands on mother, always annoying her and sometimes hurting her physically by digging her fingernails into mother's hand. She wore old worn-out clothes instead of the pretty things mother bought for her, lost coats and tore sleeves and pockets. She took things from her brothers' room or annoyed father when he was busy. She seemed to vacillate between acting like Katie, a five-year-old, very infantile friend, and Jean, a twelve-year-old domineering friend.

The second year of psychotherapy centered on the three specific emotional difficulties which had contributed to Julie's impulsivity and inner unrest in the past.

We stumbled upon the first of the three problems when Julie invited me to crawl into the igloo house which I had just helped her build. I bravely agreed, expressing my hope of having a chance to hear what she was saying aloud to herself. "That's the idea," said Julie, "Only people who live there can understand what I say." Thus, I was initiated into one of Julie's most important fantasies. She was queen. As queen, she spoke in a continuous, commanding flow of smooth speech, with no trace of stutter or stammer.

As an infant princess, she had been "grabbed away" by her present mother. Julie then became queen and had to marry the king because she thought that "to be a queen, you have to have a king." Now she saw no need for a king and this castle was all hers. She knew how to be queen without learning "from him . . . see, there are no schools for queens because the queens know how to be queens." This explanation went on for about ten minutes. Then Julie's royal speech began to deteriorate, and suddenly she tore off the coverings, and allowed the light to come into the castle. She exclaimed in a practical, this-worldly voice, "It's hot here. Let's get out of here!" I had been initiated into the regal fantasy when it was on its last leg. It had long become a burden with its guarded secrecy heavily weighing upon Julie.

The compulsive building of igloo castles was abandoned. Now Julie felt free to develop her fantasy in paintings and sculpture over the next few weeks.

Figure IV-8 is a colorful picture in chalk and crayon of a royal scene near the palace gate. The king in the foreground and the queen behind him are about to enter the palace. The queen will enter by a secret side door. The king will try to approach the gate, but will never reach the palace: he will not be killed, but will just vanish. This will be accomplished through the queen's knowledge of magic, said Julie with a twinkle in her eye.

Figure IV-8.   Chalk and crayon; King and Queen

The colors are red for the queen; brown and orange for the king; the palace is rose with black outlines; the gate green, blue, and black; and the sky is a reddish blue. The entire effect is romantic with a touch of threat in the air (see Color Plate VIII).

Figures IV-9 and IV-10 are sculptures of the queen. In the first, "the queen is mad with the king and has a red face." It is interesting that the angry queen's eyes, narrowed to long slits, look like Julie's eyes when she is angry. The queen shown in Figure IV-10 "is happy and also unhappy." Happy because she is finally alone and in power, and unhappy "because of what she had done." The face is painted yellow with black, somewhat distorted features. Julie disliked this sculpture and wondered why I wanted to keep it on the shelf.

Figure IV-11 is a painting with chalks. Against a light brown background is an interesting design of lines in orange, yellow, and violet. Below, we see a procession of dancing worshipers participating in some rite. The figures, all painted green, are depositing their offerings in a vessel or on an altar (see Color

Figure IV-9.   Clay; Mad Queen

Figure IV-10.   Clay; Happy and Unhappy Queen

Plate IX). The tall figure on the far right is the queen. She had just rescued the long-lost princess contained in one of the offerings, but it had turned out to be only her dream, and in her hand

Figure IV-11.   Chalks; The Queen's Rites

is only a potted plant. Quite interesting in design and esthetically pleasing, the painting benefited from instruction given by the visiting art teacher at school. In mood, it appeared to be a nostalgic painting about a fantasy that had been. When she completed the painting, Julie was smiling sadly but was not depressed.

Figures IV-8 through IV-11 comprise Julie's expression in art of the first of the three large problem areas: her regal fantasy. Except for the last, these productions were conscious illustrations of a story that was past.

The royal fantasy nurtured Julie's inner life and behavior over a span of at least two to three years. Most probably it reached its height when the child was first brought for psychological help. That was the time when Julie jealously guarded her "secrets." The extraordinary hold of this fantasy on the child is most intriguing. What made it so intense? What emotional ingredients went into the making of this powerful force which rendered everything outside it unimportant? And, finally, what was its function in the child's life at the time?

The most cautious way to attempt any answers to these questions might be an effort to see if we can put together into a meaningful whole what is given in the material itself provided by Julie in her psychological tests, in her art expressions, and in her verbal communication. The understanding of this experience can certainly not be compressed into one specific school of thought.

To begin with, the important emotional ingredients at the base of the fantasy were devastating feelings of deprivation: a feeling of paradise lost, a feeling of being different, and a feeling of not belonging. The overall reaction to those feelings was infantile rage, spread over the whole of personality. In order for the child to survive, some other experience, a greater one and one of gratifying value, had to arise and counteract the devastating forces. Total immersion in the royal fantasy was such an experience. It offered the gratification of power and reign over others in contrast to being forsaken and cut off.

If alleviation of the unspoken misery could be achieved at all, it would be only by magic. Magic was the answer to the child's gnawing wonderment about her unknown once-upon-a-time origin. What richer material for compensatory imaginings than tales of royalty with overtones of ancient Chinese court intrigues and with the added innovation of magic instead of cloak and dagger politics!

The infantile rage might have had its beginnings in the original, not-remembered act of abandonment by the biological parents, or in the child's intellectual knowledge that such might have been the case, or in the emotional abhorrence of having been subjected to this. The royal fantasy offered Julie a possibility of defensive displacement of the horrid deed from the biological parents onto the adoptive ones, specifically ascribing to mother the aggressive act of taking the baby away.

This, in turn, opened the way to vent suppressed aggressions and violent angers in relation to both mother and father. In reality, Julie struggled with mother about father and about power in the family, while she struggled with father for love and for mother's place by his side. This struggle was resolved in the fantasy when Julie became the absolute ruler, she alone wearing the crown. That triumph included the punishment of the king, or father who had not responded to her in reality. While she became in the fantasy both king and queen, she was also solving her struggle with each of the parents. It is of special interest that sometime near termination of the royal fantasy, Julie gave mother a picture she had painted on her own, of the family at dinner, with mother wearing a crown. The carry-over of this detail of the fantasy regalia into reality was Julie's final renunciation of her royal fantasy and of the conflict with her parents.

The renunciation might have also been a resolution of yet another conflict which made Julie's childhood even more difficult. It was the confusion of feminine and masculine identities, complicated by the child's precocious sexual impulses and excitements which were threatening, as were the impulses of aggression. Giving mother the crown was giving her the role of mother, wife, and female head of the family. It was giving up the struggle with mother for father's love. It was an acceptance by Julie of her own identity as the small girl.

The royal fantasy was also the locus and framework for the rise and fall of Julie's overwhelming sense of power, the distorted by-product of her disturbance. This was well expressed in the yellow-faced sculpture of the guilt-ridden queen. As soon as she modeled her own inner distortive forces and beheld them in the production, Julie disliked the clay model. There was more reality and less threat in the strong and clear anger of the red-faced clay queen.

Indeed, that was but one of the few instances of a mixture of the real and unreal about both Julie's life and fantasy. In this sense, Julie was overwhelmed and confused rather than schizoid. As queen, she spoke a realistic language in fantasy, but an unrealistic one in life. On the other hand, there were unmistakable echoes in life of her reigning in fantasy. The little female tyrant of the fantasy, so reminiscent of ancient Chinese queens out of a Pearl Buck novel, demonstrated her violence, in small ways, in reality. Only, what seemed bizarre in reality was logical in the fantasy. Thus, in a way, the real and unreal complemented each other. Perhaps that was the way of the fantasy, to work for the approaching unity of the child's personality.

As in dreams, so in fantasies, roles are doubled or duplicated, situations move to strange settings, and actors find themselves to be suddenly somebody else. If we look at the royal fantasy as at a dream in an ongoing reel, we see Julie as poor and forlorn, as the overpowering mother, becoming mother, removing father, becoming he, ruling supreme, feeling distorted, searching for the princess child, becoming the lost child herself. Perhaps the latter can be seen as a return of the long lost need to be child.

Exhausted, the royal fantasy played itself out when it fulfilled its two psychological functions. One was survival. The other was to gradually guide the young dreamer back to reality out of the jungle of real and unreal. Figure IV-11 was Julie's last touch of the waning dream world.

She emerged from it a little wobbly, but real. There were now real parents, real feelings, and Julie, a real child. She was ready, perhaps even eager, to acknowledge that a crown was too heavy for her.

The second problem revolved around Julie's unconscious feelings about herself in relation to her baby sister, Peggy, then two years old. According to mother's usually reliable observations, Julie had shown neither hostility nor love for the new baby. She did develop guarded curiosity, and this allowed for her participation in some routines of baby care. When the baby grew to become an outgoing personality and, to everyone's delight, showed a great fondness for Julie, Julie felt threatened and became hostile. She was seen stepping on the infant's toys. Her exaggerated manifestations of love for the little sister turned into small acts of aggression. At that time, the little sister hardly existed in Julie's therapy hours.

Figure IV-12 was produced at a time when Julie and her sister shared a room due to building alterations in the house. On the viewer's far left is the infant, standing up in her crib and screaming. Julie appears twice: first, curled up in bed asleep; then

Figure IV-12. Felt pen; Sharing a Room

jumping out of bed, awakened by Peggy's screams. Before Julie
identified the figures by name and age, it was hard to discern
which was which. As she was writing the names and ages, two
and nine, Julie was struck rather suddenly by a discovery that
"Peggy is bigger than I!" There was much distress and sadness in
her voice. She described in words and gestures what the real sizes
were and began to scribble stick figures of two-year-olds and
nine-year-olds "for size." Having covered two large sheets of
paper with couples of little and big sisters, Julie felt better.

Over the next few visits, Julie talked eagerly about her age
and height in relation to that of each of her siblings and friends.
It was the first time that she paid special attention to her ten-
year-old brother, a very bright and successful sixth-grade pupil.
It occurred to her that perhaps she could do things with him,
since both she and he were "not teen-agers yet," while their older
brother was one. Her two friends, Katie and Jean, were discussed,
and Julie observed that two-year-old sister Peggy cried less and
talked more clearly than five-year-old friend Katie, and that
perhaps Katie felt like a baby. "Feeling two years old" and "feeling nine years old" were new phrases for Julie. She began to see
herself in perspective, more realistically than ever before.

Figure IV-13, made two months later, revealed the last of

the three emotional problem areas. This painful confrontation with the unreality of another of her fantasies occurred while she was drawing a family portrait with a felt pen.

Figure IV-13.   Felt Pen; Family Portrait

Even though Julie was capable of producing relatively sophisticated paintings and of applying acquired art techniques, she would regress to a primitive artistic level whenever she drew the family. Hence, the simple round shapes for heads. The shocking confrontation came when Julie began to identify in writing who was who. She had no trouble marking the first large head on the viewer's left as Daddy, but was beset by confusion at the marking of the second large head beside father. She wrote "B" for mother's name and crossed it out, then "M" for mommy and crossed that out. Then she wrote her own name underneath the already crossed out initials, but, with deeply reddened face and growing agitation, crossed that out, too. Exasperated, Julie proceeded to draw the row of children, below. On the left, she placed the younger of the boys, the oldest one in the middle; the next space to the right was left vacant, and the baby was placed on the extreme right, almost outside the family. Julie then returned to the space she had skipped, the pen suspended in the air. The problem of placing and identifying herself, actually declaring herself, grew unbearable. Julie tried hard to hold back her tears. She finally filled the space with a female head, slightly smaller than the female head above, but with an identical hairdo. The eyes of the smaller head were made so close together that they almost suggested seeing double. But now Julie was going through the same trouble with identification. She marked the smaller head with "J" for her own name and immediately crossed it out, then printed "M" for mommy and crossed that out, too. There was complete silence and deep tension for a long time while Julie gazed at her drawing, and I, compassion notwithstanding, waited for her to find a solution. Julie suddenly and sharply turned her head away from the drawing. Tears were running down her cheeks and she quietly said, "But I am not mommy." This was very painful, but she was brave. I saw her to the door with warm reassurances about the next visit.

The next time Julie came, she mentioned a dream about "a funny house with funny windows and a funny red roof," and immediately proceeded to paint it for me. This is shown as Figure IV-14. She recalled her wonderment about the windows in disarray and her feeling of guilt in the dream. The feeling of guilt, she recalled, was vague in the absence of any specific action or deed that she knew of, yet it was as clear as when a person knows "it's my fault." Julie's mother helped her recall that the picture resembled a small, picturesque candy shop where Julie had been to shop for candy at the age of about five.

Figures IV-15 and IV-16 were scenes in the candy shop which Julie recalled two visits later. In Figure IV-15, mother is buying Julie the candy she wants. In Figure IV-16, Julie promptly throws that same candy into the wastebasket. In the ensuing conversations, Julie came to realize that she was still, years later, rejecting what mother was giving her, only now it was clothes and perhaps even education or "with growing up." Julie wondered why she had to reject what mother gave her. When I put up Figure IV-13 for a possible clue, she said, "I know: when I wanted to *be* mommy, I didn't want anything *from* mommy."

Figure IV-14.   Crayon; House in a Dream

Julie was in a good mood, as though a weight were lifted from her shoulders. She talked humorously now about the "upset" faces in the family portrait and laughed about the two identical hairdos, even though mommy's hair was really short, blond, and wavy and her own was long, black, and straight.

Now Julie seemed to want to talk about father's face on the family portrait more than about the others. Perhaps she felt that this was her chance to talk of her uneasy feelings about him. At home, she said, everybody complained that she "pestered" him continuously. She thought that this was true and supplied ample information about her ways of annoying father: interrupting, demanding, clinging, talking excessively while he was driving in heavy traffic, and being angry with him for playing with Peggy. The most upsetting incident, which caused her much anguish, had occurred the Sunday before her current visit. As always on Sunday morning, she and Peggy were allowed to spend a while

Figure IV-15.   Crayons; Choosing Candy

in their parents' bed. While Peggy remained playful and happy, Julie began to feel a strong urge to push her father out of bed. She tried in vain to control the violent impulse. She thought that her father sensed her difficulty, for he announced that the play-visit was over, much to her relief. Julie said that she had been "shook up" for days because of what she had "wanted to do." That same week, Julie came into mother's bed when father was out of town and declared that she would be mother's husband for the night.

Figure IV-17, a colorful picture made with poster paints and resembling a younger child's work, was painted over a period of time in a number of versions at school, at home, and in her therapy. "This boy in blue overalls and red hat is going up some-where on this yellow flying carpet. It would be fun to go up like this; maybe it's me," said Julie. We were now ready to gather and put up all the paintings shown in Figures IV-13 through

Figure IV-16. Crayons; Throwing It Away

IV-17, with the addition of one blank sheet of paper. I asked Julie to imagine on that paper a painting of the Sunday morning scene in her parents' bed. When she completed the task of imaging the picture, we stepped back. Julie was to look at each of the paintings and finish the sentence, "Sometimes I want to be . . . " Julie was beginning to appear fascinated with the task, but she was also growing anxious. I sought to reassure her by putting my arm around her shoulders. She began to utter her sentences and heard herself in amazement enumerate mommy, Peggy, daddy, and a boy as the persons she had wanted to be. Many memories of wanting to be a boy came back to her and she spoke of them. At the end of that hour, the feelings about wanting to be Peggy and mommy were classified by Julie as "old business." And her feelings about father and about being a boy were summed up in her practical terms. "Nobody can be somebody else, except actors on television or when we put on a play in school."

Figure IV-17.   Poster paints; Boy on a Flying Carpet

Julie's confusion about her identity and role was, of course, part of a larger confusion between the real and the unreal. There certainly were sexual overtones to Julie's broad, general problem, and some of the parents' feelings, at the time of the adoption and later, which contributed to the child's emotional difficulties. These factors were discussed with each of the parents in his separate therapy hours.

In the course of time, both parents learned to understand that through periodic regressions, Julie was repeating the overwhelming chaos originally thrust upon her when she experienced her early crisis. Most probably, it had occurred when the infant had been cut off from the familiar language in which she was ready to communicate. Overwhelmed, the child was blocked with rage. The parents learned to observe that the present regressions, which could be seen as progress in comparison with Julie's generalized retardation of the past, were usually preceded by some crisis reminiscent of the original crisis at adoption. A difficult school assignment, a house guest, any change of routine, or even a trip with the family was enough to make Julie feel overwhelmed and lost.

The parents could now see that Julie had developed as a byproduct of the whole configuration of her problems, a sense of power, at times escalating to a notion of omnipotence, really quite scary for her. Some of her actions that contributed to the sense of omnipotence were manipulating significant adults, regaining through regression to infantile behavior the status of the exotic family doll, and aggressive impositions on others by means of bizarre behavior. Thus, her retrogressions were unconsciously used by Julie as a weapon. But the parents also learned now that Julie wanted to stop this and that she had to be helped to stop and to find new, constructive ways of behaving.

Figure IV-18, a new family portrait, was made with crayons about three months after Figure IV-13. It represented a substantial change in Julie's feelings about her identity and her role in the family. Evidenced in the new portrait was also a change

Figure IV-18.   Crayons; Family Portrait

in the way she viewed the family's inner structure and the relationships among its members.

The upper row consists now of father, mother, and the elder
son. Father is looking at mother; mother has brown hair and
blue eyes, much more realistically portrayed than on Figure
IV-13; the older brother is now removed from Julie in proper
proportion to their respective ages and interests.

In the lower row are all the younger children. The younger
brother is of a realistic size in comparison with one-year-younger
Julie. Julie has her own straight hair and black eyes, and is
properly placed between the second brother and her younger
sister. Finally, the little sister is appropriately smaller, curly

haired, and restored to a place within the family. Julie described this painting as "happy" and volunteered the reason: "I didn't push anybody out of their place, and I put me between Les and Peggy where I belong."

That year Julie was promoted to a combination third-fourth grade class. She was given a long summer vacation from tutoring and from psychotherapy.

An examination of Julie's numerous paintings and of my role during her third year in psychotherapy shows that for Julie it was a year of coming to grips with her deep-seated rage and violence. Anger, blocked and dormant in her first year of therapy and bizarre in the second, finally found its expression through art in the third year. When Julie unburdened herself of some of her violent feelings, she began to experience an inner readiness as well as a need to learn as part of growing up.

Figure IV-19, "Feeling bla," expresses rather well the mood of angry, acute regression which she experienced again at school in the beginning of the third year. This was a reaction to the teacher to whom Julie had been assigned upon my recommendation, in agreement with the parents and the principal. Sympa-

Figure IV-19.   Chalks; Feeling Bla

thetic and firm, the new teacher helped Julie in her slow progress, but in contrast to other teachers of the past, she did not treat Julie as special in any way and did not feel sorry for her. This enraged Julie. Sometimes in therapy, she furiously hurled toys as of old, or made feeble attempts at crawling into an igloo house. She forgot days and dates, and there returned for a day or two the imitating of the little girl friend. But now Julie showed an ability to express and to explain, by means of painting, what was happening inside her.

Figure IV-19, explained Julie, had a dark background of gray chalk for "madness"; the few red lines were intended to indicate a classroom. Julie, represented by her torso in black and orange, was alone in the classroom because she "wanted to be special" for the teacher, but she did not succeed in her effort. It was a sad picture, Julie thought, because the corners of the mouth were turned down and because the face was "mad and worried." During the next few sessions she returned to muddy finger painting and the old puddles of paint. At one point, I stopped her from spilling and splashing paint; she was relieved and wondered why I had not stopped her sooner.

When Julie came the next time, she brought the Oriental baby caftan in which she had arrived at her adoptive home at the age of two, and the early photographs with her new family. It seemed to me that she was trying, rather deliberately, to say or perhaps to ask something. There she was, a beautiful and outgoing baby, obviously loved and admired; but what had happened that made things go wrong? Julie nodded in tears when I worded that question for her. She was able to imagine aloud how a two-year-old might have felt in such a different world, and talked with compassion about her little sister, "the same age and size I was then," and how unhappy she might feel if she were suddenly plunged into new surroundings. We also talked about pouring out old angers and Julie wondered how it was possible to store so many of them. At that time, reports from school began to inform me of Julie's good progress in all subjects. Julie now understood that this new teacher's attitude was helpful.

One time, soon after the conversations about stored-up

angers, Julie rushed in and went straight to the board to paint a nightmare she had the night before. This is shown in Figure IV-20, made with orange and blue chalks.

On the right, Julie is asleep in her bed. On the left, she found herself confined in a box. Unable to move, she was terrified, and screamed for help. The blot of deep orange around the word "help!" vividly conveys the dreamer's anguish and cry (see Color Plate X).

There were more paintings of the box dream in various versions made during the next few visits. These introduced a struggle between "old me" and "new me," supervised by a "he"

Figure IV-20.   Crayons; The Box Dream

power. In still other paintings, the struggle took place between a little girl surrounded with toys and a grown girl with an open book behind her. Julie also told about and painted dreams of piles of books which she was unable to reach.

Figure IV-21, titled "School," did not look like a school at all. Julie, marked "me," was saying to the teacher during class-time, "What is all this fighting about? Let's be friends again." This had been a dream which brought out in grotesque fashion the characteristics of Julie's reading group and the way each pupil was fighting the teacher. There was Billy the clown, Ellie the baby, and Victor the bully. When I asked Julie about her way of fighting the teacher, she answered sweetly in a whisper, "I was poor dumb Julie."

Figure IV-21.   Crayons; The Classroom

Figure IV-22 portrayed another dream which upset Julie. She described the painting: "Here [left] I ['me'] and my teen-age brother, Jay, are exchanging guns to see which is better. The classroom is full of grown-ups, all seated in all these chairs, like for a P.T.A., maybe, and we kids are fighting the grown-ups. A man, the speaker, he looks like daddy, speaks and says, 'Why fight, what for?' while I am shooting, up there, into the building." The painting was titled "Look Up" (see Color Plate XI).

Violent impulsivity and practical rationality met and mingled in this painting. Perhaps rationality was taking over,

Figure IV-22.   Chalks and crayons; Look Up

for despite the shooting, the building remained untouched and the speaker had the last word. The shooter in the painting ("me") looked quite aggressive and determined. But Julie remembered the speaker's words and repeated them a few times. When I recalled similar words in another of her recent paintings, Julie knew that I meant her words to the teacher in the first classroom dream.

Julie volunteered that there had been a lot of fighting in her dreams and I reminded her of our talks in the past about stored-up old angers. This made sense to her and she expressed a hope that they would "all get out" and soon there would be no need to fight so much. That change had already started, I reminded her, in those very dreams, in the words of the speaker and in her own words to the teacher.

Figure IV-23 is one of a group of sculptures Julie modeled at about the same time. These colorfully painted clayworks depicted birds in a variety of family situations, feeding, nestling, or learning to fly. Julie said about this sculpture, "The little bird

Figure IV-23.   Clay; Mother and Child Birds

and the mother bird are cuddling together and they both like it, because *she* is her child and *she* is her mother." Julie took all the bird sculptures home as presents for mother. Mother, in turn, reported a new warmth coming from Julie. Once, when Julie painted one of her birds and then carefully placed it in a box to take it with her, a conversation developed about her recent modeling of birds. "They are cheerful and loving," she said and added with laughter, "Maybe I am cheerful and loving, too." Thus, again she summed up in her practical way the change in her emotional life from violence to love, from anger to warmth.

Julie was promoted to a combination fourth-fifth grade class, the first time in her school career without doubts necessitating conferences and psychological reports concerning placement. After an initial brief period of regression, she settled down to a year of steady progress with no need for remedial instruction in reading. Psychotherapy was reduced to one visit per week.

Julie's visits were now different. There was more maturity

and more authentic feeling in the way she chose to spend the hour. Her paintings expressed growth and participation.

Figure IV-24, a family camping scene, tells about the family and Julie's feelings about her place in it. The crisis was centered at this time on the older son, in conflict with the parents. In the painting, he is taking himself out of the family group, his head turned back toward Julie, who looks at him and feels for him, while she is flanked securely by the two remaining siblings. The parents are together. Though engaged at the moment in a bitter dispute with their son, they seem to be confident that life will go on to be enjoyed together. Happily watching the camping children, they allow the sun to act as baby-sitter.

Figure IV-24.   Crayons; Family Camping

In Figure IV-25, Julie introduced a problem which we later named the "Growing-up Problem": "On this path, a boy walks ahead of me. I feel terribly strange. I am in a hurry because I have a music lesson, but I cannot go ahead and pass him; and this is getting worse." The way Julie went about this painting was of special interest. When she had finished the road, the green,

Figure IV-25.   Chalks; Growing-up Problem

and the sidewalk; that is, the setting for the problem, she painted a purple trapezoid on the right for the girl's skirt and added her legs, then moved toward the left to paint the pants and shoes for the boy. As she finished both figures, she was thinking aloud: "It really is the boys, not just anybody, walking ahead of me."

There we were, talking openly and freely about boys and how self-conscious they made her feel. Then, laughing and with enjoyment, we drew together many paths and on them possible solutions to the problematic situation. The next time Julie arrived, she happily reported that her problem was solved, that she no longer felt self-conscious, and she actually walked ahead of two boys.

Figure IV-26 shows a large apple tree, well rooted, fruitful, and well placed on the paper. Red apples are falling to the ground "so the family and the guests can eat them." A picnic table is ready for the party, and an owl is peeking out of his hole "to see what's going on." A next painting shows the party around the table. Compared with Figure IV-2, the miniature tree, lonely on the bottom of the page, this painting conveys an expanding sense

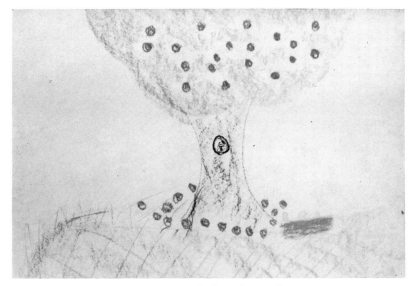

Figure IV-26.   Chalks; The Apple Tree

of security and self-esteem. In her hours, Julie now often spoke with pride of having "a mind."

Figure IV-27 is a bird in bright reds, magentas, and oranges. Well placed on the paper, the bird displays a magnificent tail, topped with an extra charmer of a plume. Julie commented, "This bird likes its tail. The wings are not big enough yet, so it can't fly very high yet, but it can hop around." Figure IV-28, the "duck with the beautiful tail," made in clay two months earlier, was a forerunner of the colorful bird.

Figure IV-29, The Clown, was made with chalks in red, blue, orange, yellow, and brown. In her search for an idea for a painting, Julie made a large scribble and found the clown in it. She was quick, inventive, and used the space well. "He is a good clown, and he is wise, and he likes kids," she said, "He could be prettier if I made a better scribble, but I like him." I saw in Julie's spontaneous way of finding and handling a painting theme her new ability to handle problems constructively.

It was Christmas time. Julie was doing well. Her mood was more stable and she was functioning better than ever before.

Figure IV-27.   Chalks; Magnificent Bird

There was no bizarre behavior at all, and the parents knew how to deal with Julie during her brief regressions. Julie worked hard and seriously at school, achieving at the fifth-grade level.

In view of these developments, I decided to see her once in two weeks, and after a while, once a month. The hint was given by Julie herself when she began, weeks earlier, to reflect upon the changes in her and to compare herself with the Julie of years ago. In one of these conversations, Julie volunteered that of all the things in her long psychotherapy, she remembered best "when I was a queen . . . , when I found out that I was not mommy . . . , and when I painted the box dream." It is interesting that she had forgotten the dream itself.

Figures IV-30 and IV-31 are a fitting conclusion for the Julie chapter. These are two self-portraits in clay, the first modeled toward the end of Julie's third year of therapy. She liked the sculpture because it made her "look like one of the kids," and took it home to keep it in her room.

Figure IV-28.   Clay; Beautiful Duck

Julie made Figure IV-31 during her very last visit before termination. Though it looks more like a mature woman than a young girl, this sculpture reflects the new seriousness and thoughtfulness which Julie had developed in recent months. The upper part of the head bears some likeness to Julie, and so does the long, straight, well-modeled hair. She needed some help with techniques and was a little uneasy about receiving it. But she accepted my help with modeling the nostrils and the neck and in giving the sculpture needed support. "This is a girl with a mind," Julie said proudly.

SUMMARY

This study presents the case of an intelligent girl who was severely disturbed, being schizoid and pseudoretarded. Her inability to learn was an unconscious resistance to learning, in part because she was afraid to grow and to face change, and in part because of crippling infantile rage.

Adopted at the age of two into a different culture, the apparently able and alert infant had been overwhelmed by the drastic change which resulted in a crisis of linguistic and emo-

Figure IV-29.   Chalks; The Good Clown

tional communication. Ready in her native country to communicate verbally with the familiar people around her whose speech she understood and successfully imitated, but suddenly removed from them, the infant had probably developed a fear and a rage which persisted through late childhood and blocked learning. She developed a concealed fantasy life which could not be reached verbally, but she readily accepted art media as a means of expression.

In the course of four years, Julie painted and modeled her rage and her fantasies. As she spontaneously discovered herself through her productions and within her relationship to me, problem areas were modified through being understood in their proper

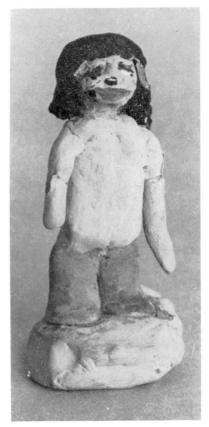

Figure IV-30.   Clay; Self-Portrait

context, bizarre forms of behavior were recognized and abandoned, and authentic feelings expressed. Through very slow and often painful work, the way was cleared for the able and vivacious preadolescent to come into her own.

FOLLOW-UP

At the time of my last contact with Julie, she had been promoted to a combination fifth-sixth grade. It was decided that she would be seen a few times in September, and two months later again for a few visits. Thus, therapeutic contact would be maintained. All bizarre behavior had been abandoned except for occasional, very brief spells of scholastic regression, now always

Figure IV-31.   Clay; Self-Portrait

specific, recognizable, and easily treated by the parents. Both at home and in school, Julie displayed good reasoning and organizational abilities, a warm attitude toward young children, sound practical thinking, much industry, and a fine sense of responsibility. Her latest triumph was being selected and trained for the school safety patrol.

Julie's hard work at school and the emotional strain due to her ambitious striving will have to be watched. Her parents were well aware of this as well as of the possibility that she may need more psychotherapy during adolescence.

V

Jeff

At the age of three and a half, Jeff, a pupil in a Montessori School, was referred for psychological help. "He goes from extreme to extreme," the teacher reported. "On his good days, he is bright and lovely and the children like him, but suddenly he turns wild, hits children, becomes unmanageable and makes strange animal like noises that scare everyone." Such extremes of behavior, from cooperation to defiance and from sociability to violence, were also reported by the parents. At home, Jeff reverted to soiling and to general infantilism, including baby talk that grew worse and worse.

One wondered about the emotional atmosphere at home, what might be its characteristic ups and downs, which might have caused the child to revert to infancy to such an extent. A conference with both parents and subsequent separate appointments with each of the parents cast some light on this question.

At the time of his decision to seek professional help, father was exasperated with mother's total inability to discipline the little boy, who was not even taught the routines commonly followed by children of his age. Father worried lest she repeat the same mistakes she had made in the rearing of her seventeen-year-old son by a previous marriage, who had needed psychological help throughout his childhood and adolescence.

Mother was obviously in need of help for herself. Her deep-seated suspicions and anxieties undermined her outer calm and erupted periodically into uncontrolled depressions. Unable to provide the child with a steady, loving, and reassuring firmness, she must have been an overwhelming and frightening mother to young Jeff.

In his first encounter with me, Jeff reached out for some boxes of toys only to scatter them, then for some crayons only to

122

break them into pieces. When the smallest pieces could not be broken anymore, he went into a fit of rage. I showed him how lines could be made with the crayon, but he did not respond; however, a demonstration of a vertical line, a horizontal line, a cross, and a circle, with an invitation after each to do the same thing, did lead to a readily successful imitation of each. This was accompanied by some apparent pride. When he copied the circle, Jeff showed a tendency to perseverate; he drew circles within and on top of circles, in a continuous movement.

This perseveration was evident also in play, which was for Jeff at that time a joyless job of putting objects in a box or on a truck, in perfect order, to fill every crevice. Anger erupted whenever an object turned over or fell, or whenever the crevice was too small for the toy assigned to it. The absence of laughter or smiles was conspicuous, and all the while he was uttering loud, roaring noises with a tone of threat. Each visit ended with a tantrum.

When Jeff became better acquainted with me and began to respond to some of my suggestions, I administered a brief battery of tests.

On the Wechsler Preschool and Primary Scale of Intelligence (WPPI), Jeff scored a Verbal IQ of 104, a Performance IQ of 101, and a Full Scale IQ of 103. He was at his best on all subtests which measured abstract thinking. Jeff's restlessness and initially aggressive refusal to cooperate made testing difficult and probably pulled down his IQ by a few points.

Jeff's responses to a small selection of cards from the Thematic Apperception Test (TAT) were his first communications about his emotional turmoil: (Card 1) "He doesn't want to play the music, he is sad." (Card 3BM) "A boy, he cries, he is shot." (Card 5) "A mommy, she says to the little boy [imitating her angry imperative], 'Put your socks on!' She is a bad lady." (Card 13B) "A boy, has no socks, he is afraid of big bear will eat him."

The response to Card I on the Rorschach was, "Big, big cow." This was followed by a stream of other mixed up and scary associations, probably out of dreams: a baby cow on his bed, daddy shooting a cow, and mommy shooting daddy. The response to Card II was, "Blood, this is blood, when you cut your finger." Finally, Jeff's response to Card X was "When I go BM in my pants," followed by a confused account of mother's reactions, with disintegration of speech.

This was a bright, but very disturbed little boy with some signs of autistic behavior. He was able to communicate, however, and in fact did communicate to me his overwhelming anger and his generally frightened state of mind, which could block normal development despite his brightness. Indeed, further development of that very brightness was now seriously endangered.

Jeff's age and the flow of change expected in a child as young as three and a half but not occurring in him, made the test findings not entirely reliable and their diagnostic implications unclear. Art expression seemed to be a more reliable method for evaluation. We can learn much through a series of drawings and paintings by comparing them with what is known about the drawings and paintings of normally developing children of the same age. Art expression seemed also to be the one therapeutic method which might enable Jeff to play like a normal child. The parents agreed to take him out of school for the time being and to bring him twice a week for psychotherapy. They also agreed to come for psychological help themselves.

Crayons and poster paints were placed in front of Jeff. Perhaps because crayons threatened to bring out his aggression and perhaps because he had been taught at school how to use paints, Jeff reached out for brush and paint. He produced ten to twelve paintings, two or three at each of the two visits per week. Of course he was never asked to name his work, nor did he choose to name it. After two or three productions, he would solemnly turn to his compulsive activity of loading a box or a truck.

Jeff's way of working with paints was significant. There was no open aggression comparable to his breaking crayons, but there were many other kinds of opportunity for Jeff to express aggression and also to try to control it. He dipped the brush with such energy that it hit the bottom of the jar and all of the handle was immersed in paint; he pressed the brush hard on the paper; he accumulated puddles of paint, and tried to paint the table beyond his paper, carefully watching for my reaction. Nevertheless, he readily accepted my reminder that painting ought to be done on the paper, and actually prided himself on his success in following such suggestions. When he painted the table by chance, he repeated the comforting reassurances I had given him.

I observed that reassurance and expressions of trust had a peculiarly soothing effect on Jeff. They seemed to give him a feeling of well-being, evidenced by his almost immediate co-operation and apparent enjoyment of his own compliance. It made me wonder again about the emotional air which Jeff had breathed all the days of his years.

The important aspect of his work with paints was how he used the colors in the available space. He would start with blue, then red or sometimes yellow, pile them one on top of the other, then heavily overlay both bright colors with black, and finally would spread the black all over the paper. Figure V-1 is representative of many such paintings. The darkest and heaviest area is the original blue and yellow covered with black on the upper right, while the rest of the paint is blackish but lighter, spread in every direction. The movements of the brush were continuous in the center and at the upper right, but staccato on the sides. They produced a mixture of vertical, horizontal, and circular lines, all vigorously smeared. Jeff would produce a painting of this kind in three or four minutes on a twelve- by eighteen-inch sheet of paper and then ask for another.

The aggression and probably also the effort at control of impulses came through in the angry insistence on piling black upon bright colors and spreading black paint to the extinction of any brightness. While he worked, Jeff's face was tense and anxious. There was none of the joy one might see on the face of a child making something new, something that was not there before and using color for enjoyable experimentation.

After a while, this diffusive painting began to change. Jeff began to place some paint in the center of the paper and to attempt to produce a more defined form. This is seen in Figure V-2. The circular blob of red paint is overlaid, but not entirely, with black. The bold brush stroke in black cuts the blob hori-

Figure V-1.   Poster paints; Dark Over Bright

zontally and extends a little beyond it on the right. The brush then returns to the top of the circle and works around it to the left, then downward and toward the right again. Thus, lines surround the red-black blob with something like a frame. These lines stop at the bottom right edge of the paper. The "frame" remains unfinished.

In Figure V-3, Jeff closed the curved, horizontal, black frame, which crossed and also enclosed some blue and red paint, only lightly smeared over with black. This time there was no insistence on completely overwhelming the two brighter colors. It did seem that Jeff was moving now toward a degree of form; he was stopping before the whole paper was covered with black.

While working with black paint on Figure V-4, Jeff was mumbling in his baby talk, "adder, adder," as he painted the elongated form at the right. He meant to say, "ladder," but

Figure V-2. Poster paints; A Partial Frame

Figure V-3. Poster paints; Framed Scribble

Figure V-4.   Poster paint; Ladder and House

had difficulty pronouncing the letter l. The ladder on the painting has one horizontal-diagonal stroke, and across it are painted eleven short strokes for steps. Jeff started to fill in the spaces between the steps, but stopped on his own. As soon as he noticed that his ladder had become attached to the form he had already painted on the left, he exclaimed excitedly, "I made a house and a [l]adder!" That was the first time he named a painting. He then proceeded to paint the well-defined frame around all four sides of the paper in one continuous line.

It is hardly possible to say that he had planned to produce the house and the ladder. Close observation led me to conclude that the ladder and the house were a chance discovery for Jeff. His familiarity with ladders, which he often saw his father use, his fascination with toy ladders in the playroom, and also his earlier painting of vertical, horizontal, and diagonal lines, all these led to the chance discovery of the ladder in his painting. The house was a connected discovery, also occurring by chance.

Jeff repeated the ladder theme on purpose (Fig. V-5) during the next hour. He started with the vertically placed ladder on the

Figure V-5.   Poster paint; Ladder and House

left, painting it quite realistically: two parallel vertical brush-strokes connected by five horizontal strokes with spaces between. Again, he proceeded to fill the spaces with black. This time, however, he did not go on indefinitely; he stopped spreading the black paint at the last space of the ladder and announced that he would now paint a house. The last features added to the house, also realistic, were two circles, each made with one brushstroke. As he painted these circles, Jeff's excitement visibly grew and he exclaimed, "Windows, I made windows, like this and like this." He ran to the windows of the playroom and pointed to the windows he had painted. He was much more excited than he had been about the chance discovery of the ladder in Figure V-4. In the course of painting Figure V-5 Jeff had discovered visual reality.

Jeff was now three years and nine months old. His change from totally inner or emotional realism to visual realism had started, indicating that his whole development was on the way back to normal. Of course, I kept in mind and made notations about the rather strange pattern of filling with paint all the spaces between the steps of the ladders. Yet, it was equally important that this stopped before the last space, that he was able to turn back to the interrupted painting which he had conceived by design.

In the fifth month of therapy, Jeff reached out for crayons again to do a great deal of up-and-down scribbling where his main interest seemed to be an infantile pleasure in the movement itself. At this time, crayons were at least something to draw with, not to break.

Figure V-6 is typical of the many crayon scribbles he produced over the next two months. Occasionally, he would return to paint and produce the half- or fully-framed dark blobs, but crayon scribbles predominated. In Figure V-6, the colors were turquoise blue overlaid with black. Both colors were used in a continuous line even though there was a change of direction. The black line was drawn with mounting pressure. It started at the top right corner with the aggressively drawn knot, and continued on to the left center where three holes were pierced

Figure V-6.   Crayon; Scribble

Figure V-7.   Crayon; Scribble

through the paper by the violent pressure of the crayon. (They show as white on the reproduction.) It is interesting that at this point Jeff was shouting, "I am not mad, I am not angry." This was probably because at home expressions of open anger were forbidden. After the holes had been made, the black crayon went up to the left in a thick line to terminate the scribble.

This act of aggression and violence was performed the day after I had seen Jeff's mother. Very despondent, she ascribed her depression to the impossibility of controlling Jeff in recent days. Mother's frequent depressive moods now regularly caused her to lose control of herself, of the household, and of Jeff. He, in turn, much as a baby responds with anxiety to mother's anxieties, sensed her loss of control and went out of control himself in his attempt to find some strength or affirmation in aggression and violence.

The scribble in Figure V-6 must also be viewed directionally; that is, in the way it relates to the painter himself, assuming that the space on the paper corresponds with his person: Jeff started the scribble from the outside, that is, away from himself; he carried most of it toward the inside or toward himself; and after the violent climax of piercing holes, proceeded toward the outside and up, again away from himself. In this sense, such scribbles were expressive, even though they resembled infantile use of art materials.

In relation to the visually realistic paintings which Jeff had begun to make in Figures V-4 and V-5, these scribbles were rather retrogressive, but not entirely so: they had much vigor as well as violence; and they were expressive.

However, in the case of Jeff, there was an additional cause of regression; that is, his participation in mother's recurrent depressions. Whenever Jeff became agitated, aggressive, and violent, his behavior was a sign of mother's regressive mood. In addition to the ordinary problems of growing up, Jeff had to cope with his reactions to mother's symptoms.

This supposition was confirmed by Jeff's ability to communicate verbally to me some of his experiences and feelings during the drawing of these scribbles. The communications consisted, usually, of a series of agitated utterances, accompanied by tense facial expressions, closing of the eyes, dilated pupils, and intense movements of the arms. At such times, Jeff's voice was high pitched and pleading rather than attacking. He was not able to tell a story; his speech was very infantile, with much stuttering and only occasional words understandably pronounced. There was some description of the painting at hand, and confused associations about experiences, real or unreal. One might say that the child loosely associated. I needed to learn his language, I realized, if I were to understand these associations.

Figure V-7 illustrates one such attempt to communicate with me. While he was drawing, Jeff's agitation was mounting and so was his fear. He was using a red crayon, talking louder and louder as he worked. The scribble consists of one continuous line, which shows up darker where more pressure was used.

Jeff started with the vertical line on the right. After descending, it turned left, then continued into the large horizontal shape. It is the darkest section. The words which could be distinguished while Jeff was scribbling this section were, "Mommy, my mommy

. . . she had a gun . . . the cow . . . running . . . daddy shoot cow . . . mommy shot daddy." At the word "daddy," Jeff moved his crayon to the upper middle part of the paper, which became the smaller area of scribbling, with darker lines inside a circular form. He then moved on to the third area on the left, which has some fierce corners, but no strong pressure of the crayon.

During the scribbling of this section, Jeff spoke a little more clearly of his sixteen-year-old brother, "my big brother, Harry. Harry says, 'That does it, get out of here or I'll clobber you,'" (pronounced, "o' a' cubbeya").

As we look at Figure V-7, we see that the space as a whole was well used. The scribble consists of three rather well-balanced sections: the one on the lower right, the strongest, is actively engaged in a struggle with the middle section; while the third section on the left is also somehow dragged into the hassle. In this scribble, more than in Figure V-6, the movements lead toward the inside. This directional aspect is the only sign of the painter's presence in the picture.

While it had not been intended as such, this scribble was actually a family portrait. Jeff had projected onto the paper an inner emotional experience, not a view of visual reality. The inner reality, though, reflected the actually contending forces in Jeff's family. Somewhere, in the turmoil of three struggling and threatening older people, the little boy was getting lost and rapidly turning in on himself in his attempt to survive. All things considered, his recent efforts to communicate through art and words were most encouraging.

Soon after making the drawing shown in Figure V-7, Jeff turned to play. His compulsive and perfectionistic loading of boxes appeared to be on the wane. He became interested in a somewhat richer variety of toys, which he had never noticed before. More and more Jeff was choosing a number of activities and taking pleasure in them during his therapeutic sessions. Soon, play became so absorbing that there was no need for him to draw. His play was of a mixed character, infantile, aggressive, and sometimes violent, along with the enjoyable play appropriate to a child his age.

Then one day Jeff came in, rushed to the painting table, and excitedly drew with crayons Figure V-8. While he was drawing, he mumbled in an agitated voice a story where the only distinguishable words were, "fire, kitchen, house, my daddy, firemen," repeated again and again. He nodded vigorously when he felt that he was understood and kept on producing one fire painting after another, nervously reaching out for new sheets of paper each time. Later, the parents reported that there had been a rather small fire on the kitchen stove, quickly extinguished by father even before the firemen arrived. They were surprised by the impact of the incident on Jeff, since he had not shown a strong reaction to it at home.

On Figure V-8, Jeff started in red and black with what seems to be the background in the reproduction: red in the center, dark red (more pressure) on the right, and a black area at the upper left (see Color Plate XII). The scribble on the right drawn vigorously in black chalk and the scribble on the left completed the painting. The use of color seemed to be intentional.

Figure V-8.   Chalk; The Fire

In the subsequent weeks, Jeff made over fourteen fire paintings. He never identified them verbally with the fire, nor did I ask him about it, but he kept producing the fire scribbles with much of the old agitation. There was a rich variety of color in this series. Some of the paintings had horizontal ovals in violet overlaying vertical ovals in orange; others were a combination of blue, red, and violet circular shapes. Still others had heavily drawn oranges, violets, blues, blacks, and magentas in a jumble of aggressive lines in all directions .The fire theme was pursued by Jeff with poster paints, also. Perhaps paint helped him express fear of the spreading of the fire, or the threat from within of his own violent feelings. This thought is, however, no more than speculation, as we have no evidence other than the visual expression itself.

It will be noticed that the transition to visual reality which had started in Figures V-4 and V-5 had ceased. Whether the process of transition had been overwhelmed by expression of the fire theme, we do not know. Nor do we have any way of knowing whether the development from emotional to visual realism would have proceeded more smoothly had there been no fire. It might also be argued that the fire paintings were indeed a combination of inner and visual realism. In children's paintings, the simultaneous production of up and down and horizontal paintings as well as expression according to inner and visual realism are not uncommon. When I reviewed all of Jeff's fire paintings, I thought, on first impression, that they were retrogressive to the stage of infant scribbling.

It will be remembered that continuous retrogression to infantile scribbling was evident in Jeff's art expression after Figures V-4 and V-5. Further examination convinced me, however, that signs of growth accompanied the retrogressive features. The retrogression to infantile scribbling in the fire paintings, including Figure V-8, can be considered in the same way. While these paintings do look like infantile scribbling on first impression, they are not the same as authentic infantile scribbles. No retrogression to an earlier stage of behavior is the same as the behavior at that stage itself, because some aspects of growth and maturation, even though distorted, have become an integral part of the retrogressive act as a whole. Such aspects can be found in Jeff's fire paintings. The choice of colors was one of them and the very theme another. Thus, paintings that seem infantile are not the same as infantile paintings. The two retrogressions in Jeff's art expression indicate a pattern, recognized by child psychologists, of a child's regressing a little just before making some new progress.

But, as noted before, another pattern of Jeff's regression, characterized by confusion, agitation, and violence, paralleled mother's moods. At such times, Jeff resisted mother's instructions, forbade her to touch him, and attacked her with whatever things that were at hand. But that situation began to change.

As mother made progress in her own psychotherapy, Jeff began to perceive her more clearly and was less threatened by her. When this occurred, Jeff abandoned violence. The change of feeling about mother coincided with Jeff's beginning to draw the human figure; that is, a first adult figure, universally named by young children, and now by Jeff, as "Mommy."

It was in the eighth month of his psychotherapy, when he was four years and four months old, that Jeff made the two crayon drawings on one sheet of paper shown in Figure-9. He named the two forms "mommy" and "my dog." This was a rather precocious development, since children generally begin to draw the human figure at the age of five.

The dog, drawn first at the upper left, was started with a triangular frame in red; next came a birdlike head and an eye, all in red; then five red lines were added for legs on both sides of the triangular trunk; and then the trunk was colored light green. The green went beyond the triangular outline and therefore the body looks undefined. While he was coloring his dog, Jeff repeated, "That's my dog, that's Barnaby. She likes to sniff."

On the right is the "mommy" figure drawn in red. The position of this recognizably human figure is horizontal-diagonal. The inner oval is the head, which Jeff volunteered to name; the larger, not quite closed oval around the head might have been Jeff's attempt at drawing a body; her right leg comes out of the

Figure V-9.   Chalk; Dog and Mommy

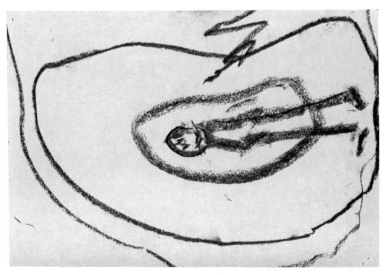

Figure V-10.   Chalk; Mommy

head, but her left leg starts from the top of the outer oval, and both legs have feet.

It was interesting to watch how Jeff drew the additional lines with the same red crayon below "mommy." First came the small, undecided line near "mommy's" right leg, as though he had wanted to attach it to the outer oval but could not. Then he made the two vertical parallel lines below, crossed by an upper horizontal line. Some small scribbles followed and suddenly, with a disturbed expression, Jeff announced that he did not want to paint any more. Among my notations made that day was this one: "Further developments may soon be expected in Jeff's drawing of the human body. He struggled today and was somewhat frustrated, but reached out in the right direction. There were no eyes or other features in the person, but the dog had an eye."

A further development did, indeed, occur a week later. This is shown in Figure V-10. Except that it lacks arms, this figure looks like a full human figure surrounded by an oval placed in another oval and framed by an outer, unfinished circle. Here is how Jeff went about this drawing: he started with the head placed horizontally and drew in it two eyes and a large, smiling mouth. Out of the head, he drew two horizontal lines for legs, and finished them with two feet, pointing down. Then he drew an oval, probably for a trunk, which frames the head and a large part of the legs, cutting across the knees or thereabouts thus creating the impression of a full human figure with a large trunk and with legs attached to it. Jeff was still struggling with the problem of the trunk when his compulsiveness and perseveration caught up with him and made his struggle more difficult. Caught in the perseverative drawing of circles around his figure, he wandered off to the upper section of the paper, beyond the figure shown. When asked to point at the head of the horizontally drawn figure, Jeff immediately turned the drawing to the vertical position and named the head, the eyes, and the mouth.

Three sessions later, Jeff drew with blue crayon Figure V-11 and immediately crossed it over many times with sharp, sweeping motions saying, "A person. I don't know how to make a person.

Figure V-11. Chalk; A Person

Here the head, here the eyes." This was a vertically drawn person lost on one side of a large sheet of paper, with a trunk much larger than the head. The trunk grew out of the head, but Jeff was thrown into confusion about the bottom part of the face and about the legs. It was, however, a vertical figure; a human figure was consciously intended, and Jeff was aware of his difficulty in drawing it.

Figures V-9, V-10, and V-11 as a group are representative of Jeff's further attempts to depict people. It was normal that humans were important to him and that the important people to him were adults. So it was "mommy," his own and the universal one, that he called his early cephalopod with the legs coming out of the head, while the trunk was ignored, as it has been by Jeff's contemporaries the world over.

As I studied all of Jeff's drawings of the human figure and observed his vexation about the location of parts of the body, it occurred to me that his, and perhaps other children's, cephalopods were not really just heads with protruding limbs. It is quite possible that these were images of the whole of the human body, perceived by the child as a whole. If that was so, then Jeff's difficulty was one of relating parts of the whole and trying to place the parts properly to make a sensible whole. This possibility calls for new observation of large numbers of children. Proper research may lead to a revision of the universally accepted cephalopod theory of the human figure in children's drawings to replace that which never explained why children draw humans in this way.

Jeff did not ignore the dog's body or the bodies of some other animals and bugs which he drew. The child's awareness of the animal's wholeness before that of the human figure is reminiscent of the pattern of animal responses preceding human responses on Rorschach examinations of children. His perception of the animal's wholeness led me to believe even more firmly in his perception of the whole of the human body.

In addition to universal aspects of the human figure drawn by children, these three drawings had about them a few individual features specific to Jeff. One of them was that the heads were, on the whole, rather small in comparison with the conspicuously large heads one usually sees on young children's productions. Another was that arms were omitted. The third feature was the way Jeff used his crayons to produce the effect of shading. He moved the crayon or chalk frequently in staccato lines while drawing his heavy lines, and this resulted in the effect of shading along the lines.

Soon after the three "mommy" drawings, Jeff drew with crayons Figure V-12. He drew in bright turquoise a number of heavy vertical lines, seven or eight, and said that he was making "the [l]egs of the horse." He counted them smoothly up to five and, in some confusion, reached the number ten. Then he made a large round line on the right, saying, "Head, the horsie has a head," and began to search for a black crayon. He tried dark green and dark violet and rejected them. When he finally found the black, he proceeded again to fill in the spaces between the horse's legs with heavy shading in vertical movements. As on the early ladder painting, he confined himself to the area of legs

Figure V-12.   Crayons; A Horse

and head only, and stopped when that area was filled in. He then noticed on the far upper left of the black mass a small diagonal line. He pointed at it with the radiant smile which recently appeared more often on his face, and said, "This is his tail, horsie has a tail." Then his eyes wandered to the far upper right. There he noticed two small linear residues on what had been the head, and announced, "Ears, that's his ears." The tail and the ears were two chance discoveries which Jeff intelligently integrated into his drawing, otherwise conceived by design. The last feature added was the series of vertical, almost oval shapes coming out of the black mass toward the bottom of the paper. These lines were made in light, indecisive strokes with little pressure and with no verbal accompaniment. As in the case of the early drawings of the human figure (Fig. V-9), this was followed by abrupt termination of the work.

As a whole, Figure V-12 makes the impression of a recognizable animal with a heavily shaded trunk. If we remember, however, that originally the horse's legs were in the place of the shaded trunk and that Jeff shaded the area with up and down lines, we must realize that in addition to his still continuing struggle with the problem of trunk and limbs, Jeff again retrogressed to the up-and-down and rather aggressive scribbling at a time when he was capable of representational production conceived by design. Figure V-12 tells us something about a certain pattern of functioning. It tells us that each time Jeff has to cope with confusion, he reverts to anxious infantile scribbling. At such times, his native capacity to proceed with his development is blocked and he even erupts into aggression or violence. This same mode of functioning, shown in Jeff's spontaneous art expression, manifested itself in all aspects of his life. It developed out of Jeff's old pattern of regression: his reaction to mother's depressions. When mother was seen after Jeff's painting of Figure V-12, she reported a fresh bout of depression, but one which was easier for all concerned, for mother was making progress now and could recover from her brief spells of depression without losing control. This allowed her to maintain steadier and calmer contact with Jeff, and she no longer needed to overprotect the child in compensation for past neglect. The interruptions to Jeff's normal development were now briefer and easier to overcome.

Thus, again, along with this regression, there was progress. For example, the integration of chance discoveries (tail, ears) into the preconceived whole; the confinement of the regressive activity to one area only; and an attempt to restore the wholeness and the meaning of the production by the somewhat feeble but successful addition of new legs on the bottom. This indicated also a new need to complete something that had been conceived as a whole.

Simultaneous occurrence in Jeff of two struggling modes of functioning became evident in the two distinct kinds of art expression which he carried on over the span of the next two or three months. Each had its specific medium and mood.

One was the production of drawings with crayons in black combined with a variety of colors. They were realistic in that they represented actual objects, and were visually representational. Jeff also was inspired to talk about them and was happy and communicative while he worked. Chance discoveries and integrative efforts were characteristic.

The other was the production of paintings with poster paints, of perseveration and the compulsive spreading of dark-colored paint. Every space was filled with a single color until the paper was covered. Jeff carefully searched out the smallest spot that remained empty and worried about it. During such activity, Jeff was serious, anxious and unwilling to stop even at the end of his hour. Though he used dark colors almost exclusively, he wanted all the jars open. Also, before starting each painting, he named the colors in succession and only then would he set out to paint. Naming colors was an achievement in itself as Jeff had had much difficulty with this at the start. Nevertheless, opening jars and naming colors in their particular sequence at a certain time had become a ritual.

By the end of the second month of this, Jeff began to use bright blue, and he was quite excited one day by a very light blue which another child had mixed. Mixing paints became his new preoccupation. He was still determined to cover the whole paper, but there were discoveries of thick and thin paint and of "funny blobs." The anxiety of the ritualistic effort began to wane slowly. The compulsion to cover the whole paper with paint gradually assumed the meaning of completing a task in order to examine it; that is, verbally describe how the paint was distributed over the paper, which parts he liked best, and so on.

The productions of the representational kind were promoted more often now by real events of which Jeff was more and more aware. A fishing trip, a camping trip, and a trip to the zoo are examples. Actually, the fire and the horse had also been examples of real objects or situations which became themes for Jeff's drawings.

Figure V-13 was made mostly with red crayon, except the light scribbles on the upper left, in blue (see Color Plate XIII). When he finished, Jeff eagerly showed it to me and described it as "a pool and a sun and also like fire." The pool, on the right, was made in one continuous movement with strong but not overly aggressive pressure and with no hesitation at the turning

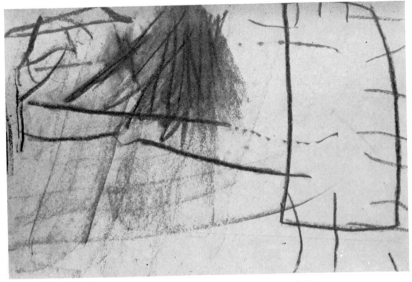

Figure V-13.   Crayons; Pool, Sun, and Fire

of corners. The path, running horizontally across the paper and apparently leading to the pool ("This where you go in the pool") was done in similar fashion, except the staccato at the end of the upper line near the pool. In the upper center of the paper, above the path, Jeff shaded heavily a roughly triangular area, carrying the shading in much lighter red almost to the bottom of the paper. For that, he used the square-shaped crayon, moving it on its side vertically and horizontally while he repeated, "The sun, this is the sun." In the process, he probably associated the red and perhaps also his strong motions with the fire which he still occasionally painted, and began to press the crayon with ever greater force in the vertical and diagonal lines at the top of the red shading.

Figure V-14, "Rhinoceros," a name Jeff found quite troublesome to pronounce, was made with black crayon. Jeff placed the round shape boldly in the center of the paper and when he drew the details at the right, he said, "Head" and "That's his eye." He also pointed out the many "legs" around the larger circle. The drawing's fierceness suggests Jeff's expression when he spoke of

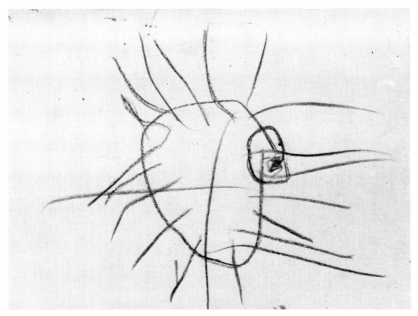

Figure V-14.   Crayon; Rhinoceros

the rhinoceros. The body is much larger than the head. The large eye truly reflects children's special fascination with eyes. That was a new development for Jeff, as he had become interested in eyes relatively late.

Figures V-15 and V-16, only two of a larger group of fish and pond drawings, were both made within one week.

Figure V-15, made with brown over yellow crayon in linear fashion, was eagerly described by Jeff as, "A daddy fish, a mommy fish, a boy fish, a big boy fish, and another fish, and a pool, and a name." He also asked me to write on the painting with a red pencil which he put in my hand, "All the fishes are alike." Occupying the upper part of the paper are two large fish, connected by a horizontal **V**; on the left, two other fish, one of them very small, are connected by a hooklike line; in the middle is a single fish, drawn with fins; on the right is the pool; and above the pool is "a name," made in staccato lines to imitate handwriting which had been fascinating to Jeff recently. Jeff might have perceived the fish group as his own family: mother

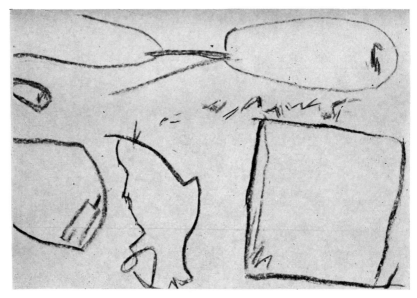

Figure V-15.   Crayons; Fish, Pool, and a Name

and father tied together, but each pulling in the opposite direction; himself and his big brother, tied again, but so different in size; and the single fish, possibly an uncle whom the parents passively hated but allowed to meddle. All the fish, except the single one named by Jeff "another fish," had facial features and rather sensible, realistic proportions. But the uncle, who is a conspicuously small man in reality, was rather large on the drawing. Since he made his presence strongly felt, Jeff made him large.

Figure V-16 was drawn with blue over yellow crayon, also in outline. In this drawing, the family situation is conveyed most eloquently. Jeff named the drawing "Big Fish Outside the Pool and Little Fishes Inside the Pool." The pool is on the right. Inside it, at the upper left, is a group of two, composed of a small fish and a larger one. Again, they are connected by a line. On the right, occupying almost the whole length of the pool, is a third, single figure drawn much like a human in profile. This figure has a large eye which is directed toward the big fish outside the pool. This can be seen more clearly when the painting is turned

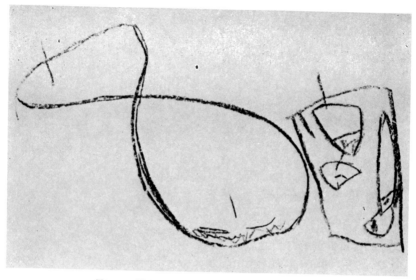

Figure V-16.   Crayon; Big Fish and Pool

upside down. The heads of the fish inside the pool are clearly defined and their bodies are much larger than the heads. The big fish outside the pool has arched eyebrows and lines reminiscent of a woman's bangs right above the eyebrows, all resembling the hairdo and head of Jeff's mother. That fish is considerably larger than the whole pool, including the three fish inside, all described by Jeff as "little fishes." The sweeping lines in the design of the outside fish and its position in relation to the pool and the in-group is of special interest because it describes so accurately and pointedly the emotional family situation, intuitively perceived and visually expressed by a little boy. From the developmental view of his art expression, Jeff combined in the recent drawings emotional or inner reality with visual reality.

SUMMARY

One year of art psychotherapy with a near-autistic four-year-old boy was presented. The use of art media opened for this child modes of expression through which he learned to communicate to the therapist. His drawings and paintings, shown in the order of production, provide an objective record of diagnostic value that goes beyond the data provided by clinical testing. When he came closer in his art expression to what is normal for a child his age, other aspects of his behavior also became more nearly normal. Toward the end of one year's therapy, he showed in his productions a new ability to combine his inner reality with visual reality.

The child's seriated paintings also reflected another important parallel. It was the rise and fall of mother's depressions as they determined Jeff's progress and regression. Use of color by Jeff in his early overlay paintings is discussed in the chapter on color in art expression in Part Two.

FOLLOW-UP

Seven months after the beginning of his art and play psychotherapy, Jeff's visits were reduced to one hour per week. Five months later, Jeff was placed in a small, informally conducted prekindergarten group which he happily attended three times a week. His psychotherapy was then terminated.

Jeff's mother increased her formerly infrequent visits to a regular weekly hour. In addition, she enrolled in an art therapy group that I conducted as an adjunct to individual psychotherapy.

VI

Ellen

Ellen's psychotherapy was brief, only thirty hours over a span of six months. Knowing they were to spend only two years in the city, her parents, both professionals centered on their careers, decided to reach out for psychologic help for their daughter six months before father's new assignment was to take them elsewhere. This drastic time limitation was described by the parents as an objective difficulty beyond their control, but when it was discussed, its highly subjective meaning to each of them became apparent.

Father realized, intellectually, that Ellen, ten and a half years old, "evidently" needed help; the evidence was that three teachers in three years had expressed wonderment about the child. However, the thought that anybody in his family needed this kind of help was emotionally unacceptable to him. He decided to give it a six month's try, including this among other items of business to be taken care of before his next move. The time limitation was, for father, a chance to get this necessary but dreaded chore out of the way. A short time after he met the psychotherapist, father went abroad to be joined later by the family.

Mother welcomed at least a chance to start something she feared, but desired very much for both Ellen and herself. She had been worried about herself more than one would guess from her happy, self-assured appearance. This had been her own secret worry, however, not shared with her husband.

Both parents talked freely and matter-of-factly about doubts and hesitations they had encountered concerning the size of their family, now complete with four children. While father talked about facts and omitted feelings, mother had much to say about her feelings in relation to each pregnancy and birth, al-

149

though she could not answer questions about her children, their smiling, crying, loving, playing in their infancy. She knew more about the fourth child than about Ellen, third of the four. She recalled that Ellen had been satisfied to be fed and cleaned and to be left alone. While the first two children were welcome, they interrupted mother's carefully planned and ambitiously followed career. The next pregnancy, with Ellen, was completely unexpected and had come as a shock. Once Ellen was there, however, both parents felt that she was loved as well as the other children. Four years later, the fourth child came, a planned last addition to the family.

The family placed a high premium on scholarship and scholastic excellence. Indeed, the two older children were "A" students, devoting all their time to school work, while the parents actively participated in their school projects and assignments. Report card days were occasions for these children and the parents to share triumph and pride.

The parents felt, however, that Ellen should be spared the pressures for scholarly achievement because she had always been, as father said, "somewhat different, perhaps not as communicative, and maybe not as bright." Consequently, she was never expected to be a particularly good student, and the average or low-average grades she brought home were considered the best she could do.

At school, the teacher wondered, however, about Ellen's true brightness, since she would sometimes come up with surprisingly good work despite a generally low level of interest and little expenditure of effort. The teacher also wondered about Ellen's silence; her brief, whispered answers to questions directed at her; her conspicuous social isolation; and the absent look on her face in class.

At home, Ellen's parents were embarrassed by her behavior rather than worried about her emotional life. It all centered on Ellen's friend, Rhoda, the girl next door, who was also a classmate. The younger child of Negro parents, professionals who were absent from home most of the day and evening, Rhoda ignored Ellen at school, seeking the popular children's favors.

She spent the rest of the day and evening, however, in Ellen's home, teasing Ellen and often allying herself with Ellen's older brother against her. Ellen, on the other hand, protected Rhoda, served her, helped her with homework, and walked her home when her parents telephoned that they had come back. Ellen's mother did not dare tell Rhoda's parents that it was a nuisance for her to always include Rhoda in her plans.

Ellen had other symptoms and habits that caused trouble at home. She had a hard time falling asleep and would get up very early, rush into the kitchen in her nightclothes, seat herself on a stool, and wait for mother. The morning encounters soon degenerated into woeful exasperation for mother and silent anguish for daughter. Ellen's watch over mother spread and grew. She kept her busy with Rhoda, demanded detailed reports about mother's routine, sat with her as often as she could, moved into the parents' bed when father went abroad, and insisted that she would not go to camp along with her siblings because she had to stay home with mother. All of this increased mother's anxiety. She realized that there was much more than an immediate behavioral problem to consider.

Ellen talked in whispers. She had a stony, determined expression, answered direct questions with one-syllable words, made no response at all to less direct expressions of curiosity, and offered no verbal comments of her own. When asked about her family, she whispered the names and ages of her siblings in chronological order.

But when I suggested that she draw or paint her family, she came to life, chose crayons, and proceeded to work in an interested way. She presented a rather eloquent picture (Fig. VI-1) of her family and of her own place in it.

On the far left are the parents holding hands; toward them walks the youngest child, a boy of five; next is another group of two, the older brother and sister, also holding hands. Next to the sister stands Ellen, alone, trying to reach for the cat, who turns away from her, toward the dog. Chronologically, Ellen belongs between the two boys, but because she finds life between them unbearable, she painted herself where she would like to

Figure VI-1.   Crayons; Family Portrait

be—near her older sister, whose first loyalties, however, go to the older boy. In the picture, the whole family turns away from Ellen but she, too, turns away from them and seeks closeness with the pets. Even they have each other.

When I suggested to Ellen that she look at her family portrait, she was able to make quite a few observations of her own: "Everybody has somebody except me." "My sister sort of wants me?" She noted that the pets, whom she considered her best friends, were not actually with her; that she had placed herself the farthest away from her parents; and that (this was added in a whisper again) her next-door friend Rhoda should be on the painting, but then, she is not exactly family.

Ellen bragged about her many friends. She tried to convince me that she indeed had many friends and offered to make a painting of all the friends at her lunch table in school. This is seen in Figure VI-2.

Ellen painted the eight girls in two rows, three in the upper row and five in the lower, and wrote their names above the painted images. She was faithful to the styles, colors, and even print patterns of dress characteristic of each of the girls except

Figure VI-2. Crayons; Lunch Friends

the two figures on the right in the upper row. The clothes of these two figures were colored dark brown, the one at the extreme right representing Ellen herself, who wore, in reality, colorful skirts and sweaters. She is holding hands with Rhoda, or rather pulling Rhoda by her hand, while Rhoda herself is leaning toward the blond girl to her left. In reality, Rhoda is taller and larger than Ellen, while in the painting Ellen is the larger of the two.

Asked to indicate who has actually to do with whom, Ellen drew circles around the related parties; to mark who would like to be friends with whom, she drew red arrows, almost invisible on the reproduction, between the interested parties. According to this scheme, the top circle includes Rhoda and the girl to her left, thus excluding Ellen, leaving her alone even though she holds Rhoda by the hand.

All the girls in the lower row are in one large circle within which one twosome is holding hands. Ellen is not included in any of the circles.

A glance at the arrows pointing from Ellen toward others shows that, of the two girls in the lower row whom she would like to have for friends, one has an intimate friend with whom she holds hands and the other, rather isolated within the group, is a visitor from abroad scheduled to leave very soon.

Arrows are pointed at Ellen by the tall girl in the red dress on the extreme left in the lower row. This is not reciprocated by Ellen. In fact, it seemed that only in the process of working out the little sociogram in her painting had Ellen become aware of this girl's interest in her as well as of the unreality of the rest of her friendship with the lunch-table girls. There were tears in Ellen's eyes when she admitted this, but there she was, able to take a realistic view of her relationships with Rhoda and with the girl in the red dress.

When she came in the next time, Ellen reported in a loud, clear voice that she had made "a new friend, a real one." It was the girl in the red dress. Ellen also decided not to "mother" Rhoda any more and not to allow Rhoda "to be the boss" any longer. Ellen's new attitude toward Rhoda had its successful counterpart in mother's recent handling of the same problem. While the two girls still maintained close contact, it had now been reduced to normal proportions.

Ellen had stopped whispering for some time now. She happily reported that she had been talking in class "like everybody else," volunteering answers and comments. Since she was speaking in a normal voice and since her concern about her brightness was growing, the time seemed ripe for the administration of psychological tests.

Ellen wished to start with the drawing tests. When she was asked to draw a house, she produced Figure VI-3. It is a narrow house, as if it were meant for one person only. It is outlined heavily with green crayon, pressed hard on the paper; the front is colored blue, the two windows green, and the door brown. There is a steep, brown roof divided in two by a strong vertical

Figure VI-3.   Crayons; House

green line. Being left open at the bottom, the little house looks like a bag turned upside down to allow the contents to fall out. Moreover, this house seems to be floating upward.

The tree, not shown here, was placed near the bottom of the paper, carefully outlined and richly colored in brown and green. Described as "a tree in spring or in summer," it represented the strong, normal aspects of Ellen's inner life.

The person, also not shown here, though a good, detailed drawing of a girl, was described merely as "a fourteen-year-old girl" and bore a resemblance to Ellen's fourteen-year-old sister.

Ellen's Full Scale IQ was 125 on the WISC, placing her in the middle of the Superior group in general intelligence. She excelled in all the subtests designed to measure capacity for abstract thinking, but fell short in noticing essential details. In a way, this repeated itself later on the Rorschach when Ellen did not produce any responses to small details on the ink blots. But her many sensible responses to whole ink blots and her responses to parts of them were imaginative, corresponding to the reality of the ink blots, and were also expressive of her individual conflicts. Many of the blots stirred strong emotions in her, such as fear and anger, but Ellen kept them under a tight control. Impulsivity and purely emotional reaction are represented on the Rorschach by color. Ellen controlled her emotionality by allowing the shape of the blot to determine her responses, rather than the color.

Here was a bright young girl who was overwhelmed by her parents and did not quite understand them or their feelings about her. There was a fear of an explosive father and worry about a distant mother, who seemed to be a little girl herself. The four siblings were struggling for the parents' recognition or love or both, but Ellen could not quite reach out. Instead of helping her to reach out to them, the parents freed her altogether from effort, thus excluding her from the in-group. It is interesting that the only response determined by a healthy combination of form and color was the one to the whole of Card IX in which Ellen fully and accurately expressed her emotional situation: "Four animals are trying to get the pink pears, but the lower animals, the orange ones, don't reach." So strong was the impact on Ellen of her emotional situation at home that in response to Card X, a card designed to draw numerous responses, she gave one response only: "The two big pink animals are holding up these two little gray animals that are climbing up here so they can reach the tree." Again, a wishful and hopeful solution, emotional by its very nature, this response was determined by shape alone, with no trace of color.

But it was the TAT challenge of testing the imagination by producing action stories that guided Ellen to focus and elaborate on the main problem. That problem, Ellen's struggle with mother for her love and for her real presence, evolved in a series of stories of anger and violence and a need to know that she, Ellen, would be missed.

The two principal feelings which came out in the psychological tests were rage and a sense of being trapped. But there was also hope, for "the outside world," the psychologist, might help now. That hope soon changed into a strong determination in Ellen, quite unusual for a child of her age, to reach for the love and recognition which her older siblings attained naturally. Early in her psychotherapy, she understood that the safest way to attain that love and recognition would be to find the real Ellen with her real feelings and her real abilities.

Immediately after the tests, Ellen turned to finger painting which she had eyed as soon as she had come in. She worked intensely and seriously over a few visits. Endless circles in thick red or black paint filled her papers. Soon she began to mix colors to produce greens and violets and oranges in various shades. While I was watching Ellen reach out for new papers to fill them with new red and black circles, it occurred to me that she was actually indulging in pure color expression. This was precisely what she was trying so hard to avoid on her Rorschach. On that test she had to control her impulsive and emotional inner drives by giving shape to every response. At the finger-painting table she was free, unconsciously, to give full reign to her impulsivity without being threatened.

The first two times, Ellen's intense finger painting was done in silence. Soon, she began to exchange expressive looks with me. Then she was uttering sounds of relief and pleasure. When they were translated for her into words, she was able to reply, "Yes, this feels good," and small conversations began about her choices of color to express certain feelings. Ellen thought she was using much red and black to express her "madness" and shyly asked whether "other kids" used the same color "for their madness."

When she had produced ten or more of the finger paintings, almost identical in the circular finger motions spread over the whole area and differing only in color, Ellen began to mark with her finger something in the center or in the middle of the lower part of the paper. Soon the mark developed into a recognizable fence. Soon after that a form resembling the human figure began to appear behind the fence. Figure VI-4 represents the clearest of these paintings, which Ellen named, "A Girl Behind the Fence."

The painting was made in deep green which Ellen had mixed with great care out of blue and yellow. The human figure

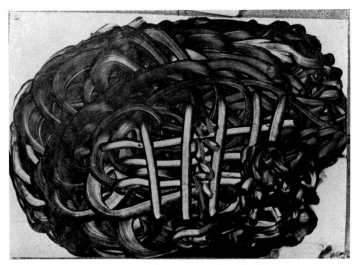

Figure VI-4. Finger paint; Girl on Fence

was first outlined in the green paint, then filled in with red-violet. While Ellen had never shown any interest in the fate of her earlier finger paintings, she took special care of this one, using just enough paint on it so it could dry to smoothness and placing it in a well-protected spot for drying. On her next visit, she proceeded directly to her painting to examine it and accentuate the human figure with pink and orange pastels. "This person," she volunteered, "is a girl behind the fence." In full color, this picture has an impact on the viewer, for the painter succeeded in expressing a few most inner feelings that were just beginning to come into her awareness: a sense of being different and isolated; a wish to be on the other side; that is, to join other people; and the paralyzed feeling of being in a "squeeze;"—also, perhaps, some suppressed anger with those on "the other side."

Soon after this, Ellen made Figure VI-5, an 18- x 24-inch crayon painting. She was in a very serious mood and wore the old solemn expression of her first visit. She worked slowly, stopping every now and then to gaze at certain areas before making some new lines.

In the center is the intersection of two roads, shaded in gray. There is a bluish, cloudy sky above and the three areas

Figure VI-5. Chalks; Lost House Dream

created by the road-crossing are green and brown (see Color Plate XIV). Houses in a variety of colors are dispersed over these areas. Some of them resemble the little lonely house which Ellen had drawn for her tests. Others give the impression of faces. The houses are not in rows; each is unto itself. Though the landscape is colorful, it gives a feeling of descending darkness. At the left side of the crossing stands a small girl in blue jeans and shirt, lost.

That was a dream, Ellen said, a recurrent dream which had come back again the night before, her dreaded dream which made her unable to fall asleep. In it, she was returning home after she had gone out in the afternoon to play (in actuality, she had stayed home for some time now after school was over). When she should have been near her house, she could not recognize it. She went up to each house, only to realize in terror that none was hers. Exhausted, she ran to one last house which looked like her home, again to experience the same thing. At the end of this dream Ellen always found herself standing, lost, at the crossroads, "just standing there," as night was falling.

Ellen wept as she related her dream in hardly audible whispers. She was anxious to find out why the dream kept coming back and why she could not find her home. Was it, she wondered, because she had allowed herself to go out to play in the dream when she would never go out in reality unless it was to shop with mother?

First of all, Ellen's whispering had to be dealt with; though it had stopped before, her whisper kept coming back whenever she was going through an emotional crisis. This time it seriously impeded any effort to talk about the painting and the dream. Figure VI-4 was put up again and the question was boldly posed: was the girl behind the fence calling for help if she so badly wished to climb over and join those on the other side?

Ellen reacted immediately. She was furious with me for asking "all these questions." When I stated her anger with me, Ellen answered in a loud and angry voice that everybody saw the girl on the other side of the fence and so they knew that she wanted to climb over, but nobody did anything about it; therefore, she kept silent and "just let them look at her." The angry silences and the whisper were put together and Ellen was able to work out a rule about what made the whispers' coming and going: when she felt isolated and angry about her isolation and when she felt misunderstood and angered about that, she kept silent, whispering only when she was required to answer. The dream brought out her isolation and her long-accumulated anger about it, so she whispered when she described the dream. "I never looked at it that way," Ellen ended matter-of-factly.

We were now ready to talk about Figure VI-5. As soon as I suggested to Ellen that perhaps she was searching for somebody in these houses, she asked with excitement and in a whisper again, "Was it my mother?" She immediately repeated her question in a normal tone of voice, chuckling. Having connected mother with the search through the houses in the dream, Ellen was able to put together a few odd things she had been doing, all associated with mother. There was her early morning rush to the kitchen, her mothering and hating Rhoda, her move into mother's bed in father's absence, and her insistence on staying home with mother each summer when her siblings went to camp. "I know," Ellen acknowledged tearfully, "but I've got to do it all. Maybe I can now go out a little to play, but I won't go to camp, I can't."

When we turned again to Figure VI-5 and I asked Ellen the question she had posed herself, what might happen if she allowed herself to take off one afternoon, Ellen said, crying, that the house would be gone and mother would be gone, that something terrible would happen to mother. She nodded vigorously and sobbed bitterly when I finished the story for her by saying, "And it would be all your fault." Clearly, the child carried a burden and was caught in an overwhelming conflict: a child's anger with mother for excluding and not understanding her and, at the same time, precocious feelings of responsibility for an immature, little-girlish mother. This conflict was acted-out in Ellen's silence and whispering, in her poor scholastic and social performances, her relationship with Rhoda, and in her vigil over mother. This was a complex problem, more complex than the usual problem of separation of child from mother. To understand it fully, mother's problems had to be considered.

These, too, were more complex than the memory of the unwanted pregnancy with Ellen eleven years earlier. Her own unsolved childhood conflicts, repeated at adolescence and re-experienced in her marriage, had been focused on Ellen, who became in many ways the bearer of mother's burdens.

Her bond with Ellen also transcended the specific problem of the at first unwanted but later accepted pregnancy of long ago. She was caught now in her own conflict about being a mother and, at the same time, in some ways a child. She also had mixed feelings about this strange child, not as brilliant as the others but so sensitively observant that her mother often felt "seen through" and threatened by little Ellen, the child with the serious face so much like her own.

Mother's important childhood difficulty, love for her brother and fierce competition with him, had now been paralleled by love for her husband and the ambitious inner push "to be no less than he." Hence, the recurrent theme of fame in her fantasies and in her art therapy paintings. When she became overburdened with her troubles, she began to drink.

Ellen, who had been keeping watch over mother originally as a result of her own pathology, saw the drinking in all its threat. In the past, she watched mother in anger. Now she watched her in fear. She hurried home from school to ask the daily question, daily dreaded by mother, "Did you drink today?" In contrast to mother's apprehensive attitude Ellen happily welcomed the news that mother was receiving help for herself.

While she did not want to take any of her paintings home for fear of her brother's teasing, she did not mind if her mother occasionally saw a painting she had made. Except for one, however, there was no need to show any of her paintings to mother.

When she joined the art therapy group for mothers as an adjunct to her individual psychotherapy, Ellen's mother found in painting the most effective way to bring out her feelings and to understand them. At the time of Ellen's dream picture, mother produced two pastel paintings (Figs. VI-6 and VI-7).

Figure VI-6, titled "No Way Out—Trapped," expressed mother's inner state at the time. At the bottom right-hand corner of an 18- x 24-inch sheet of paper stands a red figure behind a block of strongly shaded red. Out of its upper left corner rise densely intertwined circular lines in strong blue, drawn with much pressure. This section seems to be backed and pulled up by a large mass of linear and massive, heavily shaded, circular forms in dark blues and greens. As we look at this painting, we might think of Ellen's girl behind the fence. In each of the two paintings, we see a figure blocked or trapped; there is a separating object in each, one a fence, the other a block; there are green-blues with some red in each, particularly in the figures; and in

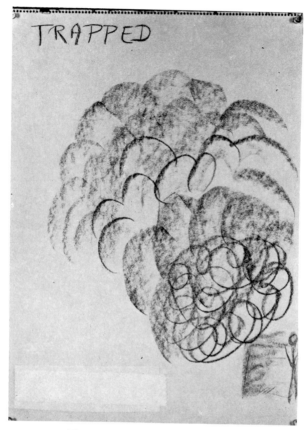

Figure VI-6.   Chalks; Trapped

each there is a muddy or cloudy mass around the main object. Each of the two paintings expresses helpless rage and despair, and this is what mother and child shared at that time of their lives.

Figure VI-7 is mother's painting of a traumatic dream she had the night before. Titled "Death in the Warehouse," the painting shows a large gray and blue building, a heavily shaded truck in green on the right, and in the oversized entrance to the building, in her favorite green dress, is Ellen, dead.

With all the anguish and tears, the dream assumed integrative meaning when mother reexperienced what she had felt

Figure VI-7. Crayons; Death Dream

in the dream. That was made possible by the conditions of group art therapy. Expression in painting, telling about the dream experience, and reacting to other viewers' thoughts to get new thoughts and feelings, these were some of the processes made possible by the use of art in a group setting.

Thus, mother was able to bring out some of her conflicts about herself and about Ellen of which she had not been aware in the past. She now understood that while Ellen annoyed her more than any of her other children did, she has held in common with Ellen some of her own moods and traits and perhaps even invested in her some residues of her own unsolved childhood problems.

Ellen was going through a phase of open anger now. This thrilled but frightened her. She was able to talk about it, though, and noticed that she had recently been starting many sentences with "I hate." At first the anger, and perhaps also the anxiety, became evident in a series of jumbled, muddy finger paintings in grays and blacks, impossible to capture in a photograph. Then, when she was able to say that her old rage was "catching up with" her, she turned to red finger paint in line with her feeling that "madness is black or red."

Figure VI-8 was the last of five finger paintings of this kind and the only one with a clear subject and a title, "The groundhog finally came out of his hole and sees everything on fire." And a fiery painting it is when seen in full color (see Color Plate XV). The blue-black groundhog and his blue-black hole are painted into the surrounding circular movements of flaming red. Dark blue lines were added with crayon on top of the dry red finger paint to accentuate the fire, and the groundhog and hole were both outlined with the same blue crayon. When I wondered how the groundhog felt seeing everything on fire, Ellen answered gleefully, "He likes it."

Figure VI-8. Finger paint; The Groundhog

The next time Ellen came, she found her groundhog painting set up and her folder handy. As she leafed through her paintings, I asked her which of them she would put next to the groundhog. Ellen searched and pulled out the girl behind the fence (Fig. VI-4). She compared the two paintings: the fence painting was very dark, while the groundhog painting was very bright, but there was "a lot of madness" in both. While she had not been aware of her anger in the earlier painting, she was quite aware of it in the later one and had wanted to express it; the girl and the groundhog were alike; but the girl could not do anything about herself, and the groundhog could. Finally, Ellen declared her dislike for Figure VI-4 and her liking for Figure VI-8.

The expression of her anger through art media did not immediately solve Ellen's problems. She was extremely worried that she might become violent, for in the past she had wanted to hit her little brother and "smash mommy's glass." Ellen needed help

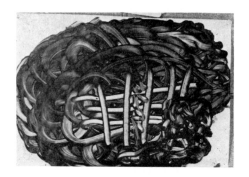

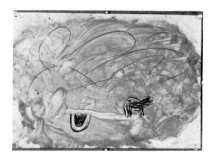

quickly, since the limited time available for psychotherapy was running out. I suggested that she make her hatreds specific. This reduction of a general, all-consuming feeling to a specific, narrower one did prove to be somewhat helpful. The most important application of this approach was in relation to mother's drinking. Ellen was able to say openly now to her, "I hate to see you drink," saying nothing aloud but repeating to herself the old gnawing, "I hate my own mother; she drinks." With great relief Ellen realized that this made it possible, also, to feel love for mother. Now that this anger had been dealt with, it was easy to bring out the other big grievance that Ellen had against both parents. That was her long-suppressed anger at them for setting her up as "the dumb one in the family," lowering their expectations of her so that no one, not even she herself, ever thought that she could do well. Her notion changed, however, soon after I told Ellen about her good intelligence and what she could do with it when she was ready to be the real Ellen, not the groundhog or the girl behind the fence. Ellen's old surprising sparks of scholarship began to appear more often, and soon she found herself among the high-ranking students.

Ellen made many paintings with pastels in her last hours of therapy. Circular or tubular, they were outstanding for their variety of color and movement. And all of them had a minute center or a tiny round spot high up above the center of the paper so as to create in the viewer a sense of perspective and depth.

Figure VI-9 is the most colorful of these paintings (see Color Plate XVI). It took most of two hour-long visits and consists of a series of large outer ovals, turning gradually into ever smaller inner circles. On a blue background, Ellen painted her ovals and circles in as many colors as she could find, leaving in the middle of the painting a very small but definite circle of light blue. At the very end, she framed the whole in a blue, green, and orange oval-rectangle. She was pleased with her production, for it came out as she had wanted, with "a little light in there." She had not intended it to be any specific object; but as she stepped back to look at it, she saw that it might be a long tunnel with the exit illuminated far away by the sunlight coming in from the outside.

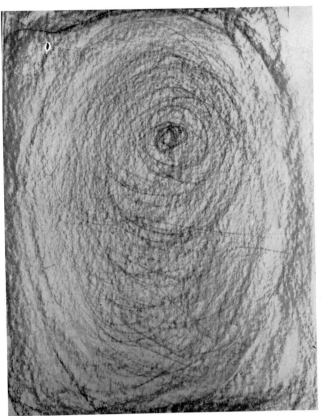

Figure VI-9.   Crayons; Long Tunnel

In her very last hour of therapy, Ellen finally reached out for clay which she had previously let alone even though she often turned her eyes to it as well as to the clay products made by other children. Encouraged to knead chunks of clay into any odd shapes, she enjoyed the activity immensely and ended up with the semi-abstract shape of an animal with a raised head. "This is my groundhog," she said as she carried it away, thus depriving this chapter of a last, most fitting photograph.

SUMMARY

A six months' span of art psychotherapy with a bright ten-year-old girl blocked by rage has been presented. The emotional difficulties of the child were focused on a complex and unproductive relationship with her mother. It was eventually discovered that the girl had become the bearer of some of her mother's conflicts. At first, I considered that the child's main problem was withdrawal in anger with mother. Soon, however, this opinion was explained by a realization that this girl had to mobilize all her resources to fight for the most important person in her life, mother. Thus, the child's disturbance was an expression of her own pathology as well as of the pathology in the relationship between mother and daughter. The same extraordinary mental energy which went into her distorted fighting behavior was invested by Ellen in her recovery. A parallel process took place in mother. Some of their most complex feelings were expressed in art therapy by both mother and daughter.

FOLLOW-UP

Ellen spent the summer which followed termination of her brief psychotherapy at home with mother. Reports received by letter indicated that it was a productive time for both despite some difficulties. They planned to look for more help as I had recommended. Since they had found the combination of psychological counseling with art therapy so helpful, they hoped to find in their new location professionals who worked in a similar way.

VII

Henry

DURING THE FIRST FIVE MONTHS of psychotherapy, eight-year-old Henry shied away from art media, from conversation, and even from using the punching bag. "Well . . . ," "I guess . . . ," and "Ask my mom" were his usual responses to any attempt at verbal exchange. He came once a week, and each time busied himself solemnly with the building of large structures and with blocking all the entrances. When he widened his building activity to include bridges, watchtowers, and garages, he was still careful to first provide entrances and then block them. Henry was an unsmiling, frightened, angry child.

Mother had been widowed six years earlier when her husband died after prolonged paralysis. She had been working as an office clerk since his death and brought Henry for psychological treatment when his school day was reduced to the morning hours only. At twelve every day, Henry found himself on the street supervised by a neighbor. This was because his behavior was too much for the school to cope with and, as the principal stated, beyond its real task. There had also been a reading problem not treated by remedial methods even though reading analysts had twice pointed out the child's need. Henry was repeating the second grade.

A brief battery of psychological tests revealed a score of 120 Full Scale IQ on the WISC, despite Henry's low motivation. There was a large discrepancy, twenty-two points, between the Verbal and the Performance IQs in favor of the latter.

In the small selections of the Rorschach and of the TAT, Henry's reluctant responses were those of a child who has almost given up even before he started. A few passages on the Verbal Absurdities of the Stanford-Binet, hilarious to some children, were answered immediately and correctly by Henry, but with no smile or spark in his eyes. For the Exciting Scene, Henry eagerly constructed one of his buildings, threw in a flexible doll, and quickly blocked the exit, saying, "He is dead now." Here was a very bright and very depressed child who was rapidly withdrawing from reality.

Mother, a guarded and suspicious lady with concealed plans of her own and a strong sense of right and wrong, was interested primarily in finding out how to "do right by this child." Her own hours were taken up with reports about Henry and about her own long speeches to Henry. She refused to be reached as a person who cared about the child. She insisted on confining herself to acting as his manager.

By the end of about five months of his almost silent, compulsive play, Henry trusted me enough to venture into some new experiences in the playroom. He made some small designs with the colorful tiles of the Mosaic Box. Soon other activities followed. He began to draw with crayons and even to play with clay. At about the same time, Henry began to punch the punching bag, at first shyly, then vigorously and aggressively.

Figures VII-1, VII-2, VII-3, and VII-4 were selected because they best represent groups of productions about similar subjects made over a span of six months, at the end of the first year and in the beginning of the second year of therapy. These particular paintings also seemed to be of special importance to Henry. He described them more eloquently than the others, charging his descriptions with more emotion. Indeed, these paintings had stronger color, more filling in, and heavier pressure of the crayon than his other pictures.

Introducing Figure VII-1, Henry said, "That's me and my new wagon with a big squash from our garden. Mom wanted me to bring it in to the kitchen. . . ." He went on to tell that he just met "the man from sun again." In previous encounters, the man would just greet him and go away and that had been scary enough. This time, the man stopped and asked to go up with him, to the sun or into space, Henry thought. On the painting, Henry was trying to hit the ground with his stick to make the man disappear. To his mother's chagrin, Henry carried the stick

Figure VII-1. Crayons; Sunman

with him wherever he went, even to church. Hitting the ground with the stick was a helpful trick, for Henry believed that the space creature did not like the earth. But the trick was not working this time. Henry "begged off," as he said, on the ground that mother expected him and that he was dressed in a suit and tie to go to church, for it was Sunday.

In color, the picture is vivid. The ground is green; the two figures and the wagon, hot pink; the squash, bright orange; the sun, pale yellow, sending its rays through the two figures. There is heavily applied color on the wagon and on the figures. Their facial features, particularly noses and lips, are prominent. There is a difference between them in that Henry looks human, but the man looks somewhat superhuman in the size of the head in proportion to the rest of his body and limbs. In this picture, Henry is in command of the situation despite his fear. He is holding on to reality and, therefore, can see himself realistically, with sensible proportions of head, body, arms, and legs. The sun man, Henry's fantasy, also shows Henry's deterioration, or at least a beginning of it. His head and body are drawn in a regressive style.

Figure VII-2 is a design on the Mosaic Box tray. "This is a spaceman," Henry said. "He is unhappy and mad, he has a ball, and this is the sky, and this is a picture frame around him."

The body of the figure is made of blue diamond shapes. A red square topped with a large black triangle forms the head. Horizontally placed on the sides of the head are red diamonds for ears or, perhaps, wings, and one arm holds a red square for a ball. Henry chose the square as a substitute for a disc, which the Mosaic Box lacks. While working on the picture frame, Henry made sure that there was a diamond in every corner. He left spaces between some of the diamonds and placed white diamonds between the red and the blue ones. As I watched how carefully Henry placed the diamonds in the frame to maintain a certain pattern, it occurred to me that perhaps the child entertained some notions of magic.

Figure VII-3 is a pencil drawing colored with crayon. There is a large school building on a deserted playground, perhaps dur-

Figure VII-2. Mosaic tiles; Man with Ball

Figure VII-3.   Pencil and crayon; Trapped in the Swing

ing class time. The building is heavily shaded in black, making the numerous windows look as though they were lit up. On the bottom at the far right is a swing, built into a structure which looks like a cage. A person stands in front of the swing. The swing structure and the person are all in red over heavy black pencil lines. There are three red flowers between the swing and the school. They are receiving a stream of black rays from the yellow sun which has a face. The sun's eyes look away from the person in front of the swing. At the top is a cloudy sky marked off from the rest of the painting and heavily colored in red, again on top of the penciled black.

Henry explained that "the boy just got off the swing and he wants to go home, but he can't get out, so he must stay there, and nobody is around, and this is the sun. She is busy 'cause she has to make the garden grow, and this is the sky." Henry used the word "she" for the sun. It seems obvious that unconsciously he meant mother. Henry's remarks about the sun reflect his confusion about mother's sex and perhaps even his own. In mythology and religion, the sun usually symbolizes the male, though this is not universal. For example, in the Agadah, the folklore part of the ancient Hebrew Talmud, the sun is referred to as both "he" and "she." Henry's mother had to some extent played the role of both parents in much of his life, and he refers to the sun as "she." He wants mother to be a mother who cares for him, not for the three flowers. This wish and the frustration of it are both further expressed in Figure VII-4.

This drawing shows two birds in flight, the smaller bird following his mother. Both birds were painted with hot pink pastel and heavily colored in with red. Tense and angry, the large bird takes off in a hurry. Scared and enraged, the little bird awkwardly tries to follow close behind. His legs and wings are much shorter than mother's, but his beak is longer and sharper than hers. "The mother is going somewhere and she doesn't want him with her, but he goes just the same 'cause he doesn't know where she goes and when she'll be back and she won't tell him,

Figure VII-4. Crayons; Flight and Pursuit

and he is mad, too," said Henry in a continuous, angry, whining sequence.

Let us now turn once again to the first of this group and follow through to the last to see what Figures VII-1-VII-4 might be telling us about the child's inner world at the time, and also how this information was put to therapeutic use.

Figure VII-1 tells us that Henry is threatened by his moments of unreality and that he struggles with the growing fantasy which begins to dominate him. Henry was given two words, "real" and "unreal," for use in a description of this picture, which he made upon my request. These two words were then adopted for use in Henry's hours whenever the situation called for such a distinction.

Figure VII-2 is Henry's cry for help. Things begin to feel less and less real. Even the ball, the only bit of Henry's reality in the picture, does not save the man from his swift movement into the sky. If his flight is not stopped, the man will disappear. Perhaps that was why Henry felt the need to frame the picture. It might have been his not-quite-conscious effort to control imminent danger.

In this picture, unhappiness, a sense of being endangered, and a wish to be stopped were expressed by Henry graphically, but not verbally. In the ensuing conversation, Henry was able to say about the man that "he wants to be pulled down, but there is no rope there." That was my moment for intervention. Henry listened with disbelief when I said that the man could be pulled down if he so wished and that I would do it as soon as I traced the shapes of the tiles that made him up. Minutes later, Henry watched me with amazement and with a big smile as I carefully put my hand over his design of the spaceman and firmly moved him down to rest his feet on the bottom of the frame.

Figure VII-3, a grim and depressing painting, conveys the dismay of being trapped, of not being heard by significant adults, of guilt and hopelessness. Henry feels forgotten by the most important adult in his life, his mother; being forgotten is the most distressing feeling a child can have. Forgotten, overwhelmed with school, with the demands of the world upon him, Henry then becomes rage itself. In the picture this is expressed in the upper section, high up in the clouds. If we cover the painting below the skyline, which Henry carefully accentuated, the red and black sky with its floating clouds becomes a painting on its own, an image of self-contained rage. Rage was confined to Henry's inner life, the one area where he could let go and still be himself. This was happening, however, at the high price of increasing separation from reality.

Figure VII-4 might be telling of Henry's feeling about mother, of unsatisfied dependency, of his fear that she might forget and leave him, and of his violent fantasies about her. But the painting also shows that Henry is still fighting, that he has not entirely given up; moreover, that he senses mother's own fear of him. In a way, the painting points at the beginning of a conflict in Henry about his masculinity and about the balance of power in the small family of two. With its flaming reds, the painting is a live and spontaneous expression of the inner dynamics of a not quite nine-year-old boy in relation to his mother.

Henry volunteered that the little bird "also wanted to stab her with his beak, but he is too scared." Then, he suddenly recalled the puzzling and most unsettling dream he had the night before when "there was a girl on my blanket!!"

This was the opening to conversations during the next few visits about hating and liking girls; about mother, who is also a girl, "but a different one," as Henry said; and also about Henry, the boy. At that point, Henry brought up mother's widowhood and his own peculiar position: "She doesn't have a husband and I don't have a daddy and everybody else has one to go fishing and to play ball." I brought out the double duty of mother, who had to be also a little bit of a father, sometimes. As this was discussed, Henry expressed a wish to have a father, "a new father." He cited examples of two children in the area whose mothers remarried happily.

When some of these themes were discussed with mother in her hours, she recalled things about Henry that she had forgotten in the initial conferences, and even volunteered some feelings of her own. In his infancy, Henry had spells of crying in rage about the paralyzed father's inability to play with him and about mother's total care of the invalid. She had been impatient with Henry and generally bitter about her lot and even toward her husband. When death came to him suddenly after two years of illness, she felt guilty of "willing it on him." She had also plunged into grossly exaggerated protection of Henry, both physical and social, never leaving him alone with the neighborhood children, rushing to him when she heard him cry, and taking him to bed with her when he cried at night.

Henry could not get along with children. They teased him and this made him act up, thereby invariably bringing mother to the rescue. She mentioned a neighborhood boy, Jerry, who became Henry's oppressor and her personal enemy.

Of course, some of Henry's difficulties were connected with her own emotional troubles, as she now acknowledged. But she was quite clearly opposed to discussing herself. Instead, she saw two problems only. One pertained to Henry's behavior in school, a problem which she thought was nearly solved since I had succeeded, two months earlier, in persuading the school principal that Henry could be restored to normal hours of attendance. The other problem was Jerry and his influence on Henry. For example, the two boys had "swapped" objects taken from their homes. Henry's mother said she had made up her mind long ago that removing Henry from Jerry was the only remedy. She had no ear for any other views and decided that she would take Henry away for the whole summer and later, if need be, think of other ways to stop Jerry's influence.

But there was also a third problem, one of her own, which she had to mention, much to her dislike, for she needed some help about dicussing it with Henry. It involved the man who had come into her life about two years previously and about whom she had doubts as well as plans. It seemed to me that testing the man's sincerity was no less important than removing Henry from Jerry; moving away for the summer seemed to be an effective double solution. My efforts to help her see that Henry needed help badly and should not interrupt therapy for almost three months were to no avail. Mother and son moved to a nearby resort for a long vacation.

When he was seen again, to start the third year of psychotherapy, Henry was quite overweight and very belligerent with mother. He was less talkative again and kept himself busy during his visits, furiously punching the bag, building very complex houses or towers with miniature bricks and shooting them down, and "messing with clay." On one occasion, I recalled his old pattern of blocking doors. Henry remembered it and volunteered that by doing that "funny thing" he was probably blocking my way to him so that I could not "succeed in finding out what was going on inside" him. Asked if he had ever had, since then, a similar need to block or to withhold information about himself, Henry answered, "Yes, like now."

He went on to say that he was now much worse than he had ever been before, that he started school "worse than ever," that there was nothing that he wanted to do, and that he really wanted to do nothing. When brought back to his theme of "withholding from" and asked to be specific and say what he was withholding from whom, he was able to make a list: "Number one, studying, from my teacher; number two, doing things, doing anything, from mother; and number three, telling about feelings and thoughts about my 'real inside,' from you." Soon, he was also able to see that he had transferred some of his hostility toward mother onto each of the two other women in his life, the teacher and the psychologist.

As previously mentioned, Henry worked with clay. Over a few visits, he built pairs of blobs in various shapes and sizes. But as obsessively as he made the pairs, he destroyed them. When I tried to put one of the blob sculptures out of the way to preserve it, Henry remembered to reach for it and to knead it furiously into a ball.

He was suddenly confronted with my question, "What goes on, Henry, what are you trying to tell me?" Henry threw the last ball of blobs into the pile of clay and informed me in a detached tone of voice that mother was planning to remarry, but that now he felt no wish or need for a father. So it was during the summer months without help that Henry particularly needed, when mother's long friendship had actually culminated in marriage to the man to whom Henry had grown attached in the past two years. Henry refused to accept the reality of the marriage and informed me of marriage plans only. Later that day Henry's mother called to make an appointment for herself to tell me about the marriage and Henry's resentment.

Three of Henry's hour-long visits were devoted to his anger at mother's marriage and to his failure to accept its reality. In addition, mother and husband were seen both separately and together. The husband had been devoted to Henry and thought of himself as the boy's father. Formal adoption was in the process.

Figure VII-5 was produced in the third of Henry's hours concerned with the event of the marriage. It was the second version of three sculptures in clay of mother and child and the

Figure VII-5.   Clay; On Mother's Back

only one preserved. Henry had destroyed the first and allowed the third to fall off the work table. All of them were about the same size, 6 x 2½ x 2 inches.

We see a bent-over woman carrying a child on her back. Her arms are folded in front. The child has no arms. He is held to mother's back by a long rope, twice wound around his back and around mother's waist. In the earlier version, the rope was much longer. Henry had persistently rolled the clay into long "snakes" to have them wind around the two figures four or five times to almost hide the child.

It is possible to view this sculpture in two ways: facing toward the left the way it was made, and toward the right, unintentionally formed. Toward the left, the woman's head is bent down, her profile on the far left. This makes the child face mother's back. From left to right, we see the mother's head forming now a profile facing the child's face and putting the whole sculpture into a forward-stepping motion. Now mother's raised eyebrows, or what seem to be eyebrows, create the impression of intention in her concentrated look at the child. Viewed this way, mother and child seem to embrace face-to-face. A glance at the sculpture from right to left again returns us to the intentionally produced image of the burdened mother and the armless child tied to her back, face to back.

Henry made no remarks about this work, but it agitated him. The agitation became more pronounced when he frantically looked for a safe place to hide the sculpture so that it would not be seen by his mother when she came for her own hour.

When I slowly turned the sculpture for Henry, he independently noticed the two views. I suggested that they represented two kinds of feelings between mother and child. From each of the two points of view, Henry was asked what the mother might be saying to the child and what the child might be saying to the mother. About the face-to-back view, Henry said, "Mother says, 'Get off my back. Don't you see I'm tired?' And the child says, "No, I won't. You've got to carry me all the time and take me places." About the face-to-face view, Henry said, "I don't know. I can't think of anything. . . . maybe she says, 'You are good, honey.' And maybe he says, 'I love you.' My mother loves me. She does." He preferred the view which he had not intended to make. He became angry when I wondered why the boy would not get off his mother's back, but gave no answer.

It was of special interest that while Henry's latest upset was about mother's marriage, there was nothing about her husband in the three hours' discussion or in Figure VII-5 "because my troubles always are with mom, not dad," Henry said. He also said that he liked his father and had begun to call him "dad." This was in accord with mother's reports about Henry's good relationship with father and about his fits of anger with her.

Figure VII-6 brought Henry's deep-seated anger with mother out into the open. He produced the blot of red paint on an old newspaper after the fashion of folded ink blots, working silently and with great care and concentration. His original intention was to develop the unpainted, oval section at the center. Much careful planning went into the preliminaries. Most of Henry's effort, however, was given to the achievement of symmetry in the spreading of the red painted blot which, I thought, was to serve only as a background for the unpainted spot. Since Henry worked in silence and offered no comments, I could only watch and wonder. When he finally opened the folded paper, he said in an imitation soprano, "This is my mom. She says, 'Oooh?' and 'What have *you* done *today?*' " The long sound of "oooh" corresponded to the oblong lip formation suggested by the unpainted center of the blot. The very beginning of the imitation of mother's tone of voice put Henry into an openly angry and aggressive mood. He began to repeat the "oooh" and the "What have *you* done *today?*" in a crescendo of the shrill, question-marked accusation many times until the words were lost and there was only shrieking. Finally, Henry burst into tears and sobbed, saying that there was "a bad" in him and that "mom knows it because she always said so."

In this blot of paint, the least artistic of his productions, Henry expresses as vividly as a child could his fear of a deep-seated evil inside him. It was the fear that mother might be right, that he was, indeed, the carrier of a germinal evil that would grow in him and overwhelm him and could not be stopped.

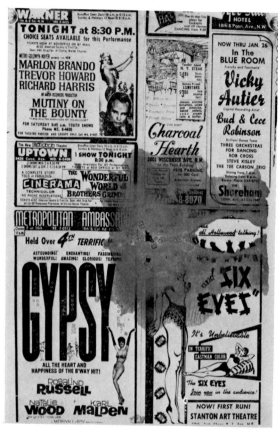

Figure VII-6. Paint on newspaper; The Inquiry

Henry's unusual expression of this combined anger at mother and fear of evil inside himself is testimony to the power of significant adults in the formation of a child's personality. Parents and others can indeed plant goodness in their children by investing full trust in them.

In the midst of his crying, I asked Henry to draw mother and himself. He drew Figure VII-7 with black crayon, starting on the right with a crawling boy with long arms and legs. He wrote above it, sarcastically adding two years to his age, "Me, Henry, 14." There was also baby talk in writing. But Henry soon crossed out both number and words and drew on the left a large figure of mother smiling at a tiny baby in her arms.

Figure VII-7.   Felt pen; Infant and Baby

The baby had a double meaning, as Henry later explained. The idea which he had planned to express in sharp sarcasm about himself was that he was regressing, first to a crawling infant and from there to the baby in mother's arms. With embarrassment and some stuttering, he was able to say that he had often entertained pleasant thoughts about being a baby and wondered what it would be like to become a baby again. To his relief, I placed the need to relive early childhood experiences in the context of human emotions that even adults sometimes feel. But Henry still had to learn to differentiate between such normal needs and the spreading of demands of this kind over the whole of a person's behavior. His sculpture of mother and child (Fig. VII-5) was brought in again to help make the point more valid. On this occasion, Henry wondered why the sculpture had not been thrown out, and the ensuing discussion brought out his embarrassment about "that boy. He is hanging on to his mother's back."

The second, unplanned meaning of Figure VII-7 occurred to Henry while he was drawing. "Suddenly it hit me," he said, and acknowledged his fear that mother might have a baby one day and would then give him up. This was an echo of the old feeling of being forgotten.

Figure VII-8, a sketch in blue and orange crayon reminiscent of the mother-and-child sculpture shown in Figure VII-5 was brought by mother when she came to discuss, rather abruptly, termination of psychotherapy for Henry because her husband's job required him to move to another town. She had found the

Figure VII-8.   Crayon; Sketch

drawing in Henry's wastebasket among many torn pictures and wondered if the boy had talent and if she should send him to art school. The significance of her notion, coming at this time, will be discussed below.

The badly creased page was ironed, dated, and placed in Henry's folder. It was an addition, perhaps a last one, to the sequence of Figures VII-4-VII-8, which encompassed Henry's complex struggle with mother and with himself in relation to her.

Figures VII-6, VII-7, and VII-8 indicated certain developments in Henry's mental health. Artistically, these productions, particularly the first two, mark a considerable regression in comparison with Henry's earlier rather precocious art expressions. The formal deterioration of the art work was a counterpart of his growing emotional disorganization. The productions follow a built-in, though invisible, arrow pointing toward an emotional breakdown.

Psychologically, Figure VII-6 is intriguing, with an inner sequence of development, even though as a product it looks like child's play. In reality, that is, in Henry's emotional reality, this production represented both his great effort to control a threatening emotional outburst, and the breakdown of that effort. The attempt at self-control included a long process of trying to obtain the "just right" shape of the blot. Four or five attempts were discarded because the red paint spread too far over the newspaper. This disturbed Henry very much, even though this should not have mattered, since he had originally intended mainly to define and emphasize the unpainted center section.

He took to marking boundaries with pencil. He turned and jiggled the paper in an agitated fashion and was quite upset when the penciled boundaries were flooded with paint. It seemed that the blot itself was becoming more important than the empty space at the center.

As I watched Henry's tense face, it occurred to me that unconsciously he was trying to check his rising rage and distress. But he succeeded better in keeping the paint within the designated boundaries than in controlling the rage itself. The verbal outburst quickly deteriorated into shrieking, and pure sound took over. This was a breakdown of the controls which Henry had tried to muster when he so pedantically toiled, early in the process, to achieve just the right shape.

Several emotional events occurred in the process of Henry's work on the blot. What he was dealing with is the fundamental stuff on which the Rorschach method is based: impulse and control. In the Rorschach cards, color represents impulsivity, and shape or form represents control. Both forces are human, both reside in the person's inner life. Only in certain circumstances an individual may take a distorted view, seeing monstrous evil in one and a prosecutor or judge in the other. Henry's impulses and controls did battle with each other long before he was mature and strong enough to combine them into a process of growth.

There was another aspect of the Rorschach system which Henry demonstrated quite naturally in Figure VII-6. He incorporated the unpainted area of the blot as a meaningful part of his graphic expression. On the Rorschach ink blots, attribution of meaning to spaces with no color sometimes indicates negativism, resistance, aggression, and also self-assertion, depending upon other responses and the proportion to the total number of responses. Henry could have painted a face with an oval-shaped mouth, or a mouth without a face, yet this important part of his very strongly felt expression about mother remained unpainted and, in fact, was made entirely in terms of form. So complex was the emotion about mother that using color would have been unbearable; using form alone was the safest thing to do. The combination of extreme negative feelings toward mother and the pressing need to control his anger at her necessitated the use of the unpainted area.

Still somewhat intrigued by the spatial relationship between the large red-colored area and the small but well-defined area free of color, and also by the importance of both areas to Henry, I tried to apply the theory of pattern and frame of reference, one aspect of the Gestalt psychology of art. In a whole configuration composed of parts, figure and ground can be exchanged, each in turn being viewed as a frame of reference for the other.

As we look at Figure VII-6, our eyes first perceive the painted area in reference to the unpainted section. If we look away and then return to concentrate on the unpainted center, that small area becomes prominent while the painted area acts as its background or frame of reference. This exercise helps us see that each of the two areas in Figure VII-6 achieved its own prominence when the other was allowed to serve as a background.

Let us consider the unpainted area as Henry's representation of mother's accusations, as it indeed was intended to be at the outset. The painted area became his unintended rage which rose up, as he proceeded, out of what started as a mere background for the unpainted section. We then understand that there was a constant exchange of foreground or intended subject matter, and background, each gaining prominence of its own.

To return to Figure VII-7, the second in the group of three, here regression is rather alarming, more so than in Figures VII-6 or VII-8. This is actually a crude expression of a person in the very state of regressing to infancy with almost no signs of strength or growth or any other redeeming feature, except for the very ability to reexperience graphically, and later verbally, some feelings about infancy apart from the old overwhelming anger. In fact, the regression, actually promoted by my request to draw himself and mother, helped Henry talk about his infantile feelings and discover his unconscious fear of a new baby and of perhaps being forgotten again. Of course, artistically and in terms of organization, Figure VII-7 is very crude and represents a serious temporary loss of talent.

Figure VII-8, the last of this group, was drawn in solitude and was probably one of many similar drawings. It appears to be a sketch for the sculpture shown in Figure VII-5. It seemed to me that the sketch was a graphic statement of his mental reviewing or re-thinking the same experience that inspired the sculpture. In that sense, Figure VII-8 has some integrative value. The drawing is placed in the center of the paper. The boy is facing his viewers. His face has features. His feet are large and strong, perhaps an indication of a dawning notion that these feet are for standing. There is an angry expression on mother's face, perhaps the beginning of a realization that she, too, has a reason to be angry. And there is a generally mocking touch about the sketch as a whole. This is best seen in the nonchalantly sweeping rounds of the rope, so loose that the boy may slip off at any moment. In some ways, this is a sophisticated, though still quite disturbed, image of self-mockery which had its beginning in Figure VII-7, when Henry ironically added two years to his age. He was much taller and larger than his friends and classmates even though he was only one year older than they.

At the time, I carefully watched Henry's states of mind because he was experiencing a rather serious crisis. Therefore, the sudden decision of his parents to move at this time was surprising. But even stranger than that was his mother's notion about Henry's talent. It seemed to me that it was an effort on her part to reject the facts about Henry's disturbance and about the crisis he was going through, as well as to shift her conscious need to do something special for her son into a less painful area.

She was becoming more and more aware of her own problems, and my effort to help her understand Henry's situation did not reach her. My attempts at urging her to seek help for Henry in the new location brought forth from her vague statements about the importance for Henry of a change of environment, about the old but long-neglected need to get him away from Jerry, and about how her husband was to start as chief of the company's section in the other town.

Two days later, the husband telephoned for a conference. He then disclosed that he had yielded to his wife's pressure to accept the company's offer but was still thinking about canceling his agreement, since he was not eager to move or take the post. He also reported that Henry had been registered for the year after next in a military academy and admitted his own uneasiness about it. This adoptive father had much more feeling for and understanding of Henry than his mother ever had. It was clear that this manipulative and perturbed lady was the manager of both her son and her husband and that there would be no change of plans. For three years after that, I heard no more about Henry.

Early in the summer before he entered the tenth grade, his parents called for a conference. The following day, Henry himself telephoned.

The family was back in the old home town. A furious dispute was taking place over Henry's refusal to return to the military academy where he had spent the last two years. The most anguishing problem for the parents, however, was Henry's re-union with old friend, Jerry, who now had a police record. They feared his influence on Henry, and felt that Henry was at present extremely disturbed. They were happily surprised when he him-self asked for permission to call me.

Both parents accepted my suggestion that Henry stay home, attend public high school, and receive psychotherapeutic treat-ment. I saw him three times a week during most of the summer, and he continued to come twice a week during the following school year.

"I am in the mud; can you pull me out?" Dirty, overweight, and extremely perturbed, Henry thus introduced me to his situa-tion after the first two weeks of his summer vacation.

He disclosed that he had not finished the school year, but had run away before exams. Jerry had met and housed him at his parents' camp site, and they spent the first week destroying abandoned cars off country roads and vandalizing apartments in new developments. After that, during a recent few days in town, Jerry coached him in the technique of "handling cops." But Henry said that "the worst thing that shook me up and made me sick" was his agreement, two nights earlier, to Jerry's wild plan to rape a girl in Henry's own house when his parents were out of town.

Before Jerry's arrival with the girl, Henry drank all the alcohol he could find in the house. He recalled only that he had wanted to be drunk so as not to hear Jerry, and that he had turned off all the lights. He remembered crawling on the floor and hoping to die. Henry broke the silence which followed his story by saying that he did not want to talk about that evening anymore. I stressed that not the events but his feelings were the important thing, and reminded him that pastels, crayons, paints, and clay could be helpful in saying without words something about what he felt.

That was how Figure VII-9 came into being. Against a background shaded black for air or space, an angular metal or wire ship is moving. In a small section on the right, a toppling figure seems to be enclosed, holding on to poles. Its pose and the position of the ship together create the impression of violent move-

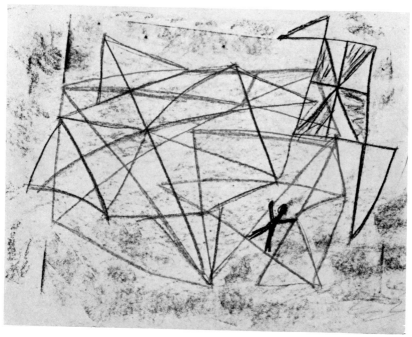

Figure VII-9. Crayons; The Space Ship

ment. The ship is very colorful, made up of red, violet, yellow, and a few black lines (see Color Plate XVII). Henry volunteered that the movement of the ship frightened him, "It puts the scare in me." At that point, I wondered if there was a resemblance between this painting and any of Henry's childhood productions. Excitedly, Henry looked through his old, worn folder, laughed at his childish work, and pulled out first the Spaceman (Fig. VII-2), then the school painting with the boy trapped in the swing (Fig. VII-3).

Figure VII-10, made with poster paints, was, in Henry's words, "a more artistic" elaboration of the scribble he drew habitually with pen and ink in his notebook during class time. Henry named it "The Flying Mattress." The rectangular grid is framed in dark blue. Underneath horizontal and vertical stripes in blue and yellow is a coat of strong red, brightly showing through the openings. On the four corners of the 12- x 18-inch paper are gray and green blobs of paint. Henry made a crescent moon, finger-painting style, on the upper right blob.

Due to its position on the paper, the whole grid seems to be

moving head-on into the sky or into space. Henry volunteered that this painting, too, was akin to the spaceman picture, only now he used the shape of the mattress because he hoped to find out why he slept so much. This was another reason for current conflicts between him and his parents. As he talked, however, he smilingly said he had "just figured out" that sleeping was the

Figure VII-10. Poster paints; The Flying Mattress

same as flying "away from it all." I challenged him to specify what the last words meant, since he had used them a few times recently, but Henry became quite angry and left a few minutes before his time was up, without explanation.

The next time, he turned immediately to work with poster paints. Very hesitantly and slowly he produced Figure VII-11, a bright, colorful painting, but one that is hard to understand at first glance and rather disturbing.

On the upper left is a simple outline in the shape of a small box. From left to right, we see a long wavy form dotted green on yellow and framed in red; above is a flower in red, blue, and yellow; below is a fruit or an insect, white outside, and inside dabbed green and black on yellow. Above and farther right is the last of the four forms, a green ball or shell split in two.

Henry was upset by this painting for he did not know what made him "paint these things," and what they had to do with each other. When he was asked to invent a story about them, he said almost immediately, "This poisonous snake came down from

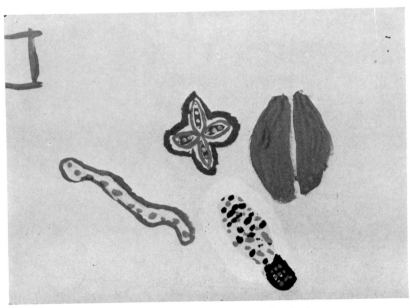

Figure VII-11. Poster paints; Unrelated Things

behind that fence [box, upper left]. He was trying to bite the flower, but didn't get to; now he is trying to eat up this here bug, but the bug is crawling away from him, so he [the snake] will get good and mad and get into this here thing [green shell] and it will close on him and he will die there or just disappear." Embarrassed and somewhat downhearted, Henry laughed at his own story, but half seriously and half humorously demanded that the "real meaning" of the disquieting painting be disclosed to him.

His own unrest about it became the basis for discussions during the next few visits about sex development, confusion, fear, reality, and unreality. Both Henry and I spoke of the "rape night" when Henry had to get drunk, and at some points I suggested a connection between adolescent fear of growing up and a desire to die. Each of these themes struck a chord in Henry's inner experience and he willingly spoke of some of these feelings, particularly of his occasional desire to die, but he remained solemn and preoccupied. It seemed that the real theme of his preoccupation still remained beyond his understanding, or perhaps it only remained unexpressed.

Figures VII-9-VII-11 form another group, centered again on disintegration of personality. While Figure VII-9 was meant to express confusion and to convey a feeling of new threats, its formal organization shows some strength. It is dramatic, it conveys the intended feelings, it communicates an imminent danger, and it is well integrated despite its disquieting theme.

Figure VII-10, however, is grim. The feeling of emptiness we sense from the flying mattress among the foreboding clouds while the moon looks on is quite depressing and reminiscent of Figure VII-3, when the sun was busy with the flowers while the little boy was trapped. But although Figure VII-10 is a depressing and unsettling picture, the painter remained in one piece. He was still able to communicate something about an intended theme and to relate the strange flying object to his actual problem with sleep.

Figure VII-11, the most regressed of the three paintings, suggests that the painter might have been experiencing a schizoid disturbance. The painting as a whole is fragmented, and in the form on the right, there is actually a split. The painter did not know why he had painted these strange images that made no sense to him or to anybody else. The bright colors did not have any redeeming effect on this inferior production by a person who had shown artistic talent.

Figures VII-12 and VII-13 are two views of a clay car Henry made at that time. It has no doors or windows; the driver sees, but is not seen. He is informed about the world via an antenna (Fig. VII-12, right) and can communicate with the world if he so desires through the little tube attached to the roof on the left. Henry pointed out that, turned to a vertical position, the carvings on the side of the car (Fig. VII-12) make a face, and the front of the car (Fig. VII-13) has another large face carved on it.

After silently working on the car most of one hour, Henry wondered if the faces could be seen. I assured him that I could recognize them and others would also be able to.

When I wondered about the driver of that very special car, Henry exclaimed, "That's a crazy lunatic driver," and was about to throw the sculpture into the pile of clay. I intervened on behalf of the smart but unhappy driver, who perhaps needed to

Figure VII-12.   Clay; The Car

Figure VII-13.   Clay; The Same Car

save himself in order to be seen by all as he was. I remarked that he was trying to hide but certainly had provided his car with a way to communicate with somebody; and somebody certainly would see him. What was he hiding from, I asked.

A change in Henry's mood of solemn preoccupation became evident, at first only in his eyes now turned toward me. He thought, Henry said, that he might be running away from Jerry, but he knew now that Jerry was not the cause of "all that trouble."

"All that trouble" included more conflict at home, more failure and loneliness at school, and more personal "messiness." Jerry had not actually been bothering him since "the night," except for occasional sarcastic looks and insulting smiles. Henry's most terrifying trouble was his recurring dreams, or perhaps even hallucinations, for he was no longer sure when they occurred, at night or in the daytime. He knew the dreams well, he said, but could not describe them in words "because they were so crazy." He knew that there were three parts that occurred in a certain sequence. He thought that these dreams showed quite clearly that he was insane and he expected me to agree. Shyly but seriously he added that it was "probably the unconscious." I commented that the unconscious may not be all that unconscious and encouraged him to paint his dreams as spontaneously as he could at the moment.

Figure VII-14 shows, at the left, a head. The triangular face has a pair of horrified Picassoesque eyes and is topped by a mass of heavily colored hair. The right eye, almost vertical, seems to be viewing the rest of the page. Out of the head, in childlike style, grow arms that resemble airplanes. Below the shoulders, where chest and stomach would be expected, a group of three intertwined one-eyed, wide-mouthed creatures appear to form the rest of a person. Antennae mark these subsidiary creatures as supernatural. This trio was drawn in black in contrast to the rest of the painting which is all in magenta (see Color Plate XVIII).

In the center of the paper is another group of three one-eyed creatures, all in motion. The upper one, turned toward a large creature on the right, bears some resemblance to a human being.

Figure VII-14.   Chalks and crayons; Creatures of the Dream

The lower ones look more like animals or fish. Of these two, the left one seems to be turning toward the two-eyed human figure.

The right side of the paper is occupied by a large image of a one-eyed person to whom the middle group of three is related. The outstanding features of this person are, in addition to the huge eye, a big, unevenly grinning mouth, many legs coming out of a round body, and a pair of ears or raised arms growing out of the head.

Viewing the painting as a whole, we notice that the composite figure on the left is the only owner of a pair of eyes and is in two colors; the images in the center and on the right form a single group, and the figure on the left is an observer of this group.

It was my impression that Henry had painted himself watching a happening about himself, but I did not share my impression with him, and he offered this interpretation of his own: "Here on this side [the left] is a boy. Inside him are these stupid devils. They make him do evil and they make him sick, too. Now you're going to laugh, but here [center] they're working on him, dancing around him and changing him so that here [right] he looks like them, only bigger. He has one eye and all these legs, and in the dream there were more legs; and he is kind of laughing, but it was scary, and the whole thing was awful, terrible and sickening." Henry remembered that in the dream the color was "like shiny pink neon light," and that was why he chose magenta. He also talked of transparency, "maybe like glass."

Henry did not know how Figure VII-15 followed in the dream. It seemed to him that it moved in on top of the fading Figure VII-14.

On a hazy red and greeen cloud, Henry outlined three heads. The center head is the largest and the fiercest; outlined in dark green, it has vertical magenta eyes with blue sockets and large orange pupils. The mouth is in the same strong blue as the eye sockets. The face is colored orange and brown. The two narrower heads might be transparent because the cloudy green and red background shows through rather clearly (see Color Plate XIX).

All three heads rest on rounded, horizontally elongated

Figure VII-15.   Chalks; Trio of the Dream

bodies. The two side bodies are orange and they overlap. Over them spreads the central body, outlined in strong red and heavily shaded with the square side of a green pastel stick, creating horizontal stripes.

Nine strong legs in brown carry the triple monster body which seems to move forward and sideways at the same time. I watched the painter attach only one leg to each of the side figures and the remaining seven to the central figure.

As in Figure VII-14, so in Figure VII-15 the space is well used. There is a central focus, and the balance is good. There is strength, too, in that the use of color, line, and varied pressure of the pastel combine to convey intense feeling effectively. The most striking features of the painting are movement and sculptural quality.

Henry turned back to Figure VII-14 and said that he knew now what he had really painted. It was his childhood belief that there was evil in him and that the evil would make him get into trouble "forever." Indeed, new troubles have always been proof to him that evil was residing inside him. Henry remembered persuading himself time and again throughout late childhood and his early teens "that there was no such thing as the devil or some evil sitting inside a person." But he also remembered being afraid of it "just the same," and praying to God for help. He also recalled that each time mother demanded that he confess what he had done wrong that day, "she was always right, because she knew, and she knew because she sort of made me." There was a special stress on the words, "she knew." This direct association of the emotional experience with its forerunner in childhood, represented in Figure VII-6, brings out the depth of Henry's old feeling of being trapped: his mother "knows" of his evil but cannot help him; therefore, his dependency upon her remains blocking and destructive.

What distressed and at the same time surprised Henry was that he still believed deep inside that there was evil in him. Indeed, in the dream pictured in Figure VII-14, he had watched with horror the destruction and complete metamorphosis of his own person accomplished by the evil.

In Figure VII-15, Henry saw the triumph of the evil, the central figure. When "he took over," Henry explained, "The real me split and was pushed open like sliding doors to make room for the fat slob." Ironically and significantly Henry, grossly overweight, was the living illustration for his own description of the painting. "Yeah, . . . got to do something about that." He smiled with embarrassment as he motioned to the folds of fat on himself, thereby allowing for the first time touching on the problem of overeating.

There had, however, been yet another part of the dream which Henry had spoken of and which I reminded him to paint.

Figure VII-16 is the production of a more relaxed painter or dreamer, certainly not of a violent one. Two fantasy creatures gently approach each other. The blue masculine one on the left is lightly touching with his yellow arm the light purple wing of the soft feminine one on the right. His whole body is turned toward her, and she is lightly turning to him, her head tilted in his direction. Her colors are delicate violets and greens and light yellows and oranges (see Color Plate XX).

Henry named the painting "the boy-girl of the spacemen." In the dream, before this scene came on, he remembered being scared of yet another scene after the first two shocking ones. But when the "boy-girl" figures appeared, it was rather pleasant and stirred warm, agreeable feelings in him. He wondered what had made him "come up with this kind of good thing" and asked if it might mean that instead of "violence and rudeness, . . . there is love?" That day, Henry went home in a very thoughtful mood.

Perhaps Henry expected that the new insights would have an instant effect on his behavior, would transform his way of life

Figure VII-16.   Chalks; Love Fantasy

immediately. If so, he was bitterly disappointed. For there still was the anticipated misery of his report card with only a part of the spring semester to go, and there were his sloppiness and his obesity, which he now hated. There were the house chores he always neglected, to the annoyance of his parents; and he craved to be Jerry's friend again "and to have some fun with him."

Henry was bitter, sarcastic, and on the whole, uncommunicative for the next two visits. When he spoke about his disappointment and anger with me for letting him down, he was also ready to realize that he had expected a magic transformation. Asked to make a brief and clear sentence about himself at that point, Henry said, "O.K., I have got to make up my mind where I am, on the side of the good or on the side of the bad."

Henry at last became able to formulate some goals for himself. His very statement about good and evil expressed, in fact, one goal. He added to it another, the scholastic one; he realized that he had to decide whether to drop out or stay and finish high school. He wanted to know something about his intelligence before deciding, and confessed that the question of how bright he really was had always worried him, perhaps as much as the fear of the evil dwelling in him.

At the age of sixteen years and five months, Henry scored a Full Scale IQ of 132 on the same Wechsler Scale on which he had scored 120 at the age of seven years and ten months. The Performance IQ, only a few points higher than the Verbal IQ, indicated a clinically important development toward unification of his personality.

Henry's reaction to the information about the level of his intellectual ability was interesting: what he deduced from it was primarily of social rather than direct scholastic significance. He reviewed at great length his past and present ties with and dependencies upon people who were not bright at all, who "could never make it anyway beyond elementary school." He understood now why his teachers had never expected better work from him: they believed that what he offered was his best and saw him as one of a group of people with quite low intelligence.

I was seeing Henry once a week now to talk about pursuing

the few specific goals which he had set for himself: to finish the
year without having to attend summer school; to lose some
weight; to look "more or less" decent; to get into better company
("I don't want the all-A boys, just the high-C kids and some B
kids who are fun, not just the goody goodies!"); to find a girl
friend; and to begin to think about how to make a living when
he would be grown up.

Figure VII-17 was Henry's last production before termination. He looked at his self-portrait and said, "That's me; that's a
dollar bill to show that I know now that I have to make a living;
that geometric thing, that's something about my interest in
science, the only subject that began to bring in my A's and B's;
and the radio, that's for electronics, that I like to play and work
with; and maybe I'll take that up for a living." When asked what
he saw in the face itself, Henry said, "There is anger around the
mouth; there is something, like one part of me, that is always

Figure VII-17.   Chalks; Self-Portrait

angry; I was never a happy kid. I never smile, maybe that's it. In the eyes there is a wonderment, a puzzlement, what will happen? What will I be?"

SUMMARY

This study deals with the course in art psychotherapy of a withdrawn and somewhat autistic boy. He received treatment at two periods: from age eight to twelve, and at the age of sixteen. In the first period, his therapy centered on the expression through the use of art media of his complex relationship with mother, who was his only parent through late childhood. In the context of this relationship, the boy developed a belief that a germinal evil resided in him and determined his actions. There were some schizoid episodes.

In the second period, at sixteen, the boy came to grips with his evil genius and also began to discover himself. This was achieved, again, with the aid of expression through art. At termination, he was beginning to face the future, and the present was beginning to make sense to him.

FOLLOW-UP

At the end of the tenth grade, Henry managed to bring up his grades to average and his science grade to B. This achievement was earned with hard work in preparation for regular exams, extra-credit assignments in most subjects, and some encouragement and even pressure from Henry's teachers who now knew about his ability. The problem of inner evil seemed to be solved for good and all, although to some extent it may have lingered on. Jerry, its outer representative in Henry's life, no longer mattered. Henry spent the summer working at a job and cultivating new friends. Playing ball and swimming helped him lose weight.

The situation at home was good, except for mother's growing "nervousness," as she herself reported. For the time being, there was no need for Henry to be seen in therapy since he was functioning rather well. If he had a problem, it was his inability to work consistently; he could not keep his average grades steady.

The first report card of the spring semester in the eleventh grade told that he was failing again, except in science. But after I talked on the telephone with him about the improvement of his grades the year before, he planned a renewed effort. He seemed to gain help particularly from a brief discussion of his question, "You don't think its the old stupid stuff, do you?"

As of this writing, Henry has started his senior year and his mother has started psychotherapy for herself. It cannot be known what lasting effect (if any) Henry's schizoid childhood experiences will have on him. His reluctance to act, in learning or at work or even at play, and his disbelief in himself certainly call for further therapeutic treatment.

VIII

Diane

THIS IS A STUDY of the first six months of art psychotherapy with a thirteen-year-old girl who suffered from anorexia. Capable of fine thinking but detached from her own feelings, Diane produced at first only mechanical pictures with a rather flat attitude toward any connections they might have with her inner life. But with only a little help she adopted art therapy and its method of spontaneous expression on paper or with clay, and soon established it as her own way of dealing with her problems. Art therapy also helped Diane communicate verbally and make her communications clear. Remarkable changes in feeling and behavior gradually developed. After the first six months, Diane's psychotherapy proceeded in much the same way with only a change in depth; therefore, the first span of therapeutic work was chosen for this study.

Anorexia, a medical term derived from ancient Greek, means want of appetite. The adjective *nervosa* in *anorexia nervosa* points at the psychopathological aspect of decrease in food intake and loss of weight. Diane was steadily losing weight as a result of diminishing intake of food when I first met her. She was then under the supervision of a physician who planned to put her in a hospital for special care if a point was reached where her health was endangered.

Diane's parents, Mr. and Mrs. Danby, were extremely anxious about her hospitalization, so much so that they failed to take into account the possibility that a course in the hospital might do their child some good. Mr. Danby, a highly qualified professional man in a medical field, had been in psychiatric treatment for some time. It was his psychiatrist who told him that Diane's anorexia might have an emotional basis and referred the family to me. In his anxiety and although he knew better, Mr. Danby expected that quick psychological treatment would save his child from the hospital. His wife, also very anxious but in general more passive, was not as vocal as he.

The anxiety of Diane's parents was, however, understandable. Only a few years earlier their older daughter, Susan, now a college freshman, had experienced a long, gruelling spell of anorexia, was repeatedly hospitalized, and at the same time, developed diabetes. Diane herself dreaded hospitalization; I had the impression that she considered it a punishment and that she would judge me by my success in averting it.

Under these circumstances, Diane's therapy began in an atmosphere of tension, fear, and unrealistic expectations on the part of the patient and her parents. These pressures hindered the therapeutic process from starting to evolve at its own pace and with the freedom essential to the development of a new relationship between patient and psychologist.

After preliminary interviews, conferences, and diagnostic testing, Diane began to come three times a week, and then was put in the hospital for twelve days. Father was seen only in early conferences as he was already in treatment and his psychiatrist kept in touch with me when necessary. Mother, who had refused professional help for herself in the past, agreed to come to me once a week for individual visits and soon joined a small group in art psychotherapy, as well.

Diane was the third of five children, four girls, and a boy one year older than Diane. She came willingly, even rather eagerly, for her first interview. A tall, extremely thin brunette with a large mass of black hair, she walked with a stoop. Prominent in her small, pale face were enormous eyes, darkly set in deep sockets and gazing into space sadly and with fear. Most impressive because of its bizarre character was her costume. The many costumes she later appeared in, a new one for each visit, were equally grotesque. They were elegant and often too big, mature-looking evening outfits, pantsuits, maxi and mini dresses with matching coats, and high-heeled shoes, all made of expensive materials. Diane's utter seriousness, her unsmiling face, and her way of speaking almost in a whisper only added to the strange impression made by this thirteen-year-old child.

She answered my question, "What brought you to me?" with a report of her "chubbiness" last year when she had grossly overeaten. At a certain point she had wanted mother to put her on a diet, but mother reassured her time and again that being chubby was becoming to her. Diane did not really believe it and plunged into a severe diet which got out of control and turned into starvation. For some vague reason, Diane connected her rapid loss of weight with the early onset of menarche at the age of eleven and a half. Much to her satisfaction, she had only menstruated once. At the time, she had felt "too fat and too young" for her rapid physical development.

During the same period, she wished to be admired for her intellectual achievement rather than for her looks, Diane said. Indeed, throughout the months of weight loss Diane worked hard and maintained A grades. At the time of her first contact with me she was heartbroken because, being unable to jump and run, she had received a C in physical education on her last report card. It did not occur to her that this might have been a result of her diminishing physical strength, as was her growing sensation of being cold. The low grade worried her mainly because it made her brother Lenny's report card better than hers; she cried herself to sleep over that. Diane said that now she wanted to eat more but could not. She complained that at home everyone watched her pick at her food, but she did not figure out anything to do about it.

The first interview, in sum, suggested bitterness toward mother, anxiety about sexual and social-sexual maturation, competition with Lenny, and some gratifications derived from her pathology.

A closer look at the parents and at the home in which two cases of anorexia had developed might, it appeared, be helpful. In separate conferences, both mother and father emerged as anxious people who loved their children with a worried love not brightened by the joy of watching them grow. These parents saw the raising of children as a hard, never-ending job; they felt an almost obsessive need to cater to them and were bitter about it. Both parents carried within a deep-seated accumulation of anger stemming from a lack of proper parental recognition in their own childhoods. Both had profound doubts about their own worth, and they had not experienced deeply loving feelings when they had met in college and decided to marry.

It had been, as Mrs. Danby later described it, "a meeting on similar problems." There was in the union, even nineteen years and five children later, the desperation of persons who have seen in each other their only chance.

Mr. Danby was rigid and depressed. Despite five children, ages five to eighteen, he reported that, "In our house, you might say, everything is dead." Unable to see his wife as a person, he was always extremely critical of her.

Mrs. Danby was repeating in her marriage the gruelling, long-suppressed childhood experience of being treated from the start as a failure who must be tolerated. She talked in a loud, whining voice, wandering from one subject to another and never finishing a sentence despite her college education and training in elementary teaching. Some months later she became aware enough of her speaking style to describe it as "rambling."

About Diane, she remembered that this baby came as a complete surprise, "right on top of" Lenny, who had been very welcome. Lenny and Diane had fought ever since they were babies. Lenny was sickly and needed much care, while Diane thrived on very little. She was always good, quiet, and healthy. Mrs. Danby thought this was why she did not remember much about Diane as a baby. Neither did she remember any of her own feelings as a child, as a student, or as a young wife and mother, and she would not try to remember. It seemed to me that she was much brighter than she appeared to be but deeply hurt, and had found long ago a safe place to hide behind her loud, whiny "rambling." This was worked through later in her own treatment, with much help from the art therapy group.

Diane scored a Full Scale IQ of 128 on the WISC, which placed her in the upper corner of the Superior group in general intelligence. This quotient was probably lower than her actual level of intelligence as evidenced by its uneven composition and certain peculiarities on a few subtests.

"Unevenness" refers to a Verbal IQ of 135 and a Performance

IQ of 114. The rather large difference between the two quotients suggested emotional difficulties. On some subtests, there were single, isolated failures on tasks otherwise successfully approached and solved. For example, failures occurred on subtests representing abstract thinking even though Diane was at her best precisely in those. At these moments, she appeared incapable of constructive action. Saying, "I can't do it," she would visibly give up and sadly withdraw. Also, despite the high Verbal IQ, Diane was often unable to express herself in words, and this also seemed to prompt a retreat into sadness. This kind of withdrawal seemed like a pattern she had unknowingly developed for dealing with emotionally threatening situations.

Diane's projective tests revealed at the time a need to arouse her parents by drastic action; a tendency to distort her original motivations into methods of manipulation; a sense of magic power over the family, along with a notion about her own unusualness (she often used the word "unusual" in her test responses). At the same time, she feared her own power and that same unusual self. There were many ambivalent feelings toward parents, siblings, and contemporaries, and much hostility expressed in passive-aggressive ways. Also apparent was a pattern of functioning in extremes: fully controlled and controlling behavior alternated with helpless yielding to impulse accompanied by complete loss of control.

But there was also a good deal of personal strength besides the overwhelmingly important strength inherent in an adolescent's very youth and the process of growth. Diane had a potential for realtistic perception, an ability to shift her point of view and the capacity to modify extreme behavior. Her need to communicate with people also constituted an asset. To be sure, there was only one human response on Diane's Rorschach, but there were many animal responses and some of those conveyed human needs, particularly Diane's own needs to be fed, caressed, and played with. While psychologists welcome a large number of animal responses on a child's Rorschach because they carry the promise of human responses later on, from an adolescent one would expect human responses in view of the importance contemporaries usually have in the adolescent's life. I concluded that because her infantile needs had not been satisfied, Diane was in some ways still immersed in childhood, and that she would turn to people as soon as the resolution of some pressing problems would free her to develop naturally. At the time, she was caught in conflict between growing up and retreating into childhood. I thought that Diane's persistent need for total care from adults might be partially satisfied if she went into the hospital.

My first goal was to help Diane express whatever she could on paper or in clay. She was offered a variety of art materials and was told that with them she might say things about herself when she did not care to say them in words or did not know how to. Diane began immediately in a style that persisted throughout her therapy, working briefly, not speculating much about her productions, but volunteering brief comments whenever she could. Gradually, she became more interested in thinking aloud about what she had made.

The earliest paintings were flat, mechanically drawn skylines, which Diane remembered from a unit of social studies at school. She repeated them a few times within the first therapy hour and finally noticed that they were "all the same." The four skylines, drawn with very light pressure were hardly visible and therefore could not be photographed. When I began to complain that I would like to see her pictures but could not, Diane began to exert more pressure with her crayons and chalks.

Figure VIII-1 was one of a small group of crayon paintings with a house as the main theme. The house was as impoverished in this painting as it was on the test drawings. An interesting feature is the distance between the two windows. But more interesting are the three upright flowers right above the house that seem to grow in the air. The flower on the viewer's left is pale blue, in contrast to the strong reds of the other two. The clouds and the sun are also very weak in color.

In Figure VIII-2, a tempera painting, Diane abandoned the house and made the flowers descend to the ground and become the main theme, with three floating clouds above. The dark reds, dark blues, and blacks of the flowers, and the clouds heavy with

Figure VIII-1.   Crayons; House

Figure VIII-2.   Poster paints; Three Flowers

red and black shading make the painting look foreboding. The picture seemed to be important to Diane, for she asked for it as soon as she came in the next time. She added the little dabs of paint around the clouds and the suggestion of trees or shrubbery on the left, and gazed at the painting without saying a word. Since there were six similar paintings with and without the house, I asked Diane to look at them as a group, together. She pointed at the flowers and said, "I do everything in threes. Why?" When I turned the question back to her, Diane showed some anger. I suggested that she might try to answer her own questions and even some questions which her paintings might suggest to me and reminded her that her fine intelligence, which I had measured in the tests, would certainly help her come up with the answers. I saw a spark in Diane's eyes when she exclaimed, speaking loudly for the first time, "I know. It's me and Lenny and Susan! I want just the three of us," that is, the three older children in the family.

Figure VIII-3 was the second of two family portraits Diane painted with colored chalks. Four weeks earlier, she had drawn with felt pen the first (not reproduced here). It consisted of

Figure VIII-3.   Crayons; Family Portrait

stick figures and included the dog. When I asked who had to do with whom, she drew only one connecting line, between Lenny and the dog.

In the second portrait, Figure VIII-3, there were no stick figures and no dog. There was color, there were persons with bodies, and there were more connecting lines and circles. The stifled atmosphere of the family was beginning to change and some feelings began to stir in Diane. From left to right we see father, mother, oldest daughter Susan, brother Lenny, Diane, younger sister Nancy, and youngest sister Jill. Father and Lenny had a connecting line, since the two had recently been doing things together. Otherwise, father is separated from his wife and from the rest of the family. The dog is not in the picture because, Diane said, "he [Lenny] is no longer so busy with the dog, he has daddy now." Mother, dressed in very pale green, is the most ineffective figure in the painting despite her size and position. Diane recognized some feelings about mother when she observed that "mommy has the weakest colors." Deeper feelings about mother's ineffectiveness were to come out much later.

In the family portrait, mother was connected with the oldest daughter by a line, and with the youngest one by another line. These lines expressed Diane's knowledge that mother identified with Susan, trying to remedy her own unhappy childhood by overemphasizing her oldest daughter's status; and also that mother was specially close to the youngest child because she always coped best with the children when they were little. Diane added that "now mother has to do with me, too," as she made a line connecting mother and herself at the bottom of the painting. The line between mother and herself was an indication of a recent change in mother's ability to relate to Diane. When Diane was fat, before she started to starve herself, the mother had been lost for ways to cope with her preadolescent daughter, "to make up to Diane" with compliments about her "chubbiness," and Diane rightly could not accept these words at face value. In the family portrait, Diane expressed her own precarious position by encircling herself with Nancy, who is also encircled with Jill. Diane really wanted to be close to the older children, but is actually separated from them. She is not even together with the younger ones.

In fact, an important link among all the family members is missing. Hands are conspicuously absent from all the figures in the family portrait. When I called her attention to the omission, Diane asked, with despair in her voice, "Why did I leave them out?" She knew now that she must try to answer her own question, and said, "When you have hands, you hold hands and you touch." She smiled when I added, "And sometimes you hit, too."

Figures VIII-4 and VIII-5 were painted with poster paints on two different visits within one week. Figure VIII-4 shows empty roads in green, red, and blue. A little black car travels alone, not quite touching the blue road. While I silently wondered if the solitary car might connote loneliness, Diane volunteered, with some triumph in her voice, that "this car has *all* the roads to itself." Figure VIII-5 is a similar painting of a boat in cinnamon brown sailing on a blue sea and, just as the car does not touch the road, the boat does not touch the water. Dark blue clouds and a muddy yellow sun look on. Diane observed that

Figure VIII-4. Poster paints; The Little Car

Figure VIII-5. Poster paints; The Little Boat

the clouds looked like two eyes and that taken together with the boat they form a face. When both paintings were hung up, Diane competently observed similarities and differences and put them into words which surprised me with their new depth of awareness.

She said that each of the vehicles was "the only one," that neither the car nor the boat "touched the ground," but that the boat touched even less and this was "weird," and also that "nobody watched the car, but somebody watched the boat." Diane had said that the boat "touched the ground" even less than did the car. The boat painting might have connoted Diane's growing distance from reality. Yet she also said that "somebody watched the boat." This might have been her way of reaching out for help as she was getting away from reality. I assured her that somebody was going to watch that boat and I also questioned half humorously just why the boat would choose to float above the water. I was not expecting an answer and was surprised when Diane replied, "Because it is afraid to be rocked." This encouraged me to ask what the car or the boat felt, being "the only one." Now it was Diane's turn to be surprised that I didn't understand that

"They feel that it's all theirs, *all* the roads and *the whole* ocean."

This was a curiously serious exchange. I knew that Diane knew we were talking about her though we continued to talk about the vehicles. I was glad I had not rushed in with assumptions or interpretations about loneliness. Had I done that, I would have found myself in one of the pitfalls of art therapy or any kind of therapy. For it sometimes is only too easy to comment on the seemingly obvious, thus putting ideas in the patient's mind but cutting off the road to his real communication.

Sometime later, Mrs. Danby joined the art therapy group. One of her early paintings depicted a boat sailing above the surface of the water; another, a bed not quite touching the floor. The group very sensitively picked up this repeated feature and helped Mrs. Danby recognize that her eyes were not quite open to see things as they really were.

It was Diane's fourth week in therapy. Even though she made two efforts to eat normally, both were short-lived. Each time, after two days of moderate success, she lost more weight. Things were getting worse; the family was watching Diane more, teasing and arguing with her more about eating. She was over-feeding her two little sisters, stuffing their lunch boxes with sweets and fattening foods. She demanded more and more shopping trips and her wardrobe of very special clothes was growing. All this was making life harder than ever for mother.

In her art productions, Diane began to express some feelings about herself directly. She was saying it with clay. She described the sculpture shown in Figure VIII-6, a black-haired, red-faced figure with the body painted white, as "a fat monster girl whom nobody likes. Her face is red, she is mad with everything."

Figure VIII-7 is a "funny rabbit" painted purple and orange. "He looks like two rabbits in one. Everybody laughs at him, but he doesn't hear it; he thinks he is cute." This was also Diane's first expression, in art and in words, of her feeling of inner duality. Her statement about the difference between what others thought about the rabbit and what he thought of himself also referred to the feeling of duality. That statement spoke of the animal's almost narcissistic withdrawal into his own cuteness and of his defensive

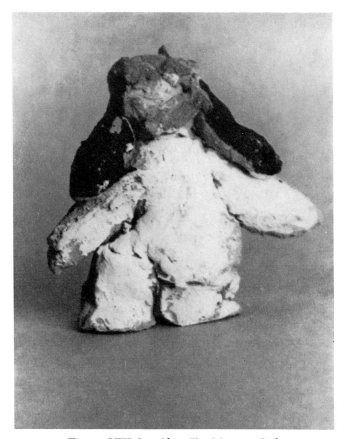

Figure VIII-6.   Clay; Fat Monster Girl

detachment from others. I asked no questions about the two sculptures and made no comments.

The feelings which Diane expressed in Figures VIII-6 and VIII-7 continued and culminated in the sculpture shown in Figure VIII-8.

That figure is composed of two parts put together. One is a large scepter. In the illustration it is at the bottom, but held upright it resembled Poseidon's fork. Diane tried to rest it on the table against the wall, then she tried other positions and places, but was quite dissatisfied.

I tried to have Diane recall what had prompted her to model

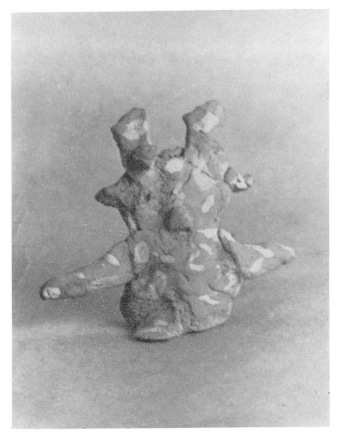

Figure VIII-7.　Clay; A Funny Rabbit

a scepter and what about it was important to her. She became quite serious and said quietly that she had felt "like a goddess" and that the scepter symbolized this feeling which was "now almost gone." She then asked for more white clay and announced that she was going to model the goddess to hold the scepter. What she actually made was a dwarfed creature with horns and a hump on its back. "See, the scepter is too heavy for her, so she put it on the floor," she said. As I was nodding agreement, Diane burst out in open anger at me for the first time. But even in this outburst, she did not shout or cry aloud. Her enormous eyes suddenly disappeared behind narrow slits and she hissed at me

Figure VIII-8. Clay; Scepter and Goddess

in an angry whisper, "First you let me make this horrible thing and then you say, 'Hmmm.' Is that all you can say? I told you that I'm not an artist, now *you* take it, *you* bake it, I won't *ever* touch clay again!"

This was a confusion of her anger at herself and at me. At me for not curing her of all the strangeness that the clay goddess brought to the fore again. At herself for bringing to light time and again all her "silliness," as she called it. When these resentments were sorted out and Diane saw that I was not offended, she followed my suggestion that she throw chunks of clay at a board and repeat anything that came to her mind, ever louder until it would sound like screaming. Diane started in a whisper to repeat the words "I am not a goddess." With my encouragement, her crescendo grew until she was shouting. When our eyes met, we laughed.

Now that Diane no longer felt like a goddess, she could tell me what she had felt earlier. She spoke quietly of her past feeling that she was superior to all her friends and that they considered her someone unusual in mind and body, someone who could get whatever she ever wanted. Her high grades symbolized her extraordinary mind. They made her tower above everyone in her class and above Lenny at home. The unusual clothes were also designed to place her above all others. At one point, Diane said, "Mom always thought that Susan was a goddess." She thought that perhaps mother's attitude toward the older sister had contributed a little to her own need to become "the most important person in the house."

The three sculptures shown in Figures VIII-6, VIII-7, and VIII-8 form a group most expressive of Diane's alarming feelings about herself.

Figure VIII-6, with distorted body and face and generally grotesque in appearance, is a first statement of the patient about her feeling of self-distortion and rage about it. This feeling became more specific and threatening with the duality expressed in Figure VIII-7, and the notion of a separateness verbally described. To counter these alarming feelings, Diane had to mobilize false feelings of specialness and greatness of a goddess. The painful confrontation with the unreality of it all came when Diane modeled a fragment for Figure VIII-8, the scepter. The troubles she encountered relating the scepter to itself, to herself, or to the modeled self-image, connoted the psychological discomforts of a person in the early stage of inner fragmentation. Diane's need to model the goddess and have her hold the scepter was an integrative effort. Painful as it was, the effort helped her get in touch with her own disturbance and actually behold it in front of her. The outburst of mixed angers was cathartic.

Artistically, the three clay works are Diane's least successful productions. Within the group, however, a decrease of artistic quality can be noticed, Figure VIII-6 being the most integrated, Figure VIII-7 still held together, but dual, and Figure VIII-8 fragmented, most distorted, and not holding together. The decrease in artistic quality is accompanied by an increase, in the same order, of psychological fragmentation.

The next time Diane came to my office, she went straight to the painting table and produced the tempera painting shown in Figure VIII-9. When it was completed, she announced that she knew what it was: "The blue dots framed on top are my parents. The black dots under that are me and my sadness. I cut myself off from the yellow happy dots [below] and am looking to the red stop sign to stop me. When will I go back to the green grass [bottom]?"

Figure VIII-9.   Poster paints; The Stop Sign

This painting is in some ways similar to Figures VIII-4 and VIII-5. All three are childlike in style, yet convey a message with a measure of sophistication. The three pictures form a sequence in terms of growing emotional urgency. Figure VIII-4 tells of the omnipotence and perhaps loneliness of the retreat from reality. Figure VIII-5 conveys a wish to be seen and watched even in this state. And Figure VIII-9 is Diane's cry about her need to stop her pathological acting out and return to a normal life.

When we view this group of paintings together with the group of sculptures previously discussed, we can see three

parallels. One is the growing pathology in both series. The other is the mounting urgency in both. And the third, contained in the last work of each group, is a cry for help, also expressed in words.

Figure VIII-10 was painted with poster paints while Diane was in a sad mood. "Kind of heavy, maybe sad, all these dark colors," she said. She had set out to paint clouds and hills, and in the process produced the figure. She observed that the face resembled a dog's, and she went on, saying, "The dog started to cross these hills. It was getting dark, and he didn't know whether he could do it."

The colors had a dark glow about them. There were strong blues, reds darkened with black, and chrome yellows. The dog had the expression of a burdened person dragging his dark yellow body, and the white face was aglow with bright red eyes. It was one of Diane's most artistically successful and expressive paintings. Color and form both carried the mood. There was a central

Figure VIII-10.   Poster paints; Dog Crossing Hills

figure cutting vertically across the horizontal lines, and the whole space was well used (see Color Plate XXI).

I told Diane about some of these opinions. She only smiled and repeated her first comment about the "heavy mood" of the painting, and so we talked about that. Diane sensed that she would soon go to the hospital, since she had continued to lose weight. She was a little startled when I speculated that she might like it there and that her stay in the hospital might help her "stop," according to the wish she had expressed in connection with Figure VIII-9.

In view of Diane's impending hospitalization, I told her parents and her doctor that I thought she was now psychologically ready for a change of attitude and behavior. I believed that a stay in the hospital would, at that point, effectively break the vicious circle in which Diane was caught. The same message was included in the psychological report sent to the psychiatrist at the hospital.

Upon his recommendation and in cooperation with the physician who administered Diane's diet on the ward, the hospital program was designed as follows: Diane's autonomy was fostered by her being allowed to choose among various foods and activities, and she was left to manage her own snacks. She was presented with her diet, but the staff refrained from showing concern about her intake and weight. This rendered ineffective her way of controlling the people around her. She was encouraged to express anger about food and toward people, including the ward staff and her family.

Diane stopped starving herself. Twelve days after her admission to the hospital and with more than the hoped for gain of weight, she was discharged with the instruction to return immediately to psychotherapeutic treatment.

When she came for her first appointment after the hospital stay, she was hardly recognizable. Her face was full and radiant. She was dressed as had now become usual, in shorts, shirt, and sandals. She said she had undergone a complete "change of mind" and mentioned the abandonment of her costumes. She talked about her clear feeling of "before and after" which she was to express later in painting.

Figure VIII-11.   Chalks; The Two Girls

Figure VIII-11, "The Two Girls," is one such image. It began with the line vertically dividing the paper in two. "Here [left] I am the goddess, remember? And I am mad, even though I got all the things I wanted. And here [right] I wear these dirty shorts and shirt and I like it," Diane said (see Color Plate XXII). There were more colorful abstractions in chalk dealing with the "before and after," and titled "The Real Me; The Unreal Me," "The Two Lives," and more.

In Figures VIII-12 and VIII-13, both made with poster paints, Diane continued to take a retrospective look at her mode of being in the last few months.

Figure VIII-12 presents, on the left, a black head surrounded with green brushstrokes. On the right, framed in red on three sides only, is a form in bright yellow suggesting children in motion. "On the left," Diane volunteered, "I, the depressed goddess, I am terribly sad. On the right, everybody is happy."

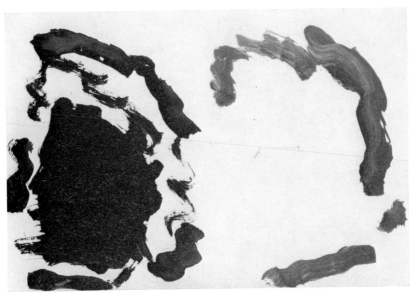

Figure VIII-12.   Poster paints; Right and Left

Figure VIII-13 was painted one visit later. Again on the left there is an animal in dark green closed off with massive maroon brushstrokes. This is balanced by a red house and a blue mass on the right. And again, Diane volunteered her rather definite ideas about the painting. "I cut myself off from the normal and the happy. That green, that's me. It looks like a horse on its hindlegs. The house is my family and the blue blot is a lake where kids have fun, maybe like camp. And I cut myself off from all this. Can I still go to camp, you think?"

Figure VIII-14 was made with blue and violet crayons during her next visit. Diane looked at it and said with desperation, "I just put the horse in a cage, I don't know why." She responded to my suggestion that she look for similar paintings made in the

Figure VIII-13. Poster paints; Right and Left

past, and took out of the folder Figures VIII-11-VIII-14, her recent productions. Looking at them as a group, she noticed that all of them except the last had a pattern of two's. Since Diane had said that the horse on the left of Figure VIII-13 was she, it occurred to her that the horse in Figure VIII-14 also represented her. When I asked her to find a painting with yet another animal, she readily found the dog in Figure VIII-10, her last painting before she went into the hospital.

At this point, Diane wondered what made her paint herself in the form of animals instead of portraying her own person, and I speculated aloud that perhaps it was easier for her to express her feelings about herself by painting her feelings about the animals. We sat and silently studied the group of paintings. Diane suddenly said, "When I was the one on the left side of each picture, I was really in a cage." This was exactly what she had painted in the puzzling Figure VIII-14.

The change in Diane, so conspicuous in her appearance, spread over to attitudes and values; for example, she was now sociable and playful. She was taking part in new activities and

Figure VIII-14.   Chalks; Horse in a Cage

surrounding herself with friends. Her attitude at home had changed. Aware of the solemn atmosphere "before," she was bringing play and laughter into the house and even got Lenny to participate at times. She stopped bossing the younger sisters and willingly took part in household chores. She was now satisfied to leave management to mother.

This was also partly the result of a change in mother. Mrs. Danby was gradually becoming calmer, able to do her job, and firmer with the children. She was also becoming more conscious of her own worth and was beginning to take a stand as mother, wife, and leader of the family. The children responded happily to these changes, while Mr. Danby was somewhat startled at his wife's new ways.

Diane's scale of values was changing. "Getting more and more things," was becoming less important, Diane said, but giving of herself to others was growing more important. She explained this to her mother when she was asking permission to invite to the family farm friends who "did not have so much." She now cared about "growing up the way everyone else is," and there was a startling change in her attitude toward grades. While she still wanted to do well, she was determined not to sacrifice everything for grades or to compete for them, especially not with Lenny.

Naturally, however, things were not all smooth and rosy. New feelings still conflicted with old ones or their residues. For example, Diane's new need to give found expression in her wish to give love to her parents. To their pleased surprise, she now liked to kiss and hug them and sit on their laps. But she was worried because she often wanted to be an infant and feared that her new behavior might contain elements of regression.

Diane was now able to talk about another related problem. It was connected, she explained, "with many things, like Lenny, and the grades and being a boy or a girl." That was how Diane brought up her old wish, "now gone," to have been born a boy. She had hoped that if she were a boy, Lenny would have been a friend rather than an enemy, and father would do things with her, too, the way he had recently been doing with Lenny. Actually, Diane said sadly, the only thing father was doing with her was taking her to some appointments and "dropping" her there. Not being a sportsman or a boy scout like Lenny, there remained only the area of scholastic excellence in which she could possibly surpass him, and even for that she had to work very hard. Now, however, she no longer wanted to compete, nor did she long to be a boy. Or so it seemed to her.

Even more disquieting was Diane's recent experience that having abandoned all her old and "childish" wishes to be a boy, she was now feeling "something different about boys," especially when her older sister brought her male friends home. These were new tensions, part of normal adolescent development but unknown to Diane because in the not-too-distant past she had tried to ward them off by fantasizing herself a goddess.

Art work had been interrupted during a few visits for the discussions reported above. Diane was able to talk about her conflicting feelings rather fluently. While her worry about a possible regression to infancy in giving and receiving love from her parents was rather easily dealt with in these conversations, she became quite upset and depressed about her new tension in relation to boys. I felt that we had come to the complex emotional background for Diane's original need to seek refuge in fantasies about being a goddess. Most probably it was based on her fear of growing up into womanhood. More specifically, it was the fear of sexual maturation, and this Diane, indeed, had tried to stop.

No longer able to talk, Diane retreated to her old mood, and art expression again assumed importance. She willingly responded to my suggestion that she do some finger painting.

Figure VIII-15 is the most expressive in a series of more than ten finger paintings which occupied Diane over a span of four hour-long visits. The early productions in the series consisted of never-ending circles produced by her fingers endlessly moving in muddy paint.

The shape in the center of Figure VIII-15 is bright red. The background gradually turns from red to violet (see Color Plate XXIII). Diane liked the painting and explained that she had wanted to make a swan, but realized upon completing her work that "it might be a snake, but not a poisonous one." She was a

Figure VIII-15.   Finger paint; The Snake

little disturbed by "the bed of weeds and thorns" in which the snake rested, but the thorns did not look very thorny.

As a finger painting, the production was quite successful. Since she had used the right amount of paint, the picture dried well without cracks. There is an interesting interplay of light and dark, and the colors are rich. Though Diane's distress about "the thorns and weeds" seemed like a minor aspect of her considerable investment in this painting, I saw in it a sign of some deeper disturbance and encouraged her to paint more.

Figures VIII-16 and VIII-17 were painted at home when Diane had an attack of the flu. In a telephone conversation with her. I felt that she had regressed. She spoke of sadness, anxiety, and of dreams about somebody attacking or being attacked. Figure VIII-16 represents an attempt to paint one of the dreams.

A jumble of heavy red, blue, yellow, and brown brushstrokes with poster paints, the painting is artistically and emotionally quite disorganized. Yet, the real disorganization is in the background, while the foreground is shaped in a rather balanced

Figure VIII-16. Poster paints; The Nightmare

manner between the assaulting, ferocious attacker and the attacked, a prone doll-like girl with a fear-stricken face.

Figure VIII-17, made during that same illness, was more completely regressive. On the back of it, Diane had written an account at my suggestion: "I felt many different feelings while I was painting this. They were not pleasant at all. First I just splashed paint, then I saw that it was a red lake, all red. Then I painted a green and blue bird flying over the lake, head down, looking for something in the lake. And there was an awful rain, all sorts of drops in red, blue, and green. I do not like this painting and, please, do not put it in my folder, Dr. B."

Diane's wish was met. I told her that I would keep the painting in another folder for a while because the unpleasant feelings expressed in it could help me understand her. This seemed to offer her some relief. I thought it advisable to have no discussion about these paintings, as talking about them would have been too threatening for Diane. The graphic expression alone had to suffice for the moment.

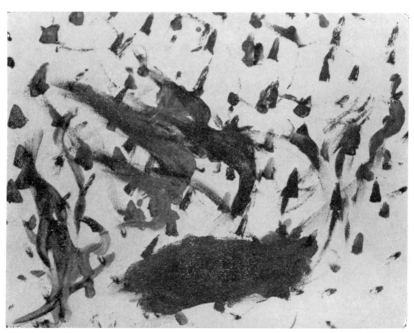

Figure VIII-17.   Colored ink; A Disliked Painting

As for my own observations, it had seemed to me that in Figure VIII-17 Diane came as close as one could to the expression of raw and violent feelings purely in color, with very little form. Her ability to see some meaning in her splash of color indicated a successful attempt at control from within. In both this painting and Figure VIII-16, she probably expressed her fear of sexual violence and perhaps also the fear that sexual maturation meant violence. If so, then that was the fear which had blocked her wish to grow up.

A few days later, Diane made the painting of a disquieting dream shown in Figure VIII-18. In front of a dark staircase or building, she stood next to her older sister Susan (far left). With them were other boys and girls, all dressed in very colorful clothes. The tall strange man on the right was shooting at the group a stream of orange-red fire by pressing a button on a machine gun. The stream of fire passed behind the three friends, ignited Diane, and enveloped Susan. Susan whispered, "Let's throw it back at him," and back went the fire to the man, this being indicated in the painting by an arrow (see Color Plate XXIV).

This painting, though it upset and puzzled Diane, repre-

Figure VIII-18.　Chalks; Fire Dream

sented recovery in comparison with the regression shown in Figure VIII-17. Her eager approach to painting the dream and her eloquence in describing it constituted an integrative effort. It was also a better painting, better organized, clearer in form and more vivid in color. The tall threatening figure was well balanced by the group backed by the solid building. Diane talked with a sense of triumph about sending the fire back to its source.

When I hung up Figure VIII-16 along with Figure VIII-18, Diane immediately compared the two. She pointed out that the latter was happier, that the girl in Figure VIII-16 "tried to kick him," but was too scared. But she, with her sister and their friends in Figure VIII-18, "fixed him." Of course she liked the colors in the newer picture. She sensed that the dark colors of the earlier one conveyed a threat of violence and destruction, while her use of bright colors carried the promise of personal strength, of her ability to cope with the stream of fire.

Diane was now willing to talk about growing up physically and emotionally, about problems and feelings shared by all adolescents. She pointed at the line of boys and girls in Figure VIII-18 and spoke of her sense that everybody shared certain feelings and said that was why she had included boys. There followed conversations about love, infatuation, sex, and the threatening aspect of sex. On one occasion, Diane recalled a dream of waking up in a dormitory and seeing a boy in the next bed; there had been no threat in that dream. These conversations led to a feeling of relief. She understood that it would be wise to postpone sexual activity until much later. For the time being, it would be enough to enjoy the company of boys and gradually learn to know them better.

Diane now appeared happy oftener than ever before. During her therapy hours, she was enjoying the games in the playroom, often laughing. But occasionally she withdrew into the old sadness, and she could neither understand nor discuss these relapses. Once, when she came in, in such a mood and asked what she should paint, I decided to suggest the theme of a hurricane or storm.

Figures VIII-19 and VIII-20, vivid and sensitive, were both

painted with chalks during that one visit. In the first, green, brown, and black branches of a tree with a black trunk, are being shattered by the hurricane. Some of the branches tangle around

Figure VIII-19.   Chalks; Hurricane

Figure VIII-20.   Chalks; The Storm

the little girl, who wears a bright tangerine and yellow dress. "She wants to run, but she can only move her feet a little bit. These branches, they look like ropes, and maybe there is also lightning," said Diane with some despair in her voice.

Figure VIII-20, "The Storm," shows a sky cut up by dynamic zigzag lines of lightning in green, black, and violet. They dance around the house, whose door seems blocked. "The people want to get out, but it's a heavy door and they can't open it. The wind won't let them. But the house won't be destroyed, it's a good building. Maybe it will only rain in through the windows." Nor was the girl in Figure VIII-19 destroyed, Diane added. She pointed to the girl's feet, explaining that "she was beginning to run."

Both paintings expressed deep fear of loneliness, perhaps of being trapped and forgotten. It was hard to know whether Diane's assurances about the survival of the house and the girl's small effort to save herself were signs of authentic strength or a device, as in happy-ending stories, to avoid the pain of a tragic conclusion. Again, I felt that graphic expression alone should suffice. Without encouraging discussion, I commented that the paintings expressed what the girl and the people in the house felt, and that as I looked at the paintings I, too, experienced some of their feelings.

Diane entered on another period marked by happy productions, happy moods, playful behavior, and laughter. She was more and more active socially, and talked freely about boys, describing her male friends and guessing which of them might like her. In her art work, she returned to clay, disclosing that she had shied away from this material ever since the scepter-and-goddess sculpture. Now she liked clay again.

This time her clay work made up a series of eight receptacles and containers in a variety of shapes and sizes and with many decorative inventions. Some of them resembled heavy, deep frying pans and were decorated with large flowers in colors. Diane was quite pleased with her pots, boxes, and ashtrays. One might look upon these productions and the pleasure Diane derived from working at them as signs of her growing readiness

to accept her femininity and her physical growth into womanhood.

Figure VIII-21, a well-integrated painting with chalks, grew
out of a scribble which Diane made when she did not know
what to paint. To begin with, she welcomed this technique of
finding subject matter, and she developed her pictorial image
with ease and pleasure, finally producing a rich painting of "a
fish with a beautiful tail, swimming among seaweeds and having
fun." The sea is brilliant blue, the fish is orange-gold, and the tail
is colored with shades of rose, red, and magenta.

Figure VIII-21.   Chalks; Beautiful Fish

Figure VIII-22, a sunny, humorous painting in chalks, received much of Diane's time and attention (see Color Plate XXV).
Oranges, greens, rose colors, and yellows bring out the bright
smile of Mr. Jeanney, a dog-person who had recently become the
hero of Diane's happy, comical paintings on a continuous roll of
brown paper. This painting, however, was special and was made
on a separate sheet of white paper. The dog-person stands in
front of a large, hot-pink flower while the sun shines.

With some hesitation, I asked Diane to find in her folder

Figure VIII-22.   Chalks; Happy Mr. Jeanney

another painting that might go with this one in some way. I thought of Figure VIII-10, the sad dog who set out to cross the hills, and I hesitated because I doubted the wisdom of possibly disturbing the happy mood of Figure VIII-22. Diane did choose Figure VIII-10, and as she looked at both pictures she said that "these [were] two girls, one exhausted, the other fresh and happy." When I read from my notes what she had said at the time about the dog who did not know if he could make it, she laughed and said, "But he could."

Figure VIII-23, Campfire, was Diane's last painting before she went to camp. She volunteered that this had been a dream she had and that if she had more space on the paper, she would paint the boys and girls around the fire. Humorously, she added, "They are coming right now, through the woods."

For myself, I associated this dream of fire with the other fire dream (Fig. VIII-18). Certain feelings had been worked through during the span of time between the two paintings. With the help of art expression and verbal exchanges, the violent threat of sexual danger had turned into security and warmth with a touch of adolescent romance. Diane could now feel herself one of a group of contemporaries who shared similar feelings and problems of growth.

Figure VIII-23.   Poster paints; The Campfire

SUMMARY

This was a presentation of the first six months of art psychotherapy with an adolescent girl stricken with anorexia. The use of painting and clay modeling helped her express and communicate a number of transient adolescent problems as well as some deeper personal difficulties. Through art expression, this patient developed a readiness to change attitudes and behavior so that the brief hospital intervention was effective.

FOLLOW-UP

Diane was happy and well liked at camp. She regained a feeling of being one among many adolescents and was often herself surprised at her outgoing attitude toward boys and girls.

After camp, she continued her art psychotherapy once a week. The general goal of therapy was now to help her recognize her real feelings and find constructive ways to cope with them in a variety of changing situations. The episode of anorexia, Diane's tendency to alternate between extremes, and her temporary sensation of duality before and during the schizoid goddess episode, all these called for extended psychotherapy. The stress on art expression continued.

IX

Lee

What they had identified as Lee's problem, smoking marihuana, was introduced to the psychologist by her parents. Their
statements of fact and their expression of their own feelings were
equally fuzzy.

They were not ready to say outright that Lee, their younger
child, now fourteen years and five months old, had indeed been
smoking pot, as had their son. While they passively condoned
his smoking, bearing their uneasy feelings and hoping for the
best, they became alarmed when Lee, too, seemed to have
adopted the habit. Yet they have never confronted her with a
direct question about it, nor have they ever told her that they
knew. Instead, they shared their worry with the son in the vague
hope that he might stop his sister from smoking. Occasionally,
they forbade Lee to attend a Friday night party, concealing their
real suspicions and fears behind feeble objections. Finally, they
dumped the entire matter of Lee into the psychologist's lap.
With much sophisticated rhetoric about the intricacies of "that
age" (adolescence) and about their own closeness ("doing things
as a family"), the parents announced that they would not take
part in the psychotherapeutic work. Thus, there was no opportunity to study the family pathology or to touch the parents'
authentic feelings and influence their attitudes.

Lee cooperated on all the tests but she was impatient to
start psychotherapy because she had "so much on [her] mind."
She was a well-informed, bright adolescent with a Full Scale IQ
of 127 on the WISC, which placed her in the upper bracket of
the Superior group in general intelligence. Yet she scored surprisingly low on Vocabulary despite her successes on most
subtests measuring abstract thinking. Within those subtests, however, there were some inadequate answers, at times in sharp

contrast to the successful responses. A considerable discrepancy between the IQs on the Verbal and the Performance parts of the test indicated emotional stress, which had to be explored through personality tests.

The brief Color-Form Sorting Test brought out Lee's confused approach to immediate problems and tasks, and probably to her own person as well.

Her production on the Drawing Tests were unrealistic and depressive.

On the Rorschach, Lee appeared either overly controlled and unemotional or at a complete loss for control, and fear stricken. Suspicious of others, even of her closest kin, she was careful to hide her real feelings, particularly the warm ones. Since she was in the midst of adolescence, a time of many bodily and emotional changes, the constant effort to conceal her feelings confused her perception of her own self and she no longer knew who she was. A gnawing feeling grew inside her that something was profoundly wrong with her. Such feelings were reflected in some of her responses: "A rock with a hole in it"; "An animal put together wrong"; and in other responses about voodoos casting powers over people, and devils with evil looks. But there were also a few quite healthy responses about animals and about people.

Complementing the Rorschach were Lee's TAT stories. These revealed areas of hostility and separation inside the family; Lee's ambivalent feelings about her brother and each of her parents; her hateful competition with mother for father's affection; her self-pity and despair.

Of special interest was Lee's response to the Exciting Scene assignment: mother just dropped the baby, the two parents and brother stand and watch, brother bends down to see "if the baby is all right," nobody picks up the baby.

The first few weeks Lee came twice a week, Saturday morning and on a weekday directly after school. On her weekday appointments she was tense and angry, but alive. On Saturdays she was "stoned," weepy, and often lethargic in the beginning, then talkative.

Lee was always extremely articulate. Eagerly and aggressively she seized her hours and never had enough time to say what she had intended to say. Her talk was complaining, angry, and bitter. It centered on home and on the boys and girls she associated with at school. Since Lee's bitterness spread from home over to her social life, she found herself in a number of strained and unproductive relationships, losing and gaining friends soon to lose them again because she demanded absolute, total mutual devotion. School days had become for Lee long hours of emotional torture during which she turned over in her mind, in class and at recess, every look and every word of each significant acquaintance and ceaselessly extracted from it the inevitable verdict that she was not liked. "Nothing changed" was Lee's unchanging opening of her eagerly anticipated appointments.

I drew for her the parallel between her unproductive relationships with friends and her unproductive hours with me. Her angry reaction betrayed the possibility that she was not altogether unaware of the similarity. When Lee realized with surprise that she was not allowing her relationship with me to become therapeutic, she reluctantly agreed to try art expression as an additional way of telling about herself. Before she started this new way of expression, she recalled her drawings on the tests, saying that she "took them very seriously," and that she had been wondering about them. We took the House-Tree-Person drawings out of the folder to have a look at them together.

Lee had had much trouble with the drawing of the house (Fig. IX-1). She could not "do it right with just a pencil." There followed much explaining and justifying of various lines and angles, much dramatic erasing, and testing of colors on many pieces of paper. She had finally decided to go over the penciled outline of the house with rust and brown crayons, which resulted in some heavy shading. When asked who lived in the house and whether it in any way resembled her own house, she asked sarcastically, "Who could live in a house like that?" and then said thoughtfully, "Not outside, but maybe inside it could be our house. It looks kind of troubled, doesn't it?"

The tree (Fig. IX-2) also made with brown shaded lines

Figure IX-1.   Pencil and crayon; House

over pencil, was large, strong, and well placed on the paper. But it was a winter tree with no leaves. Four branches were close together to the point of interfering with one another, while the branch on the observer's left "must go its own way," Lee said. My own observation, however, was that the tree is split vertically down the trunk and also horizontally by the long branch which cuts aggressively through the group of branches.

The person (Fig. IX-3) was drawn with olive-green chalk. Heavily shaded, the young angel-woman was floating in the air, smiling and shedding a tear. Lee described her as "a girl twenty-two years old."

In answer to my request that she draw a person her own age, Lee produced Figure IX-4 in bright blue crayon and exclaimed, "This nice kid just couldn't be me." She asked, with agitation and eagerness, whether that was the way I saw her, and ran to the mirror to study her face. When she came back and

Figure IX-2.   Pencil and crayon; The Tree

sat in the chair opposite me, Lee was quite upset and had to be encouraged to express some of her feelings. This brought on an outburst rich with insights. First, there was anger with me for not telling her how I saw her; then there was a moaning declaration that she surely did like Figure IX-4 because that was how she used to look, "sweet and natural," before she messed herself up, before all the "shit in grass and in words" was fed to her. Then Lee took her painting of the angel and, waving it aggressively, demanded that I choose between it and the other figure (Fig. IX-4). When she had calmed down, I helped her to accept both figures as two parts of herself, two roles she played, for the time being, of necessity. Lee took the blue crayon, en-

Figure IX-3.   Chalk; A Girl

larged the eyes of Figure IX-4, and explained, "She is saying, 'Gee, how weird can you be? Wake up!' "

But it was too soon to wake up. In the subsequent hours, Lee went right back to her resistance, expressed by verbal accounts of all the minutest injustices committed against her at home, day by day, in chronological order. She maintained that the only way to bear it was to seclude herself in her room and listen to records, for that was when she felt elated and could forget her troubles. When asked whether she could express the elation by graphic means, she drew Figure IX-5 on a large sheet of paper.

Holding green and violet crayons together, Lee drew the

Figure IX-4.   Crayon; The Nice Kid

zigzag lines on the upper half of the sheet. Some shading with the square side of a blue crayon followed, and then the short vertical lines, like commas, were scattered over the cloud form. After a long pause, Lee took a red crayon and drew the toppling stick figure below. Heavily shaded in the same red, the figure was puffing smoke and holding a cigarette in the viewer's left hand. The zigzag lines of smoke around the figure also look like strings, which tie the figure to the cloud form above, and the whole design seems to be pulled or pulling up into space.

When she finished the drawing, Lee was depressed and silent. She broke her silence very soon with the solemn state-

Figure IX-5.   Crayons; Stick Figure and Smoke

ment, "So now you know." When asked, however, to give a clear answer to my question, "I know what?" Lee worked up to a tantrum. She was furious with me for asking her to speak in sentences and for acting like a "grammar teacher instead of a psychologist." This was a sign of Lee's renewed resistance against facing and dealing with her problems. It might also have been her way of withdrawing what she had entrusted to me when she drew Figure IX-5.

There followed a number of similarly resistant visits, but now resistance took a different form. A suddenly happy Lee chatted in superlatives about "great" progress in all previously troubled areas of her life, including home. She was now being "programmed" at home with "great success." She said she was now much more "in tune" with the family, a welcome change for her mother, whose reminders, "Tune in, Lee," her daughter had often quoted to me. All this was reported with a pretense of happiness, but Lee's eyes filled all too easily with tears when I repeated her statements with only a change of pronoun.

On one of these happy visits, Lee noticed the Mosaic Box left in disarray by another child. Absorbed for a while in pleasurable play with the scattered plastic shapes, Lee settled down to serious work on a design of her own (Fig. IX-6). She called it "a clown," and commented, "I decided to be a clown—happy." It was her first candid statement about her happy and chatty self of the recent weeks.

Let us now examine "The Clown." The composition is divided into three parts. The bottom one forms the ground, the

Figure IX-6.   Mosaic tiles; The Clown

solid but rather rocky ground which Lee needed for her clowning self. The two parts above form the leaping clown. Except for two squares forming part of the ground, the picture is executed with triangles only. Its predominant colors are red with black and white. On the ground there are four blue triangles scattered in several areas, one group of yellow triangles, and one green triangle. The empty spaces between the sections are conspicuous; they create disturbing discontinuities in this production.

Lee made many more clowns with the mosaic tiles. Some were dancing, others leaping, crouching, or standing. All had a solid, rocky area under them, but none of their feet, including those of the standing ones, touched the ground. After ten or twelve clowns, both the mosaic tiles and the theme were abandoned, as was the pretended mood of radiant happiness.

The new mood was sad but not desperate, and was more authentic. Lee was still talkative, but in a more relaxed fashion. Her superlatives were gone, and gone, too, were most of her bitter complaints. She often reported small but genuine improvements in her own behavior at home, in social gatherings, and at school. These changes, however, belonged to her middle-of-the-week self and contrasted with the very confused, tense Saturday-morning self. It was obvious that pot-smoking had been given up during the week but was indulged in on Friday nights.

During this six- or seven-week period, Lee was employing two kinds of art expression, sometimes using both in one hour.

One was an infantile manner of using poster paints. These paintings consisted of muddy puddles of paint stirred into one dark, massive pool; they were impossible to photograph. The other was the projection of fantasy with crayons, chalks, and Craypas. These pictures differed very little from each other, and were all titled, "Beautiful Feelings." Figure IX-7 is typical.

It is esthetically pleasing, in delicate lavenders, blues, blue-greens, magentas, and violets (see Color Plate XXVI). Many soft linear forms in all these colors seem to move gracefully as they engage with and disengage from one another, forming loops or springlike shapes. All this movement takes place against a bluish-green background made with pastels. There is a center

Figure IX-7. Chalks; Beautiful Feelings

in the painting, the vertical, lavender-shaped form outlined in dark violet. It resembles a marine creature with the head of a whale and a body which tapers down to a graceful tail that ends with an upward flare. On the far right of the painting is a vertical magenta border with a spiral in blue-green whirling down it. On the far left is the other border in strong blue.

The whole painting may be perceived as a serene moment of life under the sea; the curved lines suggest marine vegetation slowly moving in the current. They might also represent the fleeting emotions of a lonely, longing adolescent girl.

One might also look upon the painting as a projection of not-so-serene feelings of threat along with an effort to ward it off. Oval, round, and diagonal lines converge at the neck of the vertically placed marine creature. The large whale's head seems to struggle against these converging lines. It is the head that must do the fighting.

Both the serene and the fighting views of Figure IX-7 were my immediate reactions, not shared with Lee, who seriously stared at her production and finally spoke. "Maybe," she said. "They do look like beautiful feelings, but that's when I turn on. And I saw such colors only once. But I also felt some awful things, you know; things that you can't draw or describe, you know. . . ."

When reminded, as she had been many times in the past, that her phrase, "you know," did not really help me know what she felt, Lee started crying as she talked. She said that she had beautiful feelings when she was smoking at parties, particularly with Tony, the boy with whom she shared the experience of smoking in his room while holding hands or sometimes necking. The "beautiful" feelings were followed by frightful feelings. She was dissolving and dying and screaming but not being heard and not even hearing her own screams, "because deep down in the ocean or up in space, human voices also dissolve." "So, there is no way out for you," I continued for her. She nodded and said, weeping, that she wished more than ever to smoke, to have at least a few more of the beautiful feelings. I then put up one of Lee's earlier versions of "Beautiful Feelings" and drew on it a ladder coming down to the center. It was a spontaneous gesture prompted, perhaps, by a recollection of a little boy's using ladders as a symbol for mobility, contact, and rescue. I related this association to Lee, a thought which had not occurred to me during my work with the little boy, and I wondered aloud what made me think of one patient while I was working with another. Lee immediately answered that she shared with the little boy the need "to get out of a trap." At last, Lee was willing to talk openly about smoking pot, about her horror of its possible effects, and about her dependence upon Tony for "the stuff." She saw now that she had mistaken that dependence for love, and she could also admit her anger, guilt, and confusion about her parents' attitude to her, to her brother, and to their smoking.

Figure IX-8 was the last of four paintings in Craypas which followed the ladder intervention and the talks resulting from it. Each of these four paintings was titled "Tranquil"; Lee felt a tranquility now which she had not felt for over a year, she said. She was now going to bed without crying herself to sleep, and was getting up rested every morning. The four paintings were done in a relaxed manner, with obvious enjoyment. This contrasted with the mood of Figure IX-7. While painting the latter, she was smiling in a detached, almost frozen way, which reminded one of the angel's expression in Figure IX-3.

In Figure IX-8, we see a background of rounded, fluffy shapes in light blues. Against this background, Lee drew a pattern of curved lines. The predominant color of the lines is red outlined in yellow and blue. As she stepped back to look at her painting, Lee exclaimed with delight that it was a little girl asleep under a blanket with floral design. The girl rested her head on her right arm (viewer's left), Lee said, and was having a good night's sleep. This reminded me of one of Lee's responses on the Rorschach examination (to the upper part of Card II): "These are my hands resting on my warm, white blanket while I am asleep." In this response, she had included the white of the card for the blanket.

Turning again to Figure IX-8, the linear form suggests an embryonic outline of the whole figure; and the upper oval is reminiscent, again, of the oversized heads in children's drawings, except that this head is oval, not circular.

Lee felt that she had to explain that being asleep did not mean escaping her problems. It meant to her that she was not "tranquil and confident" enough to cope with her troubles, but she knew that the coping itself would not be "so tranquil." Lee could now use her fine sense of humor. While we played with the word "tranquil," she said, with a twinkle in her eye, "Remember, I have that ladder now. I can tranquilly climb it, jump, and run, though breaking a leg or two wouldn't be very tranquil."

Both paintings (Figs. IX-7 and IX-8) also bring out a

Figure IX-8. Craypas; Tranquil

universal quality of adolescence that readily plays into an adolescent's emotional disturbance. It is the tendency to go from extreme to extreme, in Lee's case from elation to ecstasy to depression or a sense of doom. Another quality of adolescence is the very valuable ability to bounce back. Though always a source of strength, it does depend upon the degree of depression. When the adolescent is very disturbed, the extreme oscillations will block his natural bounciness. In Figure IX-8, Lee began to bounce back, to see herself more realistically.

Figure IX-9, which Lee titled "Confusion," was her first admission that she had, indeed, been confused. A question, brief

Figure IX-9.   Crayons; Confusion

and clear in its adolescent style, accompanied it: "See what a mess I really am?"

Seen in color, this production suggests the utmost confusion and violent feelings disrupting a once warm and orderly inner life. When asked why she was crying, Lee smiled with embarrassment through her tears and whispered that the crosses might mean dying. This idea had occurred to her while she was drawing "all the little things in the center," and she then felt "sort of choked"; she also told about recurrent dreams of being choked. With much relief, she accepted a suggestion that the sensation and the feeling of being choked could be understood as an unbearable pressure of some other feelings inside her, rather than as an outsile force literally committing violence against her. Lee asked about those other feelings and was encouraged to paint more in order to find them.

At about that time, Lee's two visits per week were reduced to only one, upon her parents' wish. It was not the proper time for such a change, since almost immediately after the "Confusion" painting, Lee had entered a period of angry, infantile behavior and verbal aggression. She tore paintings, broke brushes and crayons, and dropped paint-soaked papers on the floor. There were angry words about me and her family, and Lee denied all the progress she had made. There was also evidence that she was smoking more.

All this anger, in part long suppressed and in part a response to the immediate situation, came to a climax in a grand, openly furious shouting session. At this point, Lee became able to talk about her regressive behavior and to respond to a direct question, "What have you actually been doing all this time?"

Figure IX-10, "Hostility," was her first response. The large oval face, outlined in bright blue and green crayons, fills the whole paper (see Color Plate XXVII). The edges of the face are shaded in green, the cheeks in yellow-brown, and the forehead is strongly colored dark green. Heavy black and blue lines form the eyebrows, the eye sockets, and the nose. The diamond-shaped part of the nose below the long vertical black line is outlined in blue as well as black, and it is filled in with green. The area under the nose is heavily shaded in blue and black. Most outstanding in this inhuman face are the two thin, brilliant red vertical lines, standing like bloody slits in the eye sockets. The mouth is conspicuously absent. Its absence, along with the heavy shading of the area which spreads diagonally from the right nostril downward to the left, suggests both the normal adolescent sexual preoccupations and Lee's own intensified sexual worries.

The red slits in the eyes seemed most disturbing to Lee herself. "That's me," she said, pointing at them. She was talking at the time about her hatred for nearly everyone she knew, except her father. "He's the only one who understands me, but *she* [mother] won't let him do anything."

When I encouraged Lee to paint or draw something about

Figure IX-10.　Crayons; Hostility

her feelings within the family, Lee produced Figure IX-11 with crayon in heavily colored violet.

Viewed as a whole, this painting conveys the loneliness of desperate people, standing apart on a vast stage and frozen in their despair. Lee appears twice. She is the figure in the center, and she is also the smaller of the two figures at the right. The larger of these is an imaginary sister put in the place of the real brother. On the left, heavily colored in dark violet, is an angry, threatening mother who condemns the central figure. Lee turns to the imaginary sister for help, but does not get it. Underneath the painting at the right, Lee wrote in yellow crayon, "Uses me,"

Figure IX-11. Crayons; Desperate People

in lieu of a title. Father was conspicuously absent from the painting, while brother was removed and replaced.

In Figure IX-12, on the other hand, mother is the central figure. She dances on half of the double line of communication which she maintains with each member of her family. Stormy lines between mother and father are both direct and roundabout. Distant communication, mostly through mother, was drawn between Lee and brother "R." The longest lines of communication run from Lee to father; they were drawn with little pressure and look weaker than all the others. Mother was colored hot pink; brother, orange; father, green; and Lee, blue. All the lines of communication were also blue. A glance revealed that while Lee maintained contact with the others, she felt she was distant from all of the family members.

Figures IX-11 and IX-12 were hung side by side. "Now that it's all on paper, it looks weird, both of them," she remarked after

Figure IX-12.   Crayons; The Family

a long moment of gazing. It was clear that she sensed the distortions, but they were not discussed at the time.

The next time Lee arrived, she announced her parents' decision to reduce her visits to two per month. She had long been under pressure to terminate her psychotherapy and believed that she could continue only until the end of the school year. At this point there was no outburst of anger nor any regressive behavior. Instead, Lee was able to face the fact that her parents had been making a considerable financial sacrifice and to realize that she could still use the remaining five visits to good advantage. There was a new openness about her, coupled with a sense of serious urgency about using the short time that remained to learn what made her tick.

Lee felt it would be most useful to discuss her latest family paintings some more. She noted that the person most manipulated by her had always been her father, and speculated that mother would, of course, have been annoyed by her maneuvers and brother would have seen through them. She was able to see how her constant demands and competitive attitude spread from home to school and her social life, and recalled how agonizing the days at school had been for her in the past. She admitted now that grades were indeed important to her and that she was on the way back into the group of achieving students who had been her friends "before all this happened." But she knew now that to be accepted wholeheartedly by others she had to develop a different sense of companionship, free from her "poor me" attitude and from her implicit demand for exclusive possession as the proof of love. This she tried to express in Figure IX-13, her last painting, which she titled "Need for Companionship."

In this painting, two gently shaded forms, the upper a lively blue and the lower a warm pink, are moving toward each other. The upper one is larger because it represents people, Lee ex-

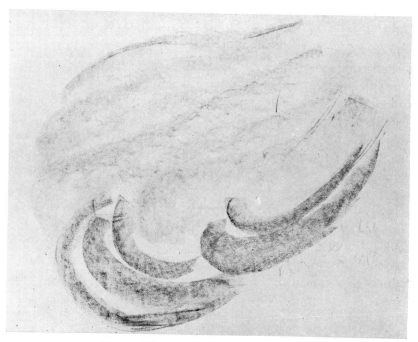

Figure IX-13.   Chalks; Companionship

plained, while the smaller form represents her own self, now much warmer than it used to be.

SUMMARY

A study was presented of art psychotherapy with an adolescent girl who suffered from a combination of transient adolescent difficulties and neurotic traits, developed against the background of some family pathology. Since this patient used her good verbal abilities mainly to fortify her system of defenses, art expression facilitated some important confrontations and helped her recognize some of her authentic feelings. In addition, art therapy offered much-needed release for her deep-seated hostilities. Smoking marihuana, the originally stated reason for psychotherapy, was treated as a symptom rather than as a cause of emotional disturbance.

FOLLOW-UP

The parents' policy of no contact with the psychologist during Lee's psychotherapy continued after termination, so there was no follow-up in the ordinary sense of the word. While perturbed adolescents must be helped to face their own problems, a parallel process ought to take place in their families. During and after Lee's psychotherapy, the family remained an unknown. Another unknown at termination was how well Lee could be expected to cope, alone, with her unresolved difficulties, burdened as she had been with the family pathology. And the third unknown concerned her psychological readiness to assimiliate her own new attitudes securely into her personality.

She had just begun to see through some of her most crippling defenses, and the importance of the future, a realistic and tangible future, had just started to play a role in her present. She had not given up smoking pot; though her use of it had been considerably reduced, it was still, at the time of termination, reserved "for special occasions."

Although therapy was terminated under pressure, young Lee's strength gave grounds for hope that she would be able to cope satisfactorily with her problems.

X

Jack

THIS IS A STUDY of eighteen months of art psychotherapy with an adolescent boy. In the course of treatment, his initial indifference grew into general resistance, and later he experienced an episode of heavy marihuana smoking. With the help of therapy and wise parents, and the flowering of his own unused musical and intellectual abilities, he began eventually to make progress toward personal and social maturity.

The parents sought psychologic help for their eldest son, Jack, because they were concerned about his apathy and general lack of enthusiasm. They brought him to me when, in their terms, he was still "pleasant to have around and not troublesome at all." He was, however, achieving at a low level in school even though he was considered bright and well informed. He showed little interest in any of his studies.

Mr. and Mrs. Dickson were wise and intelligent about the development of their family. They felt that during Jack's formative years, when they, the parents, were young and immature, he was affected by their problems. Each of them had his own difficulties, which, in turn, created trouble in their relationship with each other.

In addition, they reported that throughout his childhood, Jack was handicapped by an ailment of the muscles in his legs. Though he attended school, the prolonged treatment and his special shoes made it impossible for him to run and jump as the other children did.

For a few years he was acutely aware of being the little boy who was pushed around, and he probably carried bitter feelings about this experience into his adolescence. In psychotherapy, he could not remember having been handicapped, but recalled being lonely and angry at his helplessness in the face of his contemporaries. The parents, too, remembered that Jack had been an unhappy child in kindergarten.

Each parent was ready and willing to undertake individual treatment. Three groups of problems gradually came to the fore.

One concerned certain differences between the parents even though their marriage rested on mutual love and care. Their contrasting characters were mirrored in their two sons, Jack and Stephen. Jack, taciturn, increasingly rebellious, achieving little and insisting on going his own way, resembled father in his youth. His younger brother Stephen, like mother, cared about achievement, conformed to demands, and functioned in a generally organized fashion. At present, he also gratified father's current wish for his children's scholastic success; he was the one who supplied the good grades. The two sons were almost like Cain and Abel, one blessed, the other accursed.

Another problem centered on an unconscious alliance between mother and Jack, which made father angry with his wife. Father was so stern toward Jack that she felt compelled to defend her elder son.

The third and weightiest problem rested with Mr. Dickson, who unconsciously burdened Jack with emotional residues of his own turbulent and belated adolescence. Himself having become a philosophical and inventive professional man, he nevertheless wanted Jack to adopt manual labor as a way of life, urging that it was more sensible than today's competitive professionalism. He genuinely believed that he was being liberal with his son in not forcing him into studies.

As will be seen, Jack was not fully aware of this emotional burden, yet he keenly sensed its weight. It compounded his unsolved childhood problems and played into adolescent troubles that might otherwise have proved transient. Further, father's attitude encouraged Jack to act out the political and social unrest he shared with his contemporaries.

When fifteen-year-old Jack was asked to draw a person, he produced Figure X-1, saying that it was "a six-year-old boy, having fun, happy." Whining, he also insisted that he had no "artistic talent" and could not draw or paint. I tended to agree

Figure X-1. Soft pencil; Boy

that he was not artistically endowed, but the inadequacy of Figure X-1 by all standards of figure drawing to be expected from a fifteen-year-old stems from emotional causes.

The head is disproportionately large. Essential details, for example, hands and ears, are missing. The person has neither clothing nor any indication of sex. The figure as a whole seems to be floating. Too, there is a disturbing contrast between the troubled facial expression and the infantile body, suggesting the painter's own rudimentary body image. Last, it is very hard to accept Jack's statement that the boy is happy. On the contrary, the figure looks unhappy and awkward. Perhaps it is the awkwardness of an infant who is afraid to walk. The frozen arms without hands strongly suggest misery and an inability to cope with it. They might also suggest Jack's fear of his own aggression.

Jack produced Figure X-2 in response to my request following Figure X-1 that he draw a person his age. Even now he drew a person younger than himself, saying that "this is a boy, about fourteen; he wears a sweater and jeans."

This is a more mature version of Figure X-1. The essential details, ears, eyebrows, and hands, are there, at least after a sketchy fashion. The figure is clothed; and because the feet are near the bottom of the page, this figure seems to be resting on

Figure X-2.   Soft pencil; Boy

the ground. The placement of the figure near the bottom of the page probably caused Jack to feel no need to draw a baseline. This indicated a good measure of emotional security at home. To be sure, there is still a great deal of awkwardness about this self-portrait. But now it might be the awkwardness of an adolescent, overwhelmed with his suddenly long legs, who is, perhaps, also quite naturally worried about sex and about his own masculinity. The yearning to hold on to early childhood is suggested by the short arms with widespread fingers and by the line at the bottom. The portrait is heavily colored with crayons in red and black, black being used for outlines and red for shading.

We talked about the serious thoughts of the boy in the picture. While Jack was unable to be specific, he did succeed in conveying the boy's bewilderment about himself, his feeling different from other boys, particularly "not as successful as his brother." As he talked about the boy in the picture, Jack slipped into talking about himself and Stephen. He qualified the comparison with his brother by explaining that he spoke "according to dad's idea of success and maybe even Stephen's idea of success, because they both agree that success means good grades."

The accent on dissonance or separation is clearly expressed in the family portrait shown in Figure X-3. Jack was not concerned with details and made only slight differences in dress to distinguish men from women. He seemed primarily interested in defining his own place in relation to other members of the family.

Towering in the center are the parents; mother, tall and strong, looks challengingly at her husband. On the far left is Jack, with long hair, seeming to move away from the rest. Next to him is the youngest child, four-year-old Carla. On father's left (viewer's right) is twelve-year-old Stephen, and next to Stephen (far right) stands Eileen, a year younger than Stephen.

Jack studied his picture and complimented himself, saying that "for a lousy artist, that's not too bad. It shows how things really are right now." At first he refused to elaborate on his statement and insisted that I tell him what he meant, saying, "You are the psychologist and you ought to tell me." Then he offered

Figure X-3.   Crayon; The Family

some comments. He saw himself, mother, and Carla as a group within the family. He conceded that mother was looking away from him, but said that was because she was expecting father to say something insulting about his (Jack's) long hair. As to Carla, she was "a cute little sister" and Jack was helping mother take care of her.

The other half of the family, Jack thought, was closer to father since Stephen supplied the good grades and Eileen "hangs on to dad most of the time because she is jealous of Carla. Otherwise, half of the time she doesn't know what goes on." We talked about each member of the family, about mother's "mad look at dad" and about father's "madness." When I posed the question of a possible connection between the parents' anger with each other and with Jack himself, he was somewhat startled, admitted that he had not thought of it that way, and agreed that this was something worth thinking about.

But when Jack arrived next time, he did not remember anything about the preceding hour. He was angry and very upset about school. His eyes filled with tears and his lips trembled when he whiningly told about his troubles with some teachers and with the vice-principal, who was school disciplinarian.

Even from his highly defensive, self-righteous account, it was clear that Jack was doing all he could to provoke the school authorities. He acted as the hero and martyr of youth's struggle for freedom. His grades were extremely low. He maintained that he was faithfully doing his homework, but that no amount of homework would help him improve his grades for he could "never make it."

Jack apparently felt that he had to prove to me how the teachers misjudged his efforts. So, as he came in one day, he pulled out of his pocket a creased sheet of paper and forced it into my hands. It was the latest history test, graded very low, even though he had answered every question. He insisted that the low grade was given him for wearing his shirttail out, for his liberal ideas, and because he took part in recent protest marches.

Since the paper had been forced upon me, I accepted the implied task and examined the test together with Jack. This examination revealed either utter ignorance or a deliberately mocking attitude, and Jack had to decide which it was. This placed him in a most uncomfortable position, for he refused to be considered ignorant and was not ready to admit deliberate mockery. He solved his immediate dilemma by attacking me and the school: me for failing to do the psychologist's job of unconditionally supporting him, and the school for not meeting the true needs of today's scientifically minded, intellectual young people. Jack was quite eloquent in his anger. However, in the course of his accusations, he admitted that he might have forgotten much of the learned "stuff" because it was boring, and that he had probably developed gaps in knowledge, also, "in some other ways." When I reminded him that as "scientific-minded" people, we wanted a precise statement about the "other ways," he said "daydreaming, but I refuse to talk about it because it is my business and I can daydream anytime I want to." To his surprise, I agreed with him and suggested that he paint anything he wanted.

As he stepped away from the easel, I was startled to see

Figure X-4, the bright magenta, almost literally uttering a cry (see Color Plate XXVIII). The painting vividly expresses the deep despair felt by a boy who resisted verbal expression about his suffering. When he saw the painting many months later, Jack disclosed that he had been having frequent dreams at the time about screaming "like that," but knowing in the dreams that he had not uttered a sound. He remembered "horrible" feelings in those dreams. But immediately following the painting, Jack was unable to talk about any feelings that the screaming boy might have experienced. Over and over he insisted, "That's how it came out. I just painted it and this is what came out."

To encourage some verbal exchange about the picture, I wondered about the boy's necktie, as Jack, in accordance with his code, never wore a necktie or a jacket. "I wondered how long you would take to notice that," Jack said sarcastically. Indeed, I was slow to see that he had wanted me to notice this important detail immediately. I had underestimated his intelligence, he thought, and therefore aroused his anger.

There were three clusters of problems associated with

Figure X-4.   Chalk; The Cry

Figure X-4. One centered on Jack's emotional distress. The second became apparent from Jack's method of conveying his feelings to me by means of the necktie. Finally, there were other emotionally charged meanings, also symbolized by the necktie.

When I helped him express anger at me directly, Jack was able to sort out the problems suggested by the picture. His painted expression concerning these ideas was, at least in part, intentional.

He was gradually able to admit his distress and his inability to do anything about it, both conveyed by the boy's cry. These feelings became more acceptable to him when I spoke of them as great unhappiness. He then became able to say he felt that for him nothing could ever change, "because they don't want me to change and they won't even let me." I asked him who "they" were, but he refused to tell me. It was clear, however, that his teachers were not the chief targets of Jack's anger.

His anger at me for not immediately recognizing the intended meaning of the necktie enabled us to focus on the way he treated other people significant in his life. When they frustrated his expectation of being recognized as especially bright by only the small and concealed tokens of brightness he offered, his revenge was immediate. He would turn away from them in wrath, bitter and self-pitying, at the same time nurturing a feeling of solitary greatness.

It took five hour-long sessions to discuss with Jack these two aspects of his behavior: his inner state of distress and his revenge against those who failed to give him the recognition he expected. In spite of his reluctance, he finally was able to see that his unrealistic demands could lead to nothing but misery. Jack was bright enough to recognize that his poor scholastic performance was one of his token offerings, as was his reluctance to make himself known to others, the last exemplified by his unwillingness to talk with me, with his parents, or with his contemporaries.

Throughout these conversations, Figure X-4 was on the wall in front of us. The cry of anguish in bright magenta was a living illustration of Jack's complex emotional-social experience fixed into a pattern of hostility.

We were now ready to turn to the necktie, around which

clustered the third set of problems. Since this symbolic detail was intentionally painted, Jack spoke of its meaning more readily than about the other two problems. He began to speak in the third person about the boy in the painting but soon slipped into the use of the first person. This interesting grammatical change indicates, of course, an emotional change; he had become more committed to dealing with the problem at hand. Jack said, "The boy yells and screams, maybe because of what he does with some teachers and everyone else, but maybe also because I don't want to wear that necktie."

I sensed that we had stumbled upon an important problem and tacitly decided to take it easy and let Jack set the pace. When I asked him to tell me more about the necktie, Jack reminded me that it was intended to serve only as a symbol, since in reality, he never wore neckties in school or at home. He said, "They [his parents] never make me dress up, but see, my father, I think, would want *me* to do things that *he* would like to do, so the necktie is a symbol of that, as though he were saying, 'You must wear a necktie because I like neckties and I never had any neckties when I was your age,' and I can't do it, but its as though I must. And what I said was just an example. I am sure that my father did have neckties. Do you get it?" He looked scared and his lips quivered as he went on and on in a pleading, whining tone of voice.

I certainly did get it. For Jack, the man of few words, that was a lot to say. He went on to tell me that the problem did not even lie in "the lousy work I do in school or on the lawn or washing the car. He just doesn't want me to be *me*! Except— except when we're boating, because it pleases him to see how well I can boat, because he was the one who taught me how."

The next time Jack came, he spoke bitterly and with a sense of loss about mother who was no longer his ally. He had sensed the change for some time, he said, but had had fresh, especially convincing evidence the day before. Mother had demonstrated that she was united with father when, together, they "made" him apologize to the hated vice-principal for wearing his shirttail out, which was against the rules. Jack ascribed the change in mother to my work with her, and so I, too, was no ally. When I mentioned this implication, he nodded in agreement.

Two hour-long visits were devoted to Jack's anger at me, which he was able to tie up with his expectation of recognition. He also understood that in the past being recognized or not recognized by significant others had meant to him gaining an ally or an enemy. Yet, although father failed him in this regard, it was hard for him to think of father as a foe, and he had "long ago" decided that I was not one, either. Things were "mixed up," Jack said, and he needed to sort them out. He felt that ideas that had been "fixed" in his mind were different now, but he did not know yet what they were.

I offered him the concept of crisis that individuals or groups experience when ideas, institutions, or ways of behaving are outworn and new ones have not yet taken their place. Jack began to see himself as one of a group of troubled adolescents, but he also noticed that many of his contemporaries were not as bitter and belligerent as he was, and unlike him, could attend to their studies despite their share of emotional turmoil.

He was beginning to wonder about himself and when I suggested that testing would help me understand him a little better, he was willing to cooperate. Jack's general resistance had caused me to delay psychological testing. Shyly, he disclosed that he had been reluctant to be tested because he was afraid that I might find out how stupid he really was. At the end of that conversation, Jack painted Figure X-5 with poster paints. He said he did not know what it was.

Green and yellow spots on a bright blue background make up a semicircular form that seems to be making its way up or down a hill (see Color Plate XXIX). When the painting was hung up, Jack saw in it "a huge turtle that could be a pretty good turtle, but looks kind of beaten up because of his wanderings and because, maybe, he used to be pushed around, so he often fell off." Jack went on to say that the turtle had been moving down to see if he could find a place in the left-hand corner, but he did not like it, so he turned around and "is right now climbing

Figure X-5.   Poster paints; Turtle

up again, but it will take him ages because he will fall back and roll off a few times."

We talked a little about the turtle's predicament and Jack said seriously that whenever he sees turtles or bugs struggle on their backs, he helps them to their feet. I answered that in my work, when I see a person struggle to get back on his feet I do the same thing. This was followed by a long silence and just when I began to wonder whether my answer had been a wise one, Jack asked, "And what if the person doesn't believe that he can be helped?" I had an idea that Jack harbored a secret he found hard to bear.

Jack's Full Scale IQ on the WISC was 125, with special success in subtests of abstract thinking, but he had to be prodded and asked to repeat his answers in a louder voice. Yet, it seemed that despite his poor work in school, he had accumulated a good store of knowledge. The difference, however, of eighteen points between the rather high Verbal IQ of 131 and the above-average Performance IQ of 113 indicated the need to explore the possibility of emotional disturbance through other tests.

All personality tests brought out feelings of defeat and infantile rage at being pushed around. There were residues of unsolved childhood problems about being weaker than other children and being expected to do things that he was not ready to do.

The age of twenty-one became Jack's fantasy-haven. That would be the time of his liberation when everything would suddenly go his way; until then he would suffer and mark time. That was why Jack went to school, but once there did not do any work.

Jack struggled with father despite his admiration for him, and was bitter with mother despite deep and warm feelings for her. He seemed to carry a burden imposed upon him by father, but was unable to understand what the burden might be. The fantasy of freedom at twenty-one was becoming stronger and more frightening.

Normally, an adolescent's future becomes integrated with the present by means of realistic planning; linked with a planned future, the present takes on meaning. Not so for Jack. He day-dreamed about himself as a fantastically strong, revengeful person at twenty-one. Whatever radiance this imagined future held for him, its impact on the present was negative and only undermined his not-quite-formed ego. Thus he was unable to use his own assets, such as his interest in history or his considerable talent for music. At school, he remained on the fringe of intellectual and musical activities, leaving excellence and success to his younger brother.

Jack was not only surprised but also completely unbelieving when he was told that the level of his intelligence was rather high and that he could, if he decided that it was important, achieve above-average grades. Bolstered by the results of the tests, his parents made it clear to Jack that they were dissatisfied with his school performance even though they understood that in his present turmoil he could not be expected to raise his grades.

The personality tests with their story telling assignments and projection of images found in ink blots stirred Jack's fantasy, almost dormant before. He began to paint profusely and pro-duced numerous "nothing paintings," as he called them. They consisted of spontaneous brushstrokes in colorful poster paints. There were varieties of continuous and staccato lines, and blots of all shapes and sizes. Gradually, backgrounds and foregrounds began to appear. At the same time, Jack began to remember and tell dreams, something he had never been able to do in the past.

Figure X-6 was one of the spontaneous paintings which became, in the very process of painting, a pictorial account of a recent dream (see Color Plate XXX). Jack said, "The black lines are beams in a barn, or maybe in a huge window. All these greens and reds and golds in the background are the landscape in the hills, at sunset. The farmer just hung up this wheel on the beam,

Figure X-6.   Poster paints; Barn Dream

and left. This goat that had been standing there all the time tried
to get the wheel down, but couldn't. Trying so hard, he almost
broke his horns. He got mad and in great anger he is right now
pounding his head on this tall beam, until it hurts."

Jack disliked the dream and wondered why he dreamed it.
He liked the colors in the painting, but did not like the goat's
pounding his head against the beam since "this doesn't lead anywhere; it's stupid." As he uttered these words, he laughed and
said that perhaps he sometimes acted a little bit like the goat.

Of course, there was some sexual symbolism in the picture,
but I did not try to focus his attention on it, since I hoped to
work on Jack's sexual worries more openly and directly. Discussions bearing on them indeed often took place over the next
few months. Jack emerged as a boy of very tender feelings with
a strong, built-in morality about sex and love. With great relief
he told me of his arguments with some boys about sexual freedom
and of his own personal decision about how far he would go
with a girl if he had one and if they loved each other. He was
also pleased with my opinion that at his age he ought to know all
that could be learned about the physiology of sex, and was reassured by my saying I considered his father well able to sup-
plement Jack's discussions of these matters with me. Sometime
later Jack announced that he had decided this was the time to
learn everything about sex, but that he would postpone sexual
activity "until the girl really knows whether she wants it." This
decision apparently made it possible for him to relax for a while.

But he had new worries. Some weeks later, during three
successive visits, Jack's facial expression was strange and his eyes
would not meet mine. There were heavy silences and he refused
to paint. I suspected that his pressing secret was that he was
smoking marihuana, but I had to wait for cues from him. On the
fourth visit, Jack, very depressed and still looking tense, painted
a series of monsters, of which Figure X-7 is a representative
example.

Outlined with black crayon and lightly colored in with
orange, this monster had red eyes and a green nose. On the
viewer's right, at the bottom corner, is the outline of a house

Figure X-7.   Felt pen and chalks; Monster

with Jack behind the window, looking out at the towering creature who seems to envelope the house. Jack seemed to think that
this had been a dream, but he reported that the night before,
he thought that he saw the monster outside his window. This
sounded like an implied, but not clear hallucination.

Next time Jack reported another dream (Fig. X-8) about a
different monster. On a snowy night, Jack found himself in a
strange empty house with a bay window at the far end of a long
hall. As he approached the window and looked outside, he saw
an enormous green monster-head descending on the house (see
Color Plate XXXII). He was frozen in fear and tried to scream,

but could not hear his own voice. At that point, a lady appeared; although she was outside the house, he saw her clearly. He remembered being surprised in the dream that she did not re-semble his mother, but as she appeared, calmness descended upon him. Jack still wondered who the woman might be.

When I had him guess at her identity, Jack shyly and cautiously asked, "Was it you?" The guess led into discussion about the relationship between patient and therapist and spe-cifically between Jack and me. We also talked about his resistance and his trust, and about the monsters that had plagued him in recent weeks.

Jack wondered what psychology said about monsters ap-pearing "to a scientifically minded person who does not believe in them." He was most anxiously attentive when I speculated that perhaps when such a person feels bad deep inside, it is easier for him to place those feelings in an imaginary monster, outside himself. Jack gazed at the two monster paintings hung up on the

Figure X-8.   Chalks; Lady and Monster

wall. After much prodding from me, stammering and in a small, questioning voice, he said, "In the paintings the boy is feeling rotten and maybe guilty, and so he sees these stupid monsters. . . . You mean, maybe, I think that I am sort of a monster myself? And this is kind of bad for the whole family because the monster threatens the whole house, so I am even more scared . . . and you are there kind of to help me? But I don't need any help and I know that there are no monsters inside or outside anyone." The last words were bitter and in sharp contrast to the rest of his speech, which had conveyed a sense of discovery and hope. I thought that he was not ready to confide in me, perhaps because of his fear that I might tell his parents. Two days later, Jack was caught on the school grounds smoking marihuana.

There followed a period of about ten weeks of bitter struggle between Jack and his parents about his breach of their trust.

Both parents took a firm, united stand. They were open with Jack about their strong opposition to his use of the drug. They told their other children what was going on, and they organized other parents and their teen-age children to discuss the growing problem of marihuana smoking in the school. Unlike some other liberal parents, the Dicksons refused to make the tragic mistake of silently acquiescing in their children's self-destruction. They believed that the young boys and girls really wanted to hear the truth, and they were strong enough to bear their child's anger.

So they honestly told Jack how angry they were that he had concealed his smoking from them, as they had always trusted him to be truthful. They also told him clearly that he was too important to them for them not to fight what he was doing, no matter how independent he felt, that they were still responsible for his health, and that he was causing much anguish to the whole family. They tolerated him in the household, but the old intimacy was gone.

Jack felt acutely that his parents had shut him out; he complained that he felt like a stranger in his own home. He said he had not told his parents about the smoking for fear of being stopped, and that he could not tell me about it for fear I would tell them. Neither his parents nor I, he asserted, really understood what great things he was getting out of smoking marihuana: "a feeling of wonderful lightness, a great clarity of mind, and a new studiousness." He was certain of much better grades the next marking period.

Jack's mood, appearance, and behavior belied his exalted notion of his gains from marihuana. He had promised his parents not to smoke for the next two months, but after a few days was unable to keep the promise. He was coming to my office directly after school, moody and depressed. His eyes readily filled with tears and the old tremor of the lips was back. The happily anticipated report card was worse than ever. His tutor, whom the parents had engaged some time before, decided to quit because Jack did not respond to his efforts.

During this period, Jack was "messing around" with blobs of clay and tearing them apart. Figure X-9 grew out of this activity. Jack did not designate this bust of a grim-looking man with a white face and black hair as his father, but, somehow, he talked about father while the small sculpture stood in front of us. With pride and warmth he told how his dad had energetically intervened the day before on behalf of his two sons. Jack and

Figure X-9. Clay; A Man

Stephen had volunteered to help in the local election campaign, but although their help was badly needed, it was not accepted because of their long hair. Mother, too, had telephoned a lady on the board and given her "some real smart arguments" about it. As a result, the boys were allowed to help and their dedicated work was much appreciated.

Jack was wondering how his father could intervene for him at a time when he also treated him like a stranger at home, at best only just tolerating him ("They just feed me and let me sleep in my room.") His old notion about father wanting him to fulfill his own unfulfilled wishes changed into a question about "what dad really wants of me." Just before the big struggle about smoking erupted, father had told him that grades were not the most important thing in a person's life so long as there was an ongoing process of learning of some kind. Father had also told him about his own low grades in school to show Jack that that had not kept him from choosing a career in education at which "he is pretty good, maybe even very good."

When I suddenly asked Jack how he felt about dad that very moment, Jack said to his own surprise that he felt "pretty good about him," but wondered about that very feeling, since he had felt quite indignant "when he [father] made me feel like a criminal and a stranger at home; and even other times, when we are friends, anything wrong I do turns him against me."

I suggested to Jack that he look at the sculpture and say whatever came to his mind. Jack gazed a few minutes and said, "My father is certainly more handsome than this thing. I don't feel mad with him. I think that he cares for me, but I also think that a long time ago he made up his inner mind that come what may, I got to do things that he wants to do, but can't, or something like that. I don't know if you get this or if anybody can get this; it's kind of impossible; it's crazy. See, he hollers about the chores, but it's not that at all."

In further conversations, extended over four visits, Jack understood that what had put him at ease about the marihuana storm after the initial distress and bewilderment was his father's clear, firm attitude, the leadership he displayed throughout "the whole fuss about the smoking." Both parents had succeeded in conveying to Jack their conviction that the definitive termination of smoking was of the utmost importance for his well-being.

Even though Jack was not willing to stop smoking immediately at his parents' demand, the clarity of that demand appealed to him. This was in sharp contrast to Jack's old notion that father expected of him some special performance about which he was never to be told specifically. He could only get a vague idea, conveyed by father's biting criticisms of petty duties badly performed. Jack asked me to "find out" from his father if he actually had had any special expectations of his older son.

I challenged Jack. "Where does this leave you in the meantime?" "That I've got to face my own problem, apart from my father? That I have to make up my mind about smoking?" he asked. His voice was angry and sarcastic.

Jack tried again to resist smoking, but when he tested himself a few days later hoping to see that he no longer wanted to smoke, he only started a continuous series of "trips" which he could not stop. Soon he began to get his brother to relay messages to and from his smoking companions. He was smoking heavily.

Jack was now coming to his psychotherapy sessions visibly "turned on." He was confused, worried, and silent. Most of his time was spent at the painting table where he turned out page after page of fragmented shapes and smears that spelled disorganization and regression. In the third such hour, Jack said, "You see that my mind doesn't work today, or any day now." I decided to confront him by testing his intelligence then and there.

That day, Jack rated just above average in general intelligence, twenty-two points lower than he rated at the beginning of the school year on the same Wechsler IQ scale. He did not remember the test at all and failed at many tasks he had solved successfully the first time. Many questions had to be read to him repeatedly. He was generally passive, distracted, and apathetic.

When I told Jack the test results during his next appointment, his apathy gave way to stormy rage. For the first time, Jack shouted at me; perhaps it was the first time in his life he had ever shouted at anyone. I could not possibly know his mind, his mind was his alone and he alone knew how it worked. He had proof outside of school that his mind worked better than ever before; for example, he could make complicated repairs on bicycles, and had been doing great things in music on his own. This was the style of Jack's stormy denial of what his continuous heavy smoking had done to him recently.

When he came next time, he sat down quietly to paint with poster colors. Figure X-10 was the result. It was a colorful though hazy picture (see Color Plate XXXI). I did not expect any comments from Jack, but to my surprise he volunteered the following: "This is high up on a cliff. This small bird had fallen out of the nest, which is somewhere higher up. He chanced upon this cliff and is holding on to it. He is looking down and his head goes in

Figure X-10.   Poster paints; The Bird

circles because there is something there, like a deep abyss and water. And when he looks up, he sees the awful red sun. So he can't hardly see anything and it's awful hard to hold on, too." Jack said he had just made up the story and the painting was really "just a bunch of smears and blobs." The story occurred to him when I hung up the picture and the turquoise shape in the center suggested the bird to him and the brown and yellow areas, rocks and cliffs; the rest followed. At the end of the same hour, Jack said he often dreamed he was falling.

On his next visit, Jack was more alive, active, and direct. He painted Figure X-11 with poster paints. Against an airy background of very light reds and blues he painted two horizontal shapes, the lower in bright blue and the upper in bright red. He expanded the two massive areas to bring them close together, but carefully preserved the crevice between them, which was wider on one side than on the other. Jack did not know why he painted this picture.

I hung up a group of pictures including Figures X-8, X-9,

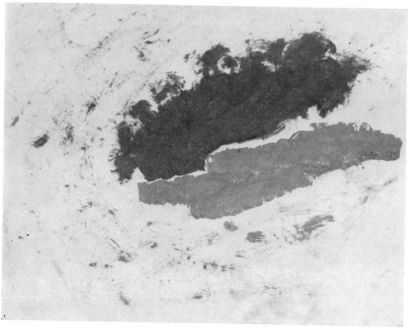

Figure X-11.   Poster paints; The Split.

X-10, X-11, and also two of the fragmented paintings not shown here, and asked Jack to see if he could say anything about them or about himself.

In connection with Figure X-8, Jack said that when he produced it he still believed that his problems were outside him and that I, his helper, was also outside him. Figure X-9, he asserted, was bad sculpture, but good for the expression of his pent-up feelings about father, especially his belief that father had wanted "something big" of him. Jack did not know, he said, whether I had worked with father to change that, but the old oppressive

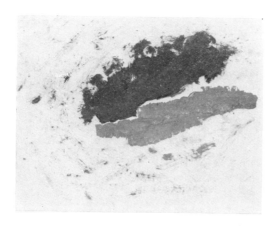

feeling was gone almost all the time. He dismissed the two fragmented pictures as his "mix-up pictures; they aren't even paintings." Figure X-10, Jack disclosed, made him "think a lot, a few days and nights," and by the time he painted it, he had come to understand that he was like the bird, and that his problems were really inside himself. Figure X-11, Jack went on, was his "inside problem" which, though not yet solved, was "getting there, and that's why there is this sky or air in light pink and blue."

I also considered Figure X-11 an expression of psychological integration, even though the split is rather conspicuous. In comparison with the other pictures in this group, however, this painting is relatively well organized. The very statement of the split is clear and strong. The two massive forms seem to move toward each other, not apart. Jack's comments show that he was actively aware of the positive meaning of this painting, and his words indicated his generally healthier state of mind.

Considering the paintings as a group, we see that Jack's sense of inner split and paralyzing conflict could not be coped with before the feelings about father were brought out. Only after he was aware of these feelings could Jack realize emotionally and intellectually how close he had come to breakdown. Thus, we can agree with the painter that in relation to Figures X-8, X-9, and X-10, Figure X-11 can be considered a first message about an approaching change for the better.

Once Jack's inner growth was somewhat less blocked, the natural resilience of a healthy adolescent could take over. Figure X-12, painted two visits later, tells the story.

The picture's general theme, the peace symbol, Jack had adopted long ago as his private emblem and frequent doodle. Here he painted four peace symbols, each on a differently colored square. From a fifth emblem in the center, rays emanated into all the squares. The whole production was secured by a sturdy frame in black, "to bring out the colors." Jack reminded me of his frequent emblem paintings in the past. He said that it had recently occurred to him that those had been the disconnected parts of him. In this picture, the parts were at last put together. Yellow was the childish and happy part of him; red, the mad part; blue, the blah part; and green, the hopeful part. These were various sides of him, but he was really one person. In the picture, he expressed this unity in the central emblem with its rays. "This isn't much of a painting, but it makes a lot of sense to me," he concluded.

When he finished the painting, Jack moved back to the

Figure X-12.   Poster paints; The Emblem

conference room and seated himself in the chair opposite me, ready to speak. There was an energy about him which I had not seen before.

"I have decided to give up smoking for good," he announced. "In fact, I have already given it up. It's not good for me. It's not good for my mind. This time, it's not a promise to my parents or to anybody; it is my own decision, for me."

Jack had indeed given up smoking for good and all. It was spring and he began to worry about promotion to the senior class. This time, however, he took some action. A few better grades resulted, enough for Jack to believe that he could do well when he tried.

This was the busy time of year in the musical community, with plans for recitals in school and elsewhere and the announcement of auditions and concerts. Jack crawled out of hiding. "I am making myself known in school as a musician," he said shyly. His music became at once focus and arena for Jack's changing attitudes and relationships.

In the past, his music had been an angry retreat, furiously guarded from others. Now it became a means of participation, something to share with others; solitary gratification was transformed almost suddenly into joy, openly though shyly expressed. Recognition, now earned, came quickly. Jack was a good and knowledgeable bass player who even ventured to transcribe songs from bass to piano. The tough music teacher, who had not previously acknowledged Jack's musicianship, was most impressed when Jack played his original composition. In the therapy hours these developments were placed for Jack in the context of his new ability and willingness to give of himself to others without worrying about recognition.

On the home front, music also became the means for Jack to cope with his old problem of helpless, angry competition with his younger brother Stephen, the excellent student and acknowledged family scholar. Jack had always stayed away from the piano, for that had been Stephen's instrument. Now he began to use it freely to play his musical transcriptions. Stephen, at first angry and shocked, then accepted Jack's challenging invitation to play duos. The parents' impression that in music Stephen was the plugger while Jack had the real ability, was confirmed. Jack admitted to me that he derived much satisfaction from his new ability to deal with Stephen and from Stephen's open admiration of his performance on the piano without formal piano training. Now they both enjoyed playing "pretty good" music. Often, the rest of the family listened and sometimes friends came to hear them play. The parents, who understood that more than music was at stake, wisely stayed away from the boys even when, especially at the start, the brothers quarreled furiously.

Jack's entry into the music community in school brought him closer to a group of boys and girls who had always appealed to him; formerly, he had thought that they looked down on him. It made him angry that he could not dare even think that he might become one of them. At the end of a therapy hour when we had discussed this change in his social life, I asked Jack to make a quick painting. He responded with Figure X-13, a self-portrait.

Referring to my past remark that he always looked away

from me, Jack said, "That's me, and I can look straight or up, now. And the blue sky is behind me." I thought for a moment of hanging up Figures X-1 and X-2 along with Figure X-13, but quickly decided it was unnecessary.

Before Jack left for a long summer vacation, he painted Figures X-14 and X-15, both pertaining to his recent transcriptions of jazz songs. I had asked him to paint a song that made him "feel a lot inside." In contrast to past resistance to tasks in art therapy that directly called for emotional expression, Jack chose a turquoise jumbo chalk and made the thick outside line of figure X-14. This was the melody, he explained, and the jumbled scribbles over this line were "some deep feelings that came with the melody itself." Inside there were more condensed, jumbled lines in green, magenta, and yellow, all compressed in a rectangular box but escaping from it in some spots. "These are more feelings," Jack said, "Kind of a mix-up, but that's how it might show in color; kind of a little wild, you might say."

Jack talked excitedly about another song, transcribed just

Figure X-13.   Chalk and crayons; Self-Portrait

Figure X-14.   Chalks; A Song

the night before, and I invited him upstairs to the piano. This was scarcely my usual practice; the thought came to me as I felt that my interest in what he was telling me generated in Jack new feelings, ready to be expressed. I also wanted to see for myself the new enthusiasm of a boy who had never shown enthusiasm for anything. Jack played the song with excitement and at the same time, with a seriousness which reminded me of the boy in Figure X-2 who, as Jack said, "is thinking about something serious."

When we came back to the office, I said, "Now try to paint it." Jack took the whole box of jumbo chalks, complimenting me for making them available at this session even though they had been there, unnoticed, for the past few weeks. He drew the basic melody again in turquoise, this time an open-ended line. Next he made a succession, starting at the bottom, of strong, horizontal areas of black, brown, magenta, green, and yellow. "These are my feelings that I felt when I worked with this song last night," he said. "They started, at the bottom, with sadness [black], then I think I had some earthy feelings [brown], then there was,

Figure X-15.   Chalks; Another Song

maybe, love, nostalgic [magenta], then all of a sudden happy [light green], and then even happier, almost like childish [yellow]."

I asked him to compare the two paintings. Saying that Figure X-14, the "Coconut Grove" song, was "not really that good" even though the teacher liked it, Jack declared that he would compare "the musicianship of the two and nothing else." He did not realize that he was being something of a psychologist and art therapist on his own.

Figure X-14 represented one of his earlier transcriptions. At the time he transcribed the song, Jack said, he was so afraid to let himself go that he had to close the whole basic melody line. "All the rest I crowded inside, and what a mess, what a mix-up!" The "Salvation Theme Song" (Fig. X-15) was "a more mature and a better piece of work," Jack thought. He was not afraid to let go and so "melody and what you would call feelings could kind of spread, and I could do what I felt. When I felt sad, I felt sad; and when I felt happy, I knew it was a happy feeling. But all the while, the melody was kind of keeping check, and I think that's why there is more order in this one, and I like this one much better than the other."

I asked Jack if he could explain exactly why he liked the second picture so much better. "Because I knew better where I was going in this one," was his reply.

To paraphrase Jack's words, in a psychological sense he was beginning to come into his own. The music was important chiefly as the medium through which he was able to start finding himself. Whether or not he had the talent to become a musician was immaterial at this point.

SUMMARY

An eighteen months' span of art psychotherapy with a fifteen-year-old boy in deep emotional crisis has been presented. Converging problems, his own and his parents', had a particularly strong impact on Jack. Early traumata remained within as the passive-aggressive young adolescent developed into an openly belligerent teen-ager.

Jack's early experience made difficult the emergence of personal identity. Hardest for him to cope with was his reaction to a problem which was essentially his father's but partly lay with both parents. Jack felt burdened and fought the poorly defined burden with irrational weapons, trying at the same time to assert himself. An episode of heavy marihuana smoking was treated within this context.

Though Jack was no artist and no ardent or easy user of art media for expressive purposes, his graphic productions became a language for him when he was not yet ready to speak. Some of the paintings which he reluctantly produced as a pastime became particularly significant in psychotherapeutic work toward personal and social maturation.

FOLLOW-UP

In the past, Jack had avoided groups, but this time he chose to spend the summer with a group of boys and girls who bicycled through some parts of the country. In this group, he emerged as a leader. He also developed a tender, romantic friendship with one of the girls.

Jack had registered for a combination program of study and work in his senior year. On his return to school, he was pleased with his courses and his teachers. His mother asked Jack whether she should make psychotherapy appointments for him. Jack said that he first wanted to find the job for his school work program and that he would then call me on his own. Both parents continued to come for separate visits, and later Jack did call to make further appointments.

Part Two
ANALYTICAL OBSERVATIONS

XI

Patient's Self-expression
in Psychotherapy

Even the early dictionary meanings of the Latin *exprimere,* the French *exprès* and the English *express,* ascribed to the word, in all its grammatical forms, a certain impact and immediacy. This word always carried the connotation of something definite and explicit. With this seed of a basic and universal meaning in it, *express* was used in relation to a variety of things, situations, and activities, human and not human.

In transportation, the verb and the noun referred to trains running rapidly to one particular place. In the postal service, it meant things delivered immediately by a special messenger. In communication, it was a piece of news worth transmitting in a special way. A news item transmitted by special means had the power of creating moods of personal, social, and political impact.

Further meanings included pressing or squeezing the contents out of an object. This, in turn, gave rise to derived meanings of extorting or eliciting. The action of expressing brought forth added meanings about that which was expressed, such as an utterance, phrase, manifestation, graphic representation, or image of, resembling, symbolically representing and revealing by external tokens.

With reference to personal qualities and feelings, the word came to indicate a state of mind as well as the very act of representing character, sentiment, action, and emotional forces by suggesting one's thoughts either in words, motions, physiognomic manifestations, or in a work of art.

Every work of art and many works in art psychotherapy express and mean something. They do something to the observer. What they do to the observer is to communicate something to him and to arouse an experience in him. Physiognomics, or the study of facial features, which never became a science, is the oldest system of correlating feelings and visible expressions of feelings. Berkeley, in the beginning of the Eighteenth century, wrote in his essay on vision of the "invisible passions . . . let in by the eye along with colors." Two centuries later, Gestalt Psychology of Art, pioneered by the late Max Wertheimer and developed by our contemporary Rudolph Arnheim, picked up the importance of the eye. The eye, instrument of visual perception, perceived expression as an equal partner to color and form, according to these scientists.

In his writings about the expression of emotions, Darwin asserted that the observer's instinct connects the outer expressions with their psychological counterparts.

This idea was differently presented by Theodore Lipps, who tried to explain in his theory of empathy how we find expression in temple columns, his example of objects which conveyed expression. Empathy or perception of expression, he said, is made possible through the action of mechanical forces such as pressures. He argued that past experience allows us to know what mechanical pressures are acting inside the columns and how we would feel if we were in place of the columns. According to that viewpoint, empathy is a projection of mechanical or kinesthetic sensations which provoke feelings. The mechanism or the nature of such provocation remained unsolved, however. Yet, this theory indicated something toward a psychology of expression and art in that it interested itself in a play of forces, later developed by Gestalt psychologists.

To the Lipps theory one might add also a mention of Benedetto Croce's ideas, at the turn of the century, that esthetic expression is necessarily expression in images and that the tangible work of art is but a copy of what the artist previously beheld in his imagination. This describes Croce's role in the history of investigations of expression. He portrayed as secondary what Darwin and Lipps had regarded as primary; namely, that expression is what enables us to connect the outer with the inner. In *The Philosophy of Art*, the American philosopher and estheticist Curt

John Ducasse took Croce quite affably to task about this approach.

All traditional approaches before Wertheimer and Arnheim assumed that expression can be put into an object only by our acquired knowledge and by feelings, projected into the object by our memory. Since none of them questioned on a scientific basis the disparity between the mental and the physical, they did not connect expression in an object with the dichotomy of inside-outside. The Gestalt psychologists of art suggest as a connecting link between inside and outside, the similarity of the object's own and that of the viewer's perception.

Expression and structure is a pair of concepts and terms that is not entirely new. Inner and outer or internal and external, mental and physical or mind and body, are its counterparts in the past viewpoints. "Structure" turns our attention to the nature of each of the two concepts.

The first thinker who questioned on a modern scientific basis the disparity between the mental and the physical was William James. He proposed that though made of different stuff, mind and body functioned in similar ways because both shared a few structural qualities.

The Gestalt psychologists elaborated on this finding by studying similarities of structure in the object and in the observer. Max Wertheimer was struck by the compelling impact of expression, too immediate and all-encompassing to be only a rendition of our memory or merely a bit of acquired information. The mood, said Wertheimer, sad or happy, is in the dancer's motions themselves, because the structure of the motions and that of the mood are the same.

Rudolf Arnheim, whose important work centered later entirely on the psychology of art, had one of his students, Miss Binney, test Wertheimer's theory. In the experiment, she asked the members of a college dance group individually to improvise, expressing such moods as sadness or strength, and found a high degree of similarity in the individual performances. Specifically, the high degree of similarity was found in the formal factors of the movements such as tension, speed, confinement, expansion, change, gravitation, passivity, and others.

To draw another example, this time from children who have less specialized and more naive emotional attitudes, Julie, whose case study is included in this book, recalled on one of her visits how she had once painted a dark background for a picture because she "was sad," how she had been thinking at the time that I might see from the dark chalk that she was sad, and how she had quickly decided to use bright orange on top of the dark background to counteract my possible impression. Curious about her thinking of colors in relation to moods, I learned from her that "sure," when I am sad I use dark grey or other dark colors and black, and I think all kids do; and when I am glad or happy, I like to use all the bright colors and I see that other kids do the same." The counterpart of the dancers' experiment in life is seen by psychotherapists when their depressed patients are slow and lacking in energy and confine their mental life to immediate interests only.

Perceiving expression is possible because all of us are constantly affected by and quite naturally interested in the forces and occurrences around us, their direction, strength, warmth, indifference, tension, any action, counteraction, etc. Such forces are at work in a rich variety of configurations in nature, in objects, in persons, in interpersonal and other social situations. Expression is the impact of such forces on the observer when he perceives them with his senses, particularly with his eyes. Expression is not only the act of expressing but also that which is expressed. The perception of the expression means more than just the visual appearance of objects. It includes the awareness of all the senses, such as kinesthetic or auditory experiences. The perception of configurations of forces, grasped by configurations of senses, is followed by emotional reactions akin to those forces. In psychotherapy this may mean that when I perceive my patients' despair, my perception is akin to his expression of despair. It follows that expression is a most important factor in art and in life.

When a psychologist perceives the play of forces; that is, the expression in a person, a family, or in any small group of two or more and is able to specify those forces, he is ready to know something about the feelings that his patient might experience and is better equipped to help the patient. As often shown in the case studies, art expression is illuminating in psychotherapy in that the patient's visual projection of his own feelings helps him discover patterns of forces inside and outside himself. From there, the way to change is at least indicated.

Expression is not limited to physiognomic factors in people and animals. Abstract shapes, natural formations of mountains, rocks, and plants, and the spheric images more familiar in recent years, have line, color, and form which can be used for expression. For their art expression, artists and children abundantly use shapes and colors of the inanimate world. This is seen in the powerful wave of abstraction that assumed the dimensions of an explosion in art. Perhaps in his search for meaning in the complex contemporary world the artist, as the sensitive pathfinder for his fellow men, finds that the inanimate world contains a more generalized law of expression, wide enough to include the physical and the mental.

That law consists of configurations of forces and occurrences. When we perceive the striving upward in a cathedral or in the Lipps example of columns, it is not that we can feel ourselves inside the towers and columns pressured by their pressures, but that we find there are forces inside us which also reside in all existence outside of us. Some of these occurrences and forces are expansion and contraction, rise and fall, activity and passivity, approach and withdrawal, discord and harmony, pushes and pulls, wants and needs, and impulses and a rich variety of others acting in a vast number of combinations. What the striving upward or holding up of the columns stirs in us is only a particle of such forces and occurrences existing and acting in the universe. This is the idea of the microcosms and macrocosms, of individual and universe, or of man in the image of God.

In art expression and also in visual expression that is not art, we often find visual resemblance among objects and persons as well as persons and animals, even though we were taught to classify them in different categories. We learned that primitives and children put animation into objects and we accepted this as an axiom not to be questioned. And, indeed, here and there our eyes will notice peculiar deviances in a child's otherwise schematic drawings of objects, such as special windows or curiously appearing doors, and precisely those deviances might convey some human expression. Now I wonder if this visual kinship between the animate and the inanimate is not expressive of the underlying configuration of forces in both. Perhaps those are the ways of true expression not marred by artistic skill.

And perhaps that is the reason the state of feelings in Henry and the appearance of the sky in his picture were the same, both heavy and foreboding. Another example that comes to mind is Barbie's House-Dog picture, which expressed the dynamic tension in the precarious situation for the house of being or not being, a situation identical with the configuration of her own inner forces. These were the forces which shaped her own human situation at the time, and this she succeeded in putting on paper in her own primitive and childish way. The visual expression opened up a vista for the child herself when she saw it.

In children's art another universal force, the child's growth, is tied in with expression. Specifically, a young child's visual or creative expression during successive stages of his mental and emotional growth can be understood only if the interdependence between expression and growth is understood. The case study titled "Jeff" provides ample material about the rise and fall of the child's growth and expression.

The emotionally burdened young artists in this book hardly ever reached the stage of artistic elaboration of their original private concepts, though some elaborated more than others. It was precisely the spontaneous presentation of the first private concept that became important in their psychotherapy. The freshness of the presentation which they could perceive with their own eyes helped them express verbally what they had felt but could not put into words. To do this they often needed help. Such help was also based on their own previous art expression. And yet, even though the therapeutic was the most important objective, some of these works conveyed true art expression in the rough.

This happened whenever the personal in an art product or in a part of one touched on some universal configuration of forces and occurrences.

XII

Art Media Used in Eliciting Patient's Self-expression

THE FEW BASIC MATERIALS which were the media for art expression played an important role in all the case studies in art psychotherapy not only by being technically instrumental, but also by virtue of their very own nature.

The spontaneous act of producing something without instruction or training for that production, helped the young persons see themselves in a process of patterning. It often helped them notice that the momentary pattern which they produced represented routine patterning in their own ways of coping with life situations. Since the spontaneous, simple, unsophisticated process of working with art materials involves visual patterning within an interaction between the person and the material used, there is reason to assume that there is a similarity between the two patterns, one inside the user of the material and the other outside him, in the product made by him with the material. In this process, the maker is also confronted by the demands of his own art expression as it grows on paper or in clay in front of his eyes.

The materials or media have something to do with this multiple interaction. By their very nature, certain materials urge us more than others, and some repel us more than others. The fluidity and consistency, yielding and resisting, shapeliness or shapelessness, softness and hardness, opaqueness and transparency, and color in all its varieties, all these qualities contain something of the universal forces found everywhere around us. This makes the materials somewhat alive, or at least not altogether lifeless and mechanical. By virtue of their kinship with universal forces, some art materials, when we willingly work them with our hands, can reach and stir deep emotional levels in us. For these reasons, I tried to provide the persons in the book with materials which are also artists' materials: paints, chalks, clay, and paper.

Of course, wood and stone are such materials, too, but because in art psychotherapy we cannot train in skills and are unable to cultivate formal standards of artistic production, these and other artists' materials were not offered. The child creates in a straightforward fashion, projecting his personality without inhibition. Standards of beauty or any other standards do not exist for him. In the same way, such standards do not exist for anyone in art psychotherapy.

The aim is to express and to discover personality in the raw. Formal standards of art work can easily become one of the pitfalls of art psychotherapy, for we know from experience that when a person becomes mindful of artistic standards, his work will reveal less of his personality.

In *Psychologie de l'Art*, Henri Delacroix finds the most important difference between art and play in the role of the materials relevant to each. He observes that while the plaything, which is the material in play, has only momentary significance for the player and is only a means for reaching the end, its nature matters little to him. In art, on the other hand, the nature of the material matters very much in that by giving of itself to the production, it may alter the course of its shaping. In art and even in art expression as used in psychotherapy, the chalk, the paint, or the clay is not being transfigured by the activity and theme as the play material would be in play. In art expression, the material fosters the inner expression itself. This paper will concern itself with materials used as art media in the reported case studies.

Finger paint is a medium which offers a primitive and direct form of expression. Knowing that this medium does not call for any training or skill, most children and adolescents felt free and often eager to dab in the paint, each according to his own need. As will be remembered from the case studies, some persons used the finger paint as a shapeless material which answered their momentary need to express diffuse feelings for which they could find no words. Finger painting taught others in a silent and non-direct way that it was possible to differentiate figure from ground and thus begin to recognize certain things about themselves. For still others, finger painting freed pent-up urges to confuse and to destroy, but later opened a flow of other, more positive feelings.

Characteristic of finger paint is that it sometimes becomes an agent of regression. When a young child becomes involved in the pastelike consistency of the finger paint, instead of normal concern of satisfying his kinesthetic energy and normal need to experience movement and rhythm, we witness a form of regression to an earlier mode of behavior. Because of its consistency, finger paint may remind even older children and adolescents of former developmental stages and may temporarily retard their behavior. When the older child involves himself with the sticky consistency of finger paint and with the activity of smearing and spilling more than with its use for expression, he is giving signals of emotional regressive stress.

In the case of some types of stress, such use of finger paint may be the advisable and necessary thing to do, for the medium then provides an important outlet. But it becomes the therapist's responsibility to watch for signs of misuse of the material, to be aware of what is actually taking place, and to help the child make verbal statements, no matter how brief or ungrammatical, about that which he is doing with the finger paint at the moment. Therapists must clearly know when they are assisting the young person to regress into earlier behavior, how and when they help the child become aware of it, and when the point arrives for termination or interruption of the regressive finger painting. Deterioration of the therapeutically regressive behavior is such a point. It may be remembered that Julie was stopped from further finger painting when her experience of regressive behavior deteriorated. It will also be remembered that she was then surprised that I had not stopped her sooner. Looking back at the experience at this writing, I do think that I had not been alert enough to sense, observe, and help her express at the most propitious moment her own dissatisfaction with the misuse of the material.

Finger painting had been employed by some art therapists as a quantitative and qualitative approach in the clinical evaluation of psychotic and schizophrenic patients and in personality diagnosis. Such work was done by P. J. Napoli (1946), H. E. Lehman and F. A. Risquez (1953), and H. E. Lehman (1957). In 1966, psychiatrist C. G. Clover and artist K. Metzler introduced a projective technique using finger painting as an activity which "fosters expression of unconscious material and reflects psychopathology in symbolic form" (*Bulletin of Art Therapy,* vol. 5, No. 3).

While I have not used finger painting as a quantitative measure for personality assessment, I have noticed similarities between poorly organized finger paintings and Rorschach responses, conspicuous for their inadequate representation and perception of form. I have also noticed similarities between primitive color symbolism in finger paintings and pure or near pure color responses to Rorschach ink blots. Of special interest to me was the transition in the process of a person's finger painting from aimless and shapeless finger work to early indications of intentionality, expressed in some differentiation between figure and ground. It often meant a transition from chaos to order and thus constituted a significant change.

None of the older children or preadolescents negatively associated finger painting with the world of childhood. On the contrary, some welcomed the long forgotten material. They readily produced kindergarten memories and positively responded to my suggestion, "See what you can do with it now." Those in need of temporary regression turned to finger paint immediately on their own in preference to other available art materials. The direct tactile experience with finger paint seemed to engage them bodily in a preverbal mode of existence which they needed to relive temporarily. A few controlling and compulsive adolescents, not of this book, chose to work with finger paint repeating the same pattern and style over and over in order to exercise control over this medium which cannot be rigidly controlled. Perhaps because of this need to control, Ellen, it may be remembered, employed crayons to emphasize details on her dry finger paintings. But, then, she may have intended to underline the difference between figure and ground.

Young persons with an affinity to art and mindful of some

formal aspects of art gained in art instruction at school, experimented with effects of consistencies of finger paint, light and dark, blended colors, and texture achieved by finger, fist, and elbow prints. Such prints are not to be confused with the playful hand prints of little children who enjoy the sense of discovery, or with the perseverance of repeatedly printing their hand by severely disturbed adult patients.

When children diluted clay to smear it, I offered them finger paint. When they used clay to force it into a two-dimensional pattern, I offered paint. These children were not ready to respond to the natural three-dimensionality which clay suggests. But when an older child or adolescent tried to work three-dimensionally with thick finger paint at its formation of peaks, I offered clay.

The young person might then break a chunk off the mass of clay, work it with fingers, and experiment with it. He or she might poke it, caress, punch, squeeze, pound, mold, or model, and finally set it down on the piece of board available for the purpose. I might then slowly turn the board base, the way a turntable slowly exposes ever new ways to see the object, or the way one might walk around a sculpture in an art gallery, to view it from various sides and then see the whole of it again.

Such activity with clay suggests to some children the multidimensionality of life itself, especially of those life situations in which the individual is personally caught when his own small, personal hurt is silenced in desperation, even before he knew what it was. Julie was reported to have constructed a number of such scenes, one in a revolving door, another crossing the street. Ricky made a scene of a flock of pigeons persecuting the smallest and weakest in their midst, and another of football players who proceeded to play on top of a player who had fallen with a broken leg. While none of these scenes could be successfully photographed because of the unskilled artists' patchwork of blobs of clay piled on top of each other, these works were very dear to their makers, who carefully carried them home and kept them in their rooms.

Beating and pounding clay without a visible purpose is parallel to the early stage of a small child's disordered scribbling.

In art psychotherapy, persons of all ages are often encouraged to do precisely this. The forming of coils and balls without aiming at working at any specific object is parallel to the next stage of the young child's art work, the controlled scribbling. And calling a blob of clay a car while imitating the engine noises parallels the naming of scribblings, the third stage in the young child's art work, when kinesthetic thinking normally changes into imaginative thinking.

But there are other qualities about clay that render its expressive and therapeutic value for persons of all ages. The impulses of formation and destruction can be easily expressed and satisfied by handling clay. As it may be remembered, continued activity of formation and destruction of shapes of clay was reported in many of the case studies. Similar processes took place in finger painting, for a production in that medium can be wiped out by a hand's single motion as easily as an object freshly made with clay can be crumpled.

Hitting and pinching and pounding of clay, akin to scratching and piercing and tearing of paper, will offer expression of negative feelings without harm or guilt and soon clear the way to a need to make something that was not there before, and to keep it. The clay object or sculpture, animal, person, or a modeled container, will help its maker at once express his feelings and desires and find in the product a much needed, soothing anonymity.

The changeability or the built-in three-dimensionality of clay often "gives" children "an idea," to quote their own words. Such an "idea" can become a turning point in the young persons' feelings about themselves. The observer and most probably also the person who works with the clay, experience a rather clear and even observable sense of "before" and "after" when such is the case. In his seemingly aimless handling of the clay before the turning point, a young person may act upon any in a number of mostly negative moods, such as aggressions and angers, vague sexual excitements, boredom, and disinterestedness. This may be followed by a "pick-up" activity, animated and alive, now structured and creative because it is "idea" oriented.

Because clay is really earth and because man has, since the

beginning of life struggled and coped with earth, there is much of the strife and resolution of that struggle in every sculpted work of art, and there is also some of that same struggle in every therapeutic art expression put forth in clay.

Then there are the jars of tempera paints in basic colors. In a program of art instruction in schools, the art teacher, knowing something about the developmental changes in his pupils and about the changes in their perception of man and environment, will supply them with appropriate materials and techniques when the pupils are ready to express those changes in their art and to cope with the difficulties inherent in the materials. Thus, for example, high school pupils will learn how to use watercolors in order to be able to paint the transparency of air and sky which they readily and sensitively perceive. In the art therapy in this book, tempera paints were the only paints available, because they are easy to control, vivid, and the closest to a primitive liquid and colorful material, suitable for brush work on paper and on dry or wet clay. Paint urges its users to spread it over areas of space. Tempera paints easily do this. While watercolors create problems that call for skill, tempera paints hardly call for any skill, its opaque colors spreading smoothly to convey expression from within as directly as possible.

I often encouraged mixing paints and dripping one color into a drop of another for the child to observe the interaction of two colors and to experiment with such change. The mixed colors seemed more dynamic and often more expressive than the solid or pure ones. Just as I found the deviances to be more enlightening for my understanding of the child's body image at the time of its visual presentation, so I discovered that deviating from the pure color and adding a bit of the color next on the color wheel added or subtracted some effect and altered the expression.

Crayons, Craypas and colorful chalks comprised the rest of the painting and drawing materials. Crayons were used by the young painters who preferred stick figures and bare outlines. Cray-pas were liked by many for the richness of colors they offered. Chalks were available in a rich variety of colors in both the round and square shapes. Though dry, their powdery substance is somewhat akin to paint. One can spread it over large areas, blend colors, use it in lines of varied width, and express moods. The extra-large chalks were found to be an enjoyable and most expressive medium by all who worked on continuous rolls of brown paper, both individuals and groups.

Paper in a variety of sizes was the basis for most of the art expression in painting and drawing. It was interesting to watch the choices of paper, where on the paper the first marks were placed, and how the production was developed on the chosen space.

Occasionally, simple techniques were briefly introduced to foster richer expression. One technique would pertain to lines, for example, with a demonstration that lines have a life of their own, that they can be quite emotional or rational in a variety of ways, and that they can relate to other lines on the same paper. Another technique would display how expressive a color can be when it "meets" another, and how different its expression becomes in relation to a third. Yet another technique was the doodle or scribble, exciting to persons who could be spontaneous, always helpful to persons who were not very spontaneous, and resourceful for persons slow in imaginative thinking.

The space selected by a person for his expression might be considered the personal universe in which he stood, or got stuck, or moved, or generally functioned at the time. The expression put forth on it might be perceived as something of himself, as he was at the time. And the materials used for the expression can be seen as something which the therapist is giving to the person who expects to be helped. The importance of this giving is the theme of the chapter on transference in art psychotherapy.

XIII

Use of Color in Patient's Self-expression

THE YOUNGEST PERSON in this book, three-and-a-half-year-old Jeff, often overlaid a patch of color on another and even doubled or tripled such overlaid colors, while other children of the same age placed their colors separately. At first, he would overlay cold colors on warm ones. According to Alschuler and Hattwick, Jeff was of passive nature. Later in his therapy, Jeff overlaid the warm colors on cold ones showing, according to the same authors, repression. Jeff, as well as some of the other young overlay artists, may have also signaled other personal patterns or temporary aspects of difficult emotional and social behavior, such as hiding, or a need to do away with a previous accomplishment or, perhaps, even a healthy curiosity for experimentation.

Jeff frequently overlaid with black. When he began to name his scribbles and to observe rather precociously similarities between his scribbles and shapes in the environment, he painted those mostly with black. And still later, when he began to do controlled drawings of objects and situations in nature, he still used black or other dark colors. Jeff's scribbling vigor, albeit aggressive, did not quite fit the popular idea about black symbolizing depressive moods. When he became more talkative and on one occasion demanded the return of the jar of black paint which I had experimentally removed, he explained that he liked black because "black is shiny; it's bright." Margaret Lowenfeld quoted similar answers about the choice of black from young children who worked with the polished, colorful shapes of her Mosaic Box.

To add to speculation about the psychodynamics of color which little Jeff might have unconsciously expressed through the use of black, the following information might be helpful. In his later development, Jeff revealed himself as a youngster of rather cheerful mood, but of a tendency to regress to the behavior of a child younger than himself who was reluctant to grow up emotionally. About one hundred and fifty or so years ago, poet and color-scientist Goethe asserted that dark objects look smaller than bright ones of the same size. At the same time, Goethe also stated that the experience of color is akin to that of affect and that the latter strikes us as color does. In size, most of Jeff's overlaid blacks happened to be the same as the underlying patches of brighter colors. It just might have been Jeff's unconscious need to assert his smallness in this way and to insist on wishing to stay little.

The choice of color or shape as determinants of responses to the Rorschach ink blots suggests a direct connection of such visual perception with either an affective or an intellectual type of personality. But, actually, all personality types perceive objects as wholes at first glance. This artificiality of the Rorschach system of determinants always made me somewhat uneasy and I was glad to find at least an idea as a solution in Rudolph Arnheim's suggestion of directionality. In the case of color vision, suggests Arnheim, the object issues action to affect the person; while in the case of perception of shape, the person's organizing mind goes to the object (*Art and Visual Perception,* Ch. VIII). Arnheim expands the approach to include inspiration, passions, and a person's general openness to the outer world, which impresses the mind through the senses.

Exhaustive studies have been made of colorimetric systems, resting on the polar structure of colors in relation to the basic universal polarity of light and darkness. Recognized by the ancients, these systems have been studied by men of the renaissance, notably da Vinci (1452-1519), Isaac Newton (1643-1727), then Goethe (1749-1832), and followed by a steady stream of research in the Nineteenth century.

But the phenomenology of the color experience still remains not quite understood and is still most intriguing. Time and again I watched with curiosity young people reach out for color. Time and again I listened to their comments, when offered, on the choice and wondered what had prompted that choice before the comment was worded.

Only when the child enters the stage of naming his scribbling does he show a desire to use different colors for different meanings. This does not mean that the child has not perceived colors sooner than he used them or even before he could name them. When he first came, little Jeff was obviously aware of colors and was obviously sensitive to them even though he did not know their names and refused to recognize them verbally. He demonstrated his perception of color early in his visits when he excitedly picked up a red-handled spoon and held it against the glass jar of red paint, triumphantly smiling to me about his discovery; and moments later angrily pulled my hand away from the jar of green paint when I held the red handle against it. Jeff could distinguish between colors, an early stage of color perception which children reach at the age of three.

Apart from his favorite black, Jeff went about the use of colors in a rather mechanical way, according to the order of the jars on his table, from right to left. In this connection, Corcoran's study on the subject comes to mind. In it, the author provides evidence that three-year-old children used colors in sequential order on the easel tray regardless of what colors they were. This might mean that the use of color at that age is related to the physical arrangement of the colors rather than to emotions.

Jeff, however, did mind the changes of orders in the placement of particular colors and rushed to restore the original order as soon as he noticed any changes. This, I thought, related to Jeff's special problems rather than to his color preferences. The problems were a compulsive orderliness and a need to control, both of which had dominated his play behavior.

On the other hand, however, the Alschuler and Hattwick study supported the assumption that children expose in painting their emotional experiences and adjustments. Those children who consistently painted in warm colors manifested free emotional behavior in warm, affectionate relations, while children who preferred blue tended to be more controlled in their behavior, and children who used black tended as a group to show a dearth of emotional behavior. To be sure, this assumption calls for articulation. When applied to Jeff, we might say that his exaggerated use of black might have indicated a dearth of warm and affectionate emotional behavior in view of his obvious angry and resistive emotional behavior.

Generally, however, color in the scribbling stages of painting by children two to four years old seems to be mainly exploratory, enjoyable, and with no conscious intention. Even in the later stage of four to seven, the choice of color shows no relationship to nature, all color choices being made according to emotional appeal. But the seven to nine group discovers a relationship between color and object. Children in this group express that relationship in certain color schemas when the same color repetitively appears on certain objects, for example the always blue sky or the forever bright yellow sun.

In this context belong the early paintings made by Barbie and Henry. At the age of eight-and-a-half, Barbie painted her "tree, two colors" in red and blue, still using color according to emotional appeal. A few months later, she caught up with the color perception of her age group and, accordingly, all trees in her subsequent paintings had brown trunks and green tops of the same kind of green. On the other hand, though he painted precociously at the age of nine, Henry's choice of color was entirely by emotional appeal. Any of his paintings of that time could serve as a good example: the flaming crimson mother-child birds in the flight-pursuit picture, the black and red school painting with the child trapped in the swing and the ominous red clouds above, or the scene of the sunman and the boy, the whole picture in hot orange.

Perception of color, however, does not develop apart from other aspects of the child's whole development. Color as well as shape or space perception and the very self are a unity, and that unity is subject of the child's total growth, within the uniqueness of personality. Being visually or haptically minded (concepts elaborated by Victor Lowenfeld in his *Creative and Mental Growth*), for example, is an aspect of the personal uniqueness. That, in turn, will influence the character of color perception.

Perception of color is more than its early stage of merely

distinguishing colors from one another. At its more developed levels, color perception means being able to notice the changes that color undergoes under different environmental conditions. This is the area in painting where striking differences may be seen between productions of visually minded and haptic* individuals. The finest of abstract expressionistic art in galleries and the crudest of art-therapeutic productions on the psychotherapist's shelves may both be recognized at a glance by crimson- or green-swept faces as in Nolde's paintings, or as in young Julie's yellow and red-faced queens, swept with a passion. Even when change of color does occur in expressionistic productions, it still is not the kind of change perceived when color appears different in light and shadow or when the surrounding colors reflect upon the focal color, and when red on a dull day will look changed on a bright day. For her painting of the weary dog making his way through the hills, Diane's first impulsive selection of colors included reds and blues of dark hue. It was the darkness of hue that determined the color atmosphere of the painting. In a much later painting, the dog, transformed by then into a happy-go-lucky character to represent Diane's new mood, appears among bright flowers in a sun-swept color atmosphere in yellow and orange chalk. These were changes in color, but they were not the changes observed by a visually minded person of the differences between bright colors at dusk and in the noon sun. Even though adolescents begin to fit colors to their visual impressions when they are visually minded individuals, Diane still depended greatly on her emotional reaction to color. While most children are between the extremes of haptic and visual mindedness, some children who are in need of psychotherapeutic help are at times in one of the extremes. The complete change of color in Diane's second painting was not due to a new visual mindedness, but due to another totally emotional state of mind.

The artist can express himself with color in one of several modes. He can do so subconsciously, partly consciously and

---

*Term coined by Victor Lowenfeld to denote emotionally determined perception, in contrast to objective visual perception. I feel that the term does not serve Lowenfeld's intentions, as it connotes a random quality.

partly subconsciously, with a variety of conscious and subconscious choices, or repeatedly altering subconscious impulses and spontaneous decisions. Expression in color might, then, be understood as a subjective correlation of emotion and ideas with appropriate colors and color mixtures to reflect and to convey the emotion and the ideas expressed.

There is expression through color in art psychotherapy, of course. But only parts of the above explanation of color expression are applicable to the art expression of psychotherapy, thus rendering that art expression incomplete in some ways. The parts of the explanation which do apply to art expression in psychotherapy are subjectivity of emotion and the need to convey it. The rest of the explanation; that is, a correlation of emotion with ideas and appropriateness of color, which actually tie up the explanation into a whole, might become a criterion in art psychotherapy of the person's mode of functioning. It is possible that an incompleteness in a person's inner and overt functioning, not in the sense of unaccomplished perfection but in the sense of missing parts (essential to well-functioning wholes such as objects, persons, or situations), can be perceived and detected through art expression, particularly color expression.

Much has been written about the psychology of color and its emotional effect on individuals. Such emotional reactions to color are determined to a large degree associatively and through the effect of experience, and also through ideas established by shared experience. Thus, horror may be red to one individual and green to another; and red may convey dread of blood, agony of pain, bliss of love, and fierceness of fury. Color becomes highly subjective in its meaning and this underlines the importance for the therapist to listen to the subjective meanings of the younger expressionists. This pertains to the haptic child who uses color in contradiction to nature as well as to the visually minded who is hiding in extreme conformity to nature. The two extremes were demonstrated in most of the art expressions reproduced in this book and in many of the children's comments about what their own colors meant to them.

Since times remembered, color has been used for symbolic

expressive purposes. To begin from the beginning, that is, with the Bible, one of the earliest acts pertaining to color was discerning between light and darkness, for without these there can be no color. Colors were the symbol for assigning parts to a whole as expressed in the rainbow, a display of God's readiness to make peace with those men who had defied His order.

The Greeks and Romans also ascribed color to light and darkness and saw color as mingling and mixing (Greek: *mixis*) and as an interacting of opposites (Greek: *synkrisis*). They noticed the constant change in the appearance of color in nature due to the incidence of light; hence, the concept of movement in their perception of color.

The importance of the number of primary or fundamental colors arose in various cultures in connection with the problem of the sharing of light and darkness. Over the question of how these two vital commodities might be apportioned or distributed according to what number of fundamental elements, the Chinese and Occidental societies of antiquity extolled the numbers five, seven, and twelve.

"They [colors] likewise produce a corresponding influence on the mind. Experience teaches us that particular colors excite particular states of feeling," says Goethe in paragraph 762 of Part VI: Sensual and Moral Effect of Color, in his *Color Theory* published in 1820.* Goethe indicates a structural correspondence, coined by Gestalt psychologists "isomorphism," between color and state of emotion and leaves the exact study of such psychodynamics of color to a later time, hopefully to our own.

---

*Arranged and edited by Rupprecht Matthaei; Van Nostrand Reinhold, 1971.

XIV

Roles of Art and Play in Psychotherapy

In his *Letters on the Aesthetic Education of Man* (*Über die ästhetische Erziehung des Menschen*, 1795), Schiller explains art as a development of the play impulse, and play as the manifestation of a superfluity of energy. This tie-in between art and play became the favored theme for psychologists, estheticists, and students of art and culture throughout the nineteenth century and in our own times. While the earlier writers tried to link art and play globally with biological and instinctual origins, using child and primitive man as sources of art and play behavior and often arriving at a point of unproductive speculation, writers of our times followed specialized research procedures in specific areas such as the play of children, the art of children at different ages, the psychology of art and play, or art as an essential ingredient of culture.

When Spencer expanded his theory in the *Principles of Psychology* about the surplus of energy located in the brain center in childhood by which play was prompted and "united with the aesthetic activities," he joined Schiller and Wundt, who viewed play also as recreation and imitation of practical life.

In *The Play of Animals* and in *The Play of Man*, Karl Groos, 1896, presented a scientifically elaborated theory based on the Schiller-Spencer-Wundt ideas. Natural selection played an important role in this theory, as it favored individuals whose "crude faculties" had more chance of cultivation when supported by parents. Those were the individuals who played. The importance of being deprived of play persists to this day and, later in the chapter, we shall discuss a few young persons who have not been able to play.

True to his biological approach, Groos linked child's play

with the play of animals and grouped play into a few major and many minor categories, such as love play and fighting play. He saw in the child's development of muscle control the same instinct which impelled animals to train themselves in infancy for the roles they were to play at maturity. As a result, Groos did not distinguish between the child's purposive bodily growth activity and his emotionally pleasurable need of play. Somewhere along a sequence of stages, the relatedness of artistic production appears when the child begins to enjoy his own productive activity. This is the time when "the higher qualities" enter play.

At the turn of the century, Stanley G. Hall came almost near a wider meaning of play when he asserted that play was a field as wide as life. But this and other promising phrases about play turned out to be only decorative overtures to a classification of organized games of teen-agers in *Youth: Its Education, Regimen, and Hygiene.*

It was I. Sully, the British psychologist, who, in 1896, put play in the context of childhood proper without attaching to it any of the Spencer-Groos functions. He spoke of play as the child's expression of imagination and ideas and as something incomprehensible to adults. Sully did note a connection between art and play in the child's impulse to realize a bright idea. But, while he revealed the child's expression and spontaneity in play, he did not elaborate on the aspect of art.

At the same time, elsewhere in Europe, F. Froebel began to publish his writings, which originated the European Kindergarten movement known as the Froebel Schools. In his *Pedagogics of the Kindergarten,* 1895; *Education of Man,* 1906; and *Writings on Education,* 1912; the noted educationist spoke of play in the totality of the child's life. He lifted play out of the limited scope of recreation or games and elevated it to a most important aspect of childhood, but did not ascribe any role to art expression of children. Though his writings were interspersed with brilliant observations and comments about play, this important material did not include any specific considerations about art expression in childhood. Nor did his material compound a systematic theory and classification of play. Thus, the old and inadequate classifications of Groos and Hall remained the only systematic theories of child's play until well into this century when British psychiatrist Margaret Lowenfeld published her well-known work, *Play in Childhood.*

This first modern and competent work on play barely touches on the child's art not only because play was the author's chief interest but also because of her cultural-anthropological view of play and art. Margaret Lowenfeld finds that the connection between designs of pottery, sculpture, etc. throughout the ages and the people who made them, repeats itself in children's play. She considers art expression of children a form of play, much as Johann Huizinga and others considered art an outgrowth of play in culture.

One year before World War II, Huizinga, deeply discouraged with Homo sapiens, published his *Homo ludens* (*Man, the Player*), 1938. He believed that play was as essential to the nature of man as was his ability to make things, that art grew out of play, and that play and art were both features intrinsic to culture.

After World War II, art therapy came into its own and the problem of art expression of the emotionally disturbed gathered interest. Art teaching also became a specialized field with theories and disciplines of its own. In relation to children, however, the study of play and play therapy excluded art, while the study of art and art therapy excluded play. As in all social sciences and interests, modern specialization and research procedures caused a discontinuity between art and play. While we are now richer than ever before in information about each, art and play in childhood, we are also aware of a separation between them. It seems relevant, therefore, to turn to some thoughts in the history of ideas of our days to see what bearing they might have upon the art psychotherapy in this book, where art and play meet again, interact, and sometimes touch upon the universally human.

In his *Philosophy of Art,* Curt John Ducasse points at a very real difference between art and play by the reintroduction, in Greek tradition, of a telic quality of each. Telic, from the Greek *telos*, means purposive, tending or being directed to a definite end. Ducasse defines play formally as a systematic pursuit of an end. The end pursued in play is actually a means to pursuing activities which constitute play. The immediate enjoyment of these activities is the true end of play. Play is thus an activity, telic in form, and performed for its own sake. It is, therefore, autotelic. In this sense, play is not really creative, Ducasse thinks, but art is. While the purpose or end of play is the very activity itself, the purpose or end of art is more real than that of play, Ducasse asserts when he says that the end of art is not as "trumpery" as that of play. For, he asserts, while play is pursued freely, art is pursued by "an obligation" that springs from within. To borrow and apply the concepts of Ducasse to this book, where art expression often mingles and interchanges with play, the endotelic quality of art often supersedes the autotelic quality of play. Proper examples for this are Henry in his childhood paintings and play and Barbie in her childhood paintings and play.

Started by Freud in *Beyond the Pleasure Principle*, the psychoanalytic theory of play was developed by that school of thought in psychology, particularly by Melanie Klein and M. N. Searl. In that context, play, like art, is understood as a representation in symbolic forms, of wishes, ideas, and thoughts, related to infantile sexuality. Many psychologists acknowledge now that while art and play of this kind do exist in some cases, found even in this book, such examples are only a part of the total field of art and play. In *The Savage Mind*, 1966, Claude Lévi-Strauss unraveled the complexity of the "savage" mind and placed art halfway between science and mythical thought, which he likened to "bricolage." He explained that the "bricoleur" was a do-it-yourself man who enjoyed his freedom to make things out of odds and ends and to put something of himself into what he made, all of which might be called poetry or art. While in the Lévi-Strauss theory mythical thought, not science, was the intellectual "bricolage" which fitted together the odds and ends of events, we might find at least one real "bricoleur" of our own in this book. He was Ricky, who fitted together an art production out of materials found when he made his self-portrait in nails on an odd piece of board.

Within its limited scope, art and play had much to do with

each other in this book, in a variety of ways. Both were spontaneous and self-generated. Both were self-expressive. And each was practiced by children according to their age, intelligence, emotional maturity, stress of emotional problems, and the total life experience.

In cases of children under ten, play and art always interacted, even when play was blocked. Within one hourly visit a child would freely move from one to the other and back. Sometimes art provoked play; other times play was abandoned in favor of art. Often one helped unblock the other and free the burdened child from his burden. The child who could not play was a child of special interest.

Little Jeff's perserveration was so acute that he could not spontaneously enjoy playing with toys. At that stage of his development Jeff's play showed only that he was blocked in his overall self-expression. Work with art media, self-defeating at first, soon became Jeff's self-expressive, diagnostic, and also therapeutic facility. This activity helped Jeff himself from the acute perseveration and helped him discover the joy of spontaneous play.

Another child who could not play was Barbie. Early in her therapy, she took to finger painting. Entirely isolated and personal in that activity, she was in great need of the shapeless play of motion in the sticky material. Her prolonged work with this art medium offered enough release for the emotional tensions to help her play with bricks and snap blocks. What she made with snap blocks enabled her, in turn, to combine art with play. It was within that combination of art and play that the child was able to express her problem of sexual identity and worry. Barbie went from inability to play to isolated and shapeless art play, to play with definite materials and specific objectives, to rich emotional expression with art media.

Ricky, also unable to play for enjoyment, developed richly expressive artistic activity with art media. Then, emotionally aroused by the art expression and in need of a more immediate and dramatic medium, he turned to toys and pinpointed his problem. Only then was he able to open up to free "bricolage" and to spontaneous investment of the self in it.

Julie was inspired by her painting to act-out her relationships at home in dramatic play. Later, playing with constructive materials led her to the expression of one of her most important fantasies, parts of which she subsequently painted and sculpted. She seemed to use art and play for the expression of low and high points of the regressive and integrative stages in her development.

And Henry, who had played but did so compulsively and with no enjoyment, began to express himself more freely when he began to use crayons, paint, and clay. This helped him communicate some feelings about himself.

But Ellen, whose whisper indicated her complete disinterestedness in communicative play, also indicated that daydreaming was her kind of play. This was extremely isolated and entirely shapeless play. Some of the shapelessness of her kind of play was expressed in Ellen's early ceaseless finger painting.

Diane, Lee, Henry (at sixteen), and Jack followed different courses in their play-art expression because they were the adolescents in the book. Preadolescents and certainly adolescents are most of the time not interested in child's play with toys. At best they play with construction materials such as bricks. Art expression gradually becomes their only mode of expression for, with their art work, they can give us signs of their inner experiences which they want to share indirectly.

In psychotherapy, the signs of inner experiences are often signs of not very smooth development. There may be regressions into childhood or a leap into adulthood as in the case of Sally or Diane. Disturbed feelings about parents are another area of inner experiences, expressed by adolescents in art work. Jack's sculpture of an anonymous male bust helped him talk about his feelings in relation to his father. He needed that anonymity. The same sculpture drew strong reactions from Ricky in relation to his father when he voiced feelings which he had never before allowed to come through. Or take the concept of one's body at which the young boy and girl arrive at various stages of their general development and, most importantly, the deviations from that concept, usually expressed by a child in art more clearly than in play. The exaggerations of certain parts of the body, the omissions of parts, and the symbols for added importance, all these are expressions in painting or sculpture of inner experiences of the young person in psychological treatment who is also going through the normal changes in growth and in the formation of concepts about themselves, other people, and environment.

Barbie painted her figures first without legs and with only slight indications of sleeves or arms, then with tiny arms pressed to the body. Diane was surprised to discover that she had been omitting hands on all members of her family. Sally drew blank faces; and when she did paint facial features at a later time, she scratched lines over them. Ricky painted a dot for a self-portrait and when he did dare paint a person, he produced a dwarfed body, marked with crossings and scratchings to indicate bodily deficiencies and ugliness. And Jack consciously invested deep inner experiences in the necktie symbol, the Gestalt meaning of which turned out to be much more complex and integrative than the Freudian symbolism would have it.

The closer preadolescents in the book moved to adolescence, the more art expression became their vehicle for the communication of the inner experience. Interestingly, play would then also find its expression through the art media in the form of playful images, lines, and colors. Diane's development of art expression provided a good example of this. When some of the weightier problems had been visually expressed by her and when they had helped modify her behavior, the seriousness of her art expression gave way to playful characters and dancing lines in bright colors. This coincided with verbal humor, laughter, and warmer relationships at home and with friends.

Some of the adolescents in the book were endowed with a flare for art and an ease of visual expression. Lee's natural ease at art expression helped her psychologically to counteract her profuse verbal affability used by her as escape from the necessity to state authentic feelings. Such authentic feelings stared at Lee out of her imaginative paintings. Lee was also playful, but hers was neurotic play which she invested in the activity of spinning and disrupting friendships. There was, however, also some healthy play in her truly adolescent romance of the daydreams, visually expressed with art media in the course of her therapy. She had no difficulty in translating both her child play and her neurotic adolescent play into visual expressions of lines, shapes, and colors on a given space. In the process of doing this, she learned a few authentic things about herself.

Henry, in his adolescent span of therapy, was also endowed with a talent for art expression, as his precocious childhood drawings had indicated. Unlike Lee, he was not verbally expressive, but was hiding and finding haven in his silences. The expressive aspects of Henry's art work in childhood and the depressive aspects of his childhood play met in his adolescent art expressions. Henry had actually never played spontaneously or for the sake of enjoyment. He realized this himself when he examined his last self-portrait of a serious young man in which he saw the forecast of himself in the not-too-distant future, a man who had never played.

Also, there was Jack, who, for different reasons, never playfully played as a child. He struggled through his early and middle adolescence, through much of his psychotherapy and, in it, through most of his art expression. Not helped by talent for painting, he developed the visual mode of expression and benefited from it as some of his overcontrolled feelings were brought out, objectified, and verbally shared with one other person. Jack's smoking marihuana might have been a deviant bit of his play. The music which he had practiced all the time without real commitment was his external play. Not before he unburdened himself of the most pressing problems, however, did music become his real self-expression on an inner, personal level. When that happened, Jack was also able to express music and some real feelings about it in lines, shapes, and color.

These few examples show that adolescence is the time when play and art expression assume a very personal style and that each adolescent is unique in his style despite the few developmental facts shared by all.

Cutting across the general development and along with the individual uniqueness is a discernible general difference in the mode of art and play expression between visually minded and nonvisually minded individuals. The difference pertains to the role and place of space and environment in the adolescent's art and play expression. In the extreme, the visually minded adolescent prefers to be a spectator who describes the environment with line and color. Diane did this in an exaggerated way, because it was detached from all feeling, when she started her art expression with a series of skylines. The nonvisually minded person will concentrate on the expression of the self and the emotions. For this person, space and environment will be significant only to the extent to which they will serve expression. Diane's later development in therapy shows that she had become entirely self-expressive and nonvisually minded, this also in the extreme, in line with her emotional problem. Victor Lowenfeld observed and studied these two types of perception among his many art students in schools and termed them as the visually minded and the haptically minded. He noticed that whereas the visually minded individuals included environment in their visual concept and projected the experience of the self into it, the haptically minded individuals absorbed in their visual perception of the environment only those qualities which derived from their subjective experiences. He found, however, that generally, the art work of his students stayed between the extremes.

Looking at the art expression of preadolescents and adolescents in this book from the point of view of haptic and visually minded perception within the context of the interaction between art and play, it is noticeable that most of the art expression was haptic in the extreme when the young persons were emotionally most disturbed. When they recovered from their disturbances, their visual perception was able to absorb qualities of the environment. They were then able to project themselves into the environment and express this ability in the organization of the given space. Jack's painting of the goat in the barn backed by a vista-type mountain landscape is an example of such a change.

In connection with this development, the neurotic adolescent's isolated and shapeless play of daydreaming attains visual shape in the process of art expression and thus becomes objectified. What happens then is that an inner, highly personal and diffuse experience of unreal dream quality becomes an object of real, visual quality. To put to art-therapeutic use Victor Lowenfeld's concept, the extreme locked-in haptic experience comes out and becomes visually perceptive in his art expression to its haptic maker. What then occurs to the haptic person is discussed in the chapter on psychological processes in art psychotherapy.

Most students of childhood play include the child's art in it and consider it a part of play. The nurseries' and kindergartens' paper and crayon and paint are materials to do with, just as toys are. But soon enough the child senses and discovers that by the stroke of the hand, things happen on paper that will not happen with toys and playthings. On paper or with clay, something is made that was not there before. This something is new and akin to a small act of creation. The little child who cannot play will benefit from an opportunity to experience such acts of creation. He is the child who was not given the experience of play, or the child too full of fantasies to play; he is the naturally slow child, the child stricken by perseveration, the child whose deep angers are threatened by play, and the child for whom nothing works at play.

We have seen in this chapter how art and play interacted to support and develop each other in the younger and older child. And we have shown how, for preadolescents and adolescents, art became the chief vehicle of self-expression and was pervaded by individual, more mature versions of play. For some of the adolescents, art expression often became a conscious, secretive way to dispatch messages to the receiving station, the therapist, and to watch if the message had been received. In such cases this was the adolescent's little play of his own.

XV

Psychological Processes Occurring in Art Therapy

I N THE COURSE OF HIS ART WORK and when the expression assumes the form of an art production, its maker may experience something which I like to call a psychological occurrence.

To be sure, there are more meaningful and less meaningful art expressions. The more meaningful ones are those which bring forth a psychological occurrence. Such an occurrence has an impact upon the person and can serve as a basis for change in thinking, feeling, and behavior.

Depending upon its intensity, a psychological occurrence will arouse in the person a stirring experience at once physical, rational, and emotional. Physically, the experience will produce sensory impulses such as quickened or slowed heartbeat; a rush of sweat; a lump or dryness in the throat; tears, blush, or pallor; uneasiness in the area between the heart and the stomach; a weakness in the knees, changes in the pupils, or changes in speech and tone of voice. Rationally, the experience will rush an activity, with or without the psychologist's intervention, of putting together bits of heretofore piecemeal thoughts and notions into a cognitive act, usually perceived about one's own self or about his interrelating with significant others. Emotionally, the experience will touch the person's inner core through an arousal of some strong feeling or feelings about the cognitive perception which had just occurred. Such feelings can also be verbally specified.

The three-way experience can be likened to a personal overall perception, visual and cognitive, about the product of one's own hands, which pertains to what was implicitly going on inside him over a span of time. There is a unity in this three-way arousal and, because focus is on the tangible art production, the experience is real and the patient has a sense of its being real. As such, the experience assumes and generates additional qualities. These are a vitality, an importance, and a direction toward change. By virtue of these characteristics, the felt experience may be described as a psychological occurrence.

All psychological events are anchored in awareness. Awareness is a conscious psychological experience. It owes its rise to interaction, at a moment of the present, between subject and environment. The experience of awareness combines feeling and thinking and can be clearly stated in words. Art expression fostered and promoted the experience, as was shown in most of the case studies, by first giving rise to awareness on a preverbal level and then on a verbal level, in an act of communication of the rising awareness to the therapist.

Observing children in play therapy during my own training as child psychotherapist and watching them play with crayons and finger paint offered to them for "release," I became aware of their expressionistic work. I also wondered what to do with release and with that which was being released. I then became aware of the importance of awareness and of the possibility of channeling the emotionally released material into the patients' awareness.

Over the years, I found that in the lives of all age groups awareness was an essential force which could be blocked and unblocked. Awareness or unawareness of body, feelings, thoughts, environment, and social situations, I learned, could constitute the difference between a well-functioning person and one so profoundly disturbed as to be unable to function. Experience in psychotherapy still teaches us that people's problems often arise from lack of sufficient awareness and from blocking of all awareness.

In a more or less well-functioning life, awareness is always present, acting along with ongoing behavior. Such a person is able to know his own needs and to see what choices reality offers. By virtue of his well-functioning stream of awareness, he can try to alter some aspects of reality and arrive at solutions acceptable to himself and to others. This does not exclude conflicts, frustrations, and often true suffering. But then a person whose awareness is alive takes his suffering for what it is, does not land in fantasies and does not allow the fantasies to dominate him. We have seen how Julie's fantasies dominated her development, how Diane's fantasy dominated the whole of her behavior, and how Henry's fantasy took over all of his decision-making.

An ongoing emotional-rational process *in statu nascendi,* or in the making, is constantly taking place within us. Some people bring such processes to completion as they quite naturally combine the piecemeal thoughts and feelings into wholes. Others, for a variety of reasons inside and outside themselves, are unable to do so. In their solitary, most inner being, such persons are perturbed and worried about themselves. They do not know, however, how to put their fragmented thoughts and feelings together, let alone how to express them or to communicate them to others. Sometimes the very speech, tone of voice, and the general mode of verbal expression are manifestations of a person's inner difficulty of this kind. In outstanding cases, patients do not finish their sentences. They speak as though they were sending disconnected bits of messages interspersed with three-dot punctuation, to no receiving station at all. These are persons with blocked awareness.

It is these persons who experience psychological occurrences in the process of gaining their stream of awareness, with the help of art expression. In art psychotherapy, the task of communicating an expression in paint or in clay involves having to look at it. Indeed, the very act of art expression has to do first with its own maker's perception of it in the very act of the making, and then with his wish and ability to express his rising awareness in words. Thus, art and words interact in art psychotherapy, art most often preceding words, together to comprise an exercise in awareness which attains full clarity in the act of verbal communication.

In the spirit of Gestalt psychology of art, the process of looking at an art product is akin to the process of looking at a situation at hand, or at a person, or at the world. There is an ongoing interaction in such a process between the aspects of the whole of the observed object and those of the whole of the observing subject. Seeing something means seeing it located or placed within a wider whole. Thus, we can see a problem, a person, an art expression, each in the pertinent whole. When the therapist is able to locate an art expression within the wider whole of its maker's personality or within the configuration of problems, he is ready to help the patient become aware of the proper connection between the expression and the specific problem. This may become one of the patients' first psychological occurrences.

Feelings often elude us, even when we think that we are conscious of them. But, elusive as they may be, they implicitly pervade some of our actions. While this is true for most of us, it is more so for persons with emotional difficulties. The visual expression of their own making helps such persons make implicit feelings explicit. When that happens, they experience a psychological occurrence.

While the trait theory of personality assigns the individual into a diagnostic category and predicts his future behavior, and the psychodynamic personality model leans on the unconscious, both theories neglect the rich and illuminating variety of states of the conscious, quite potent in relation to the human ability to change. Between the subject's utterance, "I can't think of anything; I don't know," through, "I guess," and "Perhaps," to "That's it; I never thought of it that way," lies a wide field of possibilities for the discovery of the self and its many abilities to cope and to do things. Each of the cited utterances can bring forth a new thought, a new feeling, while each new thought and feeling is a bit of growth. An art expression renders the occurrence of new thoughts and feelings more readily than exclusively verbal psychotherapy because the patient is more sure of himself when he talks about an object, even though and perhaps because, the object is of his own making. The art expression also helps its maker take responsibility for his own thoughts and feelings. These are opportunities for psychological occurrences.

Sometimes the process of becoming aware of a new thought or feeling takes time. In art psychotherapy, we learn that the

patient is taking time when he produces art expressions of repeated sameness, or with striking similarity. The example of
Diane, the girl with anorexia, comes to mind, when she worked
"in three's," or when she kept producing enclosed figures on the
same side of the paper. At one point, when the process of repeating fulfills its function, the patient states his wonderment
about his own repetitive pattern, or is helped to do so. When
he is given an opportunity to view his repetitive productions as a
group, the pattern becomes striking and he is able to state
verbally what his eyes perceive about that which his hands
repeatedly made. Since every wonderment contains a question
mark which challenges an answer, the patient provides the
answer, often to his own surprise. That is another psychological
occurrence.

While akin to the act of discovering a new thought or feeling, this psychological occurrence has a certain magnitude about
it. It sums up a pattern of thought and conduct that had been
prevalent over a long span of time, sometimes even years. It also
brings out the falsehood and futility of the principle which was
guiding the old conduct. This adds a new dimension to the
occurrence. There is the freshness about it and the spontaneity
of the "Aha" experience, so vividly depicted and coined by Max
Wertheimer. In the series of his own repetitions in art expression,
the patient perceives, at once visually and intellectually, a certain
fact about his own doing. Indeed, it often happens in art psychotherapy that patients say in amazement, "Aha, so this is what
it was; this is what I have been doing all along; that's it." The
experience then becomes an important confrontation and therefore a valuable psychological occurrence.

Some other aspects of repetitive art work must not be over-
looked. If the child continually draws or paints the same thing,
he may be doing this because he is specifically interested in the
one item, for example, airplanes, or his mind is not flexible enough
to explore and imagine other possibilities. A small child, two to
four, who continues to paint the same movements with crayons
on one side of the paper only, indicates some emotional in-
flexibility.

Repetition also offers a certain form of security to a child in that he knows there will be no need for him to face new situations if he continues to draw that way. In this sense, repetition is an escape, the same way that tantrum is an escape from having to cope with a situation that is emotionally difficult for the child to accept. It is therefore important to watch the degree to which a child is fixed at one representation. The degree of such fixation will help in the choice of therapy for such a child. Of course, another important thing is to observe and understand how the repetitive or perseverant drawing of the child corresponds with the rest of his behavior. An example of some perseverance was given in the case study of young Jeff.

As soon as the patient declares his art expression finished, it becomes the object of his immediate perception. As such, it is, of course, an objective reality. The importance of visual perception mediated by the eye as the instrument of perception cannot be overestimated. As he views the objective reality of his art work which usually pertains directly or indirectly to personal life situations, the patient specifies and clarifies both the art expression and the experience of his perception of it verbally within the act of communication with the therapist.

In the process of this communication, he experiences a cognitive and emotional process about his subjective reality. Thus, the object of the patient's perception is also the object of his consciously experienced subjectivity. The case studies in this book supply many examples of what seemed real but was actually not, and what actually was real but appeared to be unreal. The cognitive process, based on visual perception, leads the patient to a grasp of objective reality about this subjective situation. Not before Julie visually experimented with the family portraits could she cognitively grasp the objective reality of her family and of her own place in it. That confrontation, painful as it was, channeled Julie's mental life and social orientation in the direction of growth.

In this case, as in other cases, the finished art expression became a stimulus for the patient. Not in the sense of the behaviorist stimulus-response psychology, but in the sense of its own phenomenology, the art expression stimulated its maker to thinking and to feeling and to guiding his own psychotherapeutic situation toward change.

Visual perception and cognitive or recreational perception are both accompanied or immediately followed by emotion. It seems, at least in art psychotherapy, that feelings are often created by the cognitive act or come so quickly on the heels of the conscious grasp that we cannot say when they occurred. But we can specify them and say what they are. To pursue another example, when Diane cognitively grasped that she had wanted only the three older children in her family, she could say that she felt embarrassment and shame. But feelings can also influence cognitive acts and become the source of change.

This underlines the interdependence between cognition and emotion. Such interdependence takes place through art expression in the fine arts as well as in psychotherapeutic art work. Actually, the interdependence pervades human life in general. Perhaps this is the meeting point of personality and art.

The three forces — visual perception, cognitive perception, and emotion — form a configuration which acts together. While it acts together, it gains an additional quality, characteristic of its very wholeness. This can be a vividly felt quality. It will enrich the patient's inner life and spur him on to become aware of his own capacity for inner growth. It is a tangible quality felt by patients in many concrete situations, such as being able to make decisions or reacting to other people in new ways. Patients often hear about their own change through other peoples' verbal reactions to their appearance, facial expression, or a generally assertive quality new to the observer.

Whenever, in the case studies, a patient was helped to specify what he saw in his art expression, then thought and felt about it, the so-called irrational unconscious became rational cognitive. "Perhaps the unconscious is not altogether unconscious," I had to say to an adolescent in this book when he tried to lean on the all-controlling, powerful unconscious in order to free himself from the responsibility of hard cognitive work.

One of the vehicles the young persons used for the attainment of awareness and for communication of feelings was dream material. In many of the case studies, children and adolescents painted their dreams even before they reported them verbally. In the approach of this book, dreams were considered a valuable means for the restoration of awareness.

Dreams and fantasies and works of art are the same in many ways. The images which appear in dreams are creatures of the dreamer's relaxed body and mind. They represent bits of his awareness even when they are in the form of joy or surprise or anxiety and worry experienced by himself or by another figure in the dream. Dreams borrow overt forms and symbols from reality routines and speak to the dreamer about his real self and about his real place in life situations, as various elements of the dream represent specific feelings in the dreamer. Perceived as statements about authentic feelings and attitudes, dreams can be startling, but they can startle the dreamer into integrity, since the exaggerated and overstated dream images and situations sharpen his awareness.

The children and adolescents in the present work quite naturally included their dream material in their art expressions. They sensed that what they dreamed was somehow part of the business of their visits, that it somehow belonged there. Once their dreams were painted, the young painters perceived them as objectified situations of the present, challenging enough for the dreamers to find meanings of their own. Julie's painting of the box dream was so challenging to her that she acted out how she felt in the box during the dream and, in subsequent sessions, how the box "felt" in its effort to lock her in. In a series of paintings about that dream, Julie richly expressed her inner struggle between a wish to withdraw for fear of growing up, and a need to become part of life. This appeared in the dreams and in her paintings in the form of two roles, one pushing her into the box, the other pulling her out of it. These two roles were the centers of awareness, but in the dream they acted as two states of being. They represented Julie's progress in the process of psychological change.

The uniqueness of each individual and his particular

phenomenology are the most striking features in the art expressions of the patients in this book. The phenomenology includes, above all, being human and social and expressive. Each person is a phenomenon capable of observing phenomena. He thinks and has a need to share his thought and expression with another human. He is uniquely capable of experiencing psychological occurrences and psychological growth.

The psychological occurrence is not usually a sudden turning point followed by dramatic change, though occasionally it comes close to this. Rather, it is something meaningful to refer to in times of regression and throughout the process of psychotherapy. Change does often follow, but not always dramatically. Sometimes a psychological occurrence will only draw a line of demarcation between old and new performance for change slowly to move along that line. The psychological occurrence contributes at all times to the restoration of the normal stream of awareness.

XVI

Transference in Art Psychotherapy

IT IS WIDELY ACCEPTED that transference feelings, including the understanding of one's own transference experiences, are crucial to the therapeutic process of change. But transference has all too often assumed different meanings, and there is no longer one concept of transference applicable to all therapeutic situations. In a general way, the variety of the accumulated meanings of transference may be grouped into positive and negative feelings in relation to the therapist on the one hand, and reviving past relationships and experiences, on the other. Both groups of meanings are related to distortion of reality according to the present view of transference.

In the two-person therapeutic situation of the present work, transference functioned in a special way of its own because of a new factor, the art expression. A few facets of transference in the art therapy setting will now be considered.

Though mostly present-oriented, certain art expressions often led to recall of memories loaded with feelings. Those were experiences when the past moved into the present. Such memories were considered important in the person's art psychotherapy, but not as events which had determined the patient's subsequent life. When past events were reexperienced through a painting or a sculpture, that art production became instrumental in helping the young expressionist specify old, lingering feelings which had originated in the past events, but had been carried in patterns of mechanistic transference into subsequent situations, objectively different from the historical ones. Such lingering feelings carried on a life of their own in the young person's fantasy, strong enough to block development. This kind of transference-fantasy was revealed in Julie's paintings and sculptures as well as in other children's art expressions.

Transference in the form of feelings about parents transferred onto the therapist was also treated in art psychotherapy as a vehicle for bringing the past into the present, to reexamine it in the light of the present.

Transference was always considered an ongoing aspect of the psychotherapeutic process which was not to be terminated upon clarification of the relationship between patient and therapist. The patient's negative or positive feelings about me were brought out in the open as soon as they became apparent. Art expression was quite helpful in making such feelings clear, since children and adolescents freely painted portraits in caricature, abstract, and realistic styles, sculpted masks and modeled faces and heads of the psychologist. In addition, many of the young patients occasionally dreamed about the psychologist or about an anonymous figure representing her in some ways. Such dreams, subsequently painted, usually introduced the transference theme. On the verbal level, the theme would be introduced by utterances such as "You talk just like my mother," "My mother would never look at it this way," or "If you only sat at our dinner table . . . ." Such introductions were followed by a scrupulous examination by the youngster, with my assistance, of the differences between his parent and me until he or she was able to concede all distortions.

Additional transference material was often supplied by family portraits and individual portraits of family members, volunteered by most children and many adolescents. Some adolescents, when they were at the developmental stage of viewing their parents as men and women, would paint or sculpt anonymous figures and speak their feelings more readily. Jack, for example, found the anonymity of his sculpture of a man safe enough to talk of his feelings about father. He then also made an attempt to draw me into the father-son struggle as he used to do so often with mother. That same sculpture later drew from Ricky reactions to threatening fathers represented by the clay figure. Ricky, too, tried to get my sympathy for sons of such fathers, true to his practice of manipulating mother into his father-son hassles.

In their expectation that the psychologist has special formulas for being the right kind of parent, young persons often do fantasize about the therapist as their parent. Yet, they make their acceptance of the therapist as a parent quite difficult. It will be remembered that some of the children and adolescents in the reported case studies tested me to see if I qualified; that is, if I lived up to their fantasy-image of a parent better than their own. Such was the case of Barbie when I, with some luck, passed her test. Such was also the case of Jack, whose test I failed to pass.

These "tests" brought out, as an additional feature of transference, the conditional acceptability of the therapist by the young patient. Jack put me to the test in a situation in which his father failed him most when he did not understand his son by that son's minimal token communications. Such crises of transference were pointedly discussed by Joe Fagan in "The Tasks of the Therapist" (*Gestalt Therapy Now*, Harper & Row, Ch. 7).

A new aspect of transference, placing the relationship at a different angle, comes from the art media made available by the therapist. In the form of art materials,* the therapist gives something to the young patient. By the act of giving such tangible and challenging materials, the therapist says, in effect, "I am here to assist you, but you can be on your own if you choose. Here are these materials. You can do something with them now. You can say something with them now."

While many children and adolescents readily come for psychotherapy, many others resist this assistance in their struggle with the parents, and thus bring an initial transference of angers and resistance into the therapeutic relationship. When the unknown, feared, or dreaded therapist gives them the art materials, a new dimension is introduced into the initially difficult relationship. Sally's general angry resistance and her repeated accusations, "You are not helping me," is one example of such negative transference, imported into the initial relationship.

In art psychotherapy, the therapist appears almost immediately as a person who can emotionally afford to give.* The

---

*See Ch. XII.

*The rescue interventions in Chs. II, VII, and IX were also forms of giving.

giving is done with no wordy or bribing promises, no prying inquiries, and no instructions of what to do. It is a calm, matter-of-fact presentation of art materials, yet to be accepted by the suspicious or fearful and unsure young person. Indeed, it may be remembered that Sally rejected, at first, all materials given to her.

The materials immediately tend to accomplish two things vital to transference. They bring the whole emotional-social situation, hitherto experienced by the child, into the present through the very act of self-expression, however small or simple, on paper or in clay. And they transform the reluctant recipient into an actor who finds himself doing something in the present, acting with the materials on his own, while the therapist stands by, only indicating directions for the young person's energies. Transference suddenly becomes three-dimensional.

The new dimension features the young person in the act of self-expression with brush, chalk, or clay, put to work by his own hand-eye-feeling-thought energy. The relationship is no longer locked in the struggling interdependence within the dyad of woe-fully unequal partners. The materials are challenging and pointing at new directions. The art expression develops and grows. When difficulties arise, there is always the therapist's encouragement to paint more, to sculpt more, and to communicate. Patient and therapist visually perceive the production. The patient takes responsibility for his work and often volunteers comments about it. Soon he discovers patterns evident in series of his own art expressions. He begins to connect these with patterns of his behavior and begins to take responsibility for those. This process is permeated with ever-changing feelings of transference, relating to distortions of reality of any kind, simply and openly dealt with as they surface in the communicated art expressions or in direct verbal exchange.

The paintings and sculptures of this book, even those which seem at first glance not directly related to the everyday life, were at all times a specific and beneficial means for the patient to relate his cognitive perception to his own specific life situations. The best therapeutic transference occurred when the treatment situation was related to actual behavior in a life situation. That relatedness had been facilitated by the art expression in the first place. References to broad characterizations and general dispositions such as hostility or aggression were hardly used. Instead, as the patient looked at his own art expression, he was helped to specify just when or how he or anybody else was hostile, in relation to what and to whom, and when there was less or more of the hostile behavior and feeling. This method opened a way for the patient constantly to react to his own behavior on the one hand and to environmental events and changes on the other, particularly to changing relationships among people of importance to him. Such environmental changes were also worked through separately with the significant others whenever it was possible.

The therapist's contributions to the psychotherapeutic process and his gains from it comprise an experience much richer than some definitions of good therapy as good technicianship would have it. Such enrichment occurs when the therapist gives of himself as a person, in addition to and beyond the professional knowledge and experience.

Without being swept by ego involvements, I had concern for the persons who came to me for assistance, and cared for them on a personal and emotional level of compassion. I was able and willing to give my own direct personal responses to these persons as well as occasional accounts of my own experiences when they were relevant. These attitudes grew out of a recognition that life is harder to bear for some than for others. Child or adult, whoever asks for psychologic help, is most often trying to find his authentic self, lost or hidden or given up in the process of such search, and replaced by an assumed self as a pseudosolution. My limited task was to help these children and adolescents gain a clearer awareness of what they really felt inside and about themselves. Fostering their awareness enriched my own. Somehow, this widened the boundaries of transference and also changed its climate.

XVII

Limitations of the Use of Art in Psychotherapy

Spontaneous art expression through the use of art media may become misunderstood, lightly taken and misleading. To be therapeutic, art expression must be fitted into a system of carefully guided psychotherapy. But even when such a system is provided, it must be kept in mind that art therapy has its limitations.

For certain patients, art materials may give beneficial contact with some aspects of reality or a taste of freedom in using their hands and eyes and in making choices. These patients may begin to regain a sense of mastery over the environment. But in others, if they are severely disturbed and not supervised by trained art therapists, using art materials may touch off explosive impulses and release outbursts of formless and irrational energies with no redeeming value and no one to offer solutions or support.

In this book about children and adolescents in psychotherapy, art expression was presented as an integral part of the psychotherapeutic process. With the help of art expression, psychotherapy can be rendered perhaps more fruitful, but not necessarily speedier than other therapies. Becoming aware of immaturities, relinquishing them while normal maturation is struggling with its own blocks, and integrating slowly developing new maturities, is a time-consuming process which cannot be hastened by the magic of self-expression with paint or clay.

All art expression in this method of art psychotherapy must be raised to the level of awareness by means of verbal statements, communicated to the therapist by the patients themselves. That is the way to put them in touch with their own personal behavior. Intelligently guided, this may initiate a change. But before this happens, the subconscious material expressed in the art production must be brought into the awareness of both the therapist and the patient. Of the two, the therapist bears all the professional responsibility for the process and its procedures.

The therapist must not be eager to prove the effectiveness of art therapy. His casual manner and quiet interest will create an atmosphere of trust. The therapist must know when to be active and participant, and when to stand by but not interfere. He must not rush to supply words when the patient gropes for words or to translate art expressions into meanings. There will be times for the therapist to convey understanding and compassion with words, and other times for silence.

In art psychotherapy with preadolescents and occasionally also with children and adolescents, it may happen that one who had expressed himself richly in many art productions will abruptly stop the stream of art expression and refuse to resume it. A number of reasons may explain this development. One pertains to the developmental onset of self-criticism and self-consciousness about inadequacy of artistic talent. This reason is sometimes used by the patient for the concealment of feelings about the therapist. Having gained a new awareness about himself, the youngster may fear that he has given himself away. He may regret the loss of a manipulative power. He may even suspect the therapist of having set up art expression as a trap. This, of course, is a form of transference. But the reason for withholding self-expression could also be that the awareness gained might have been prematurely fostered, or that such awareness was too overwhelming, and a pause was needed.

This brings up the related problem of pace in art expression. The pace will be set by the inner need of the person in therapy and also by the degree of his involvement in therapy. Even if not pressed or hastened by the therapist's own eagerness, the pace may be accelerated by the patient himself from within when his emotional burden urgently needs to be unburdened. On the other hand, however, there are lulls in the art therapeutic process when art expressions trickle slowly and infrequently, presenting incomplete images somewhat akin to incomplete thoughts. Such art expressions are usually disliked by their creators, who name them "nothing paintings," "dumb things," or "just messing." Yet, something may slowly be ripening toward completion in such incomplete expressions. Again, it is the therapist who must be aware of the nature of such lulls and be able to differentiate the incomplete art expressions from fragmented forms signaling inner disorganization or from regressive art expressions representing behavior of a younger child.

Some people have less ability than others to express inner experiences in visual form. Some are less spontaneous than others. In fact, lack of spontaneity will, at times, constitute a person's major difficulty. This applies to adults more often than to children, but is also characteristic of some persons in the younger age groups. Such resistance to art media is not necessarily a resistance to therapy or the therapist. These patients must be helped to experience the pleasure of spontaneous experimentation and play with lines, shapes, and colors. Spontaneity can be fostered by physical warm-up exercises whose free motion the patient then transfers with chalk onto paper.

The art expressions reproduced in this book are not art, even though some of them touch on universal feelings and others show a promise of talent. These paintings and sculptures must be understood in terms of their specific role and meaning in the psychotherapeutic situation. They are visual art expressions of children and adolescents caught in emotional crises at various points of their developmental growth. Because inner growth was the primary goal of therapy and because art expression was a means to that goal, the art productions have limited meanings within that context only.

Color Plates

	Title	Medium	Size (in Inches)
1. Plate I.	Fenced Tree	tempera	18 x 24
2. Plate II.	Divided Monster	crayon	18 x 24
3. Plate III.	Dwarfed "Me"	crayon	12 x 18
4. Plate IV.	A Terrible Creature	tempera	9 x 12
5. Plate V.	House on Fire	tempera	6 x 9
6. Plate VI.	House on Fire	tempera	9 x 12
7. Plate VII.	The Monster Dream	tempera	12 x 18
8. Plate VIII.	King and Queen	chalk	18 x 24
9. Plate IX.	The Queen's Rites	chalk	18 x 24
10. Plate X.	The Box Dream	chalk	18 x 24
11. Plate XI.	Look Up	crayon and chalk	18 x 24
12. Plate XII.	Fire	chalk	12 x 18
13. Plate XIII.	Pool, Sun, and Fire	chalk	12 x 18
14. Plate XIV.	Lost House Dream	crayon and chalk	18 x 24
15. Plate XV.	The Groundhog	finger paint	12 x 16
16. Plate XVI.	Long Tunnel	crayon	18 x 24
17. Plate XVII.	Spaceship	crayon	18 x 24
18. Plate XVIII.	Dream Figures	chalk	18 x 24
19. Plate XIX.	Trio of the Dream	chalk	18 x 24
20. Plate XX.	Love Fantasy	chalk	18 x 24
21. Plate XXI.	Dog Crossing Hills	tempera	12 x 18
22. Plate XXII.	Two Girls	chalk	18 x 24
23. Plate XXIII.	The Snake	finger paint	12 x 16
24. Plate XXIV.	Fire Dream	chalk	18 x 24
25. Plate XXV.	Happy Mr. Jeanney	chalk	18 x 24
26. Plate XXVI.	Beautiful Feelings	crayon	18 x 24
27. Plate XXVII.	Hostility	crayon and chalk	18 x 24
28. Plate XXVIII.	The Cry	chalk	12 x 18
29. Plate XXIX.	Turtle	tempera	12 x 18
30. Plate XXX.	Barn Dream	tempera	12 x 18
31. Plate XXXI.	The Bird	tempera	12 x 18
32. Plate XXXII.	Monster Dream	crayon and chalk	18 x 24

COLOR PLATE I

"The Split Personality"

COLOR PLATE II

COLOR PLATE III

COLOR PLATE IV

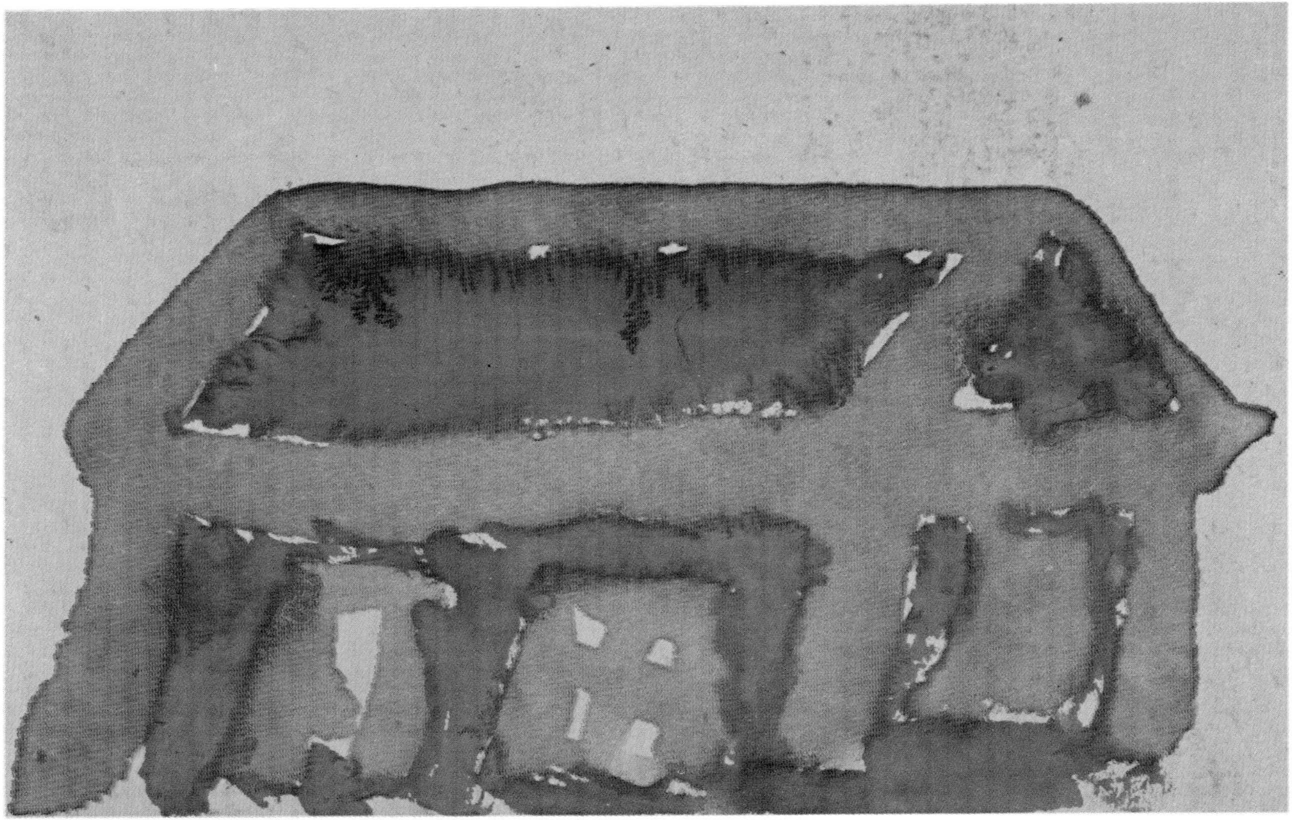

COLOR PLATE V

COLOR PLATE VI

COLOR PLATE VII

COLOR PLATE VIII

COLOR PLATE IX

COLOR PLATE X

COLOR PLATE XI

COLOR PLATE XII

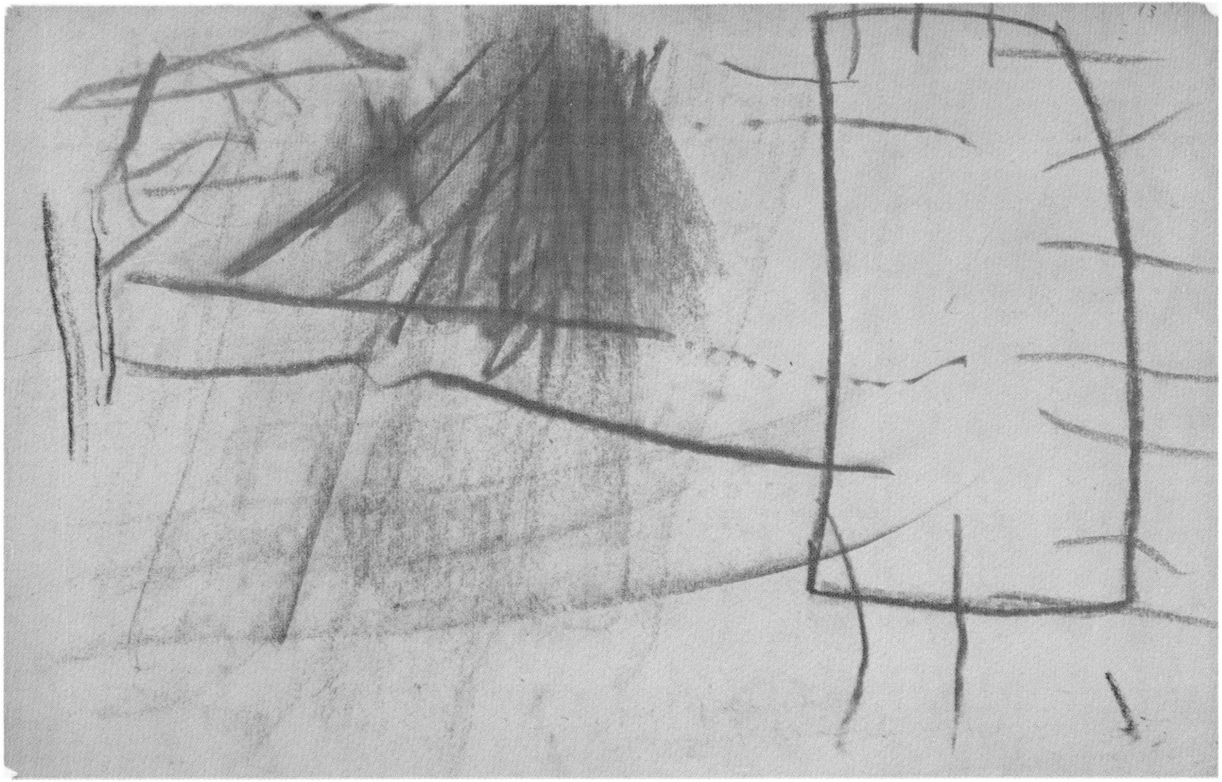

COLOR PLATE XIII

COLOR PLATE XIV

COLOR PLATE XV

COLOR PLATE XVI

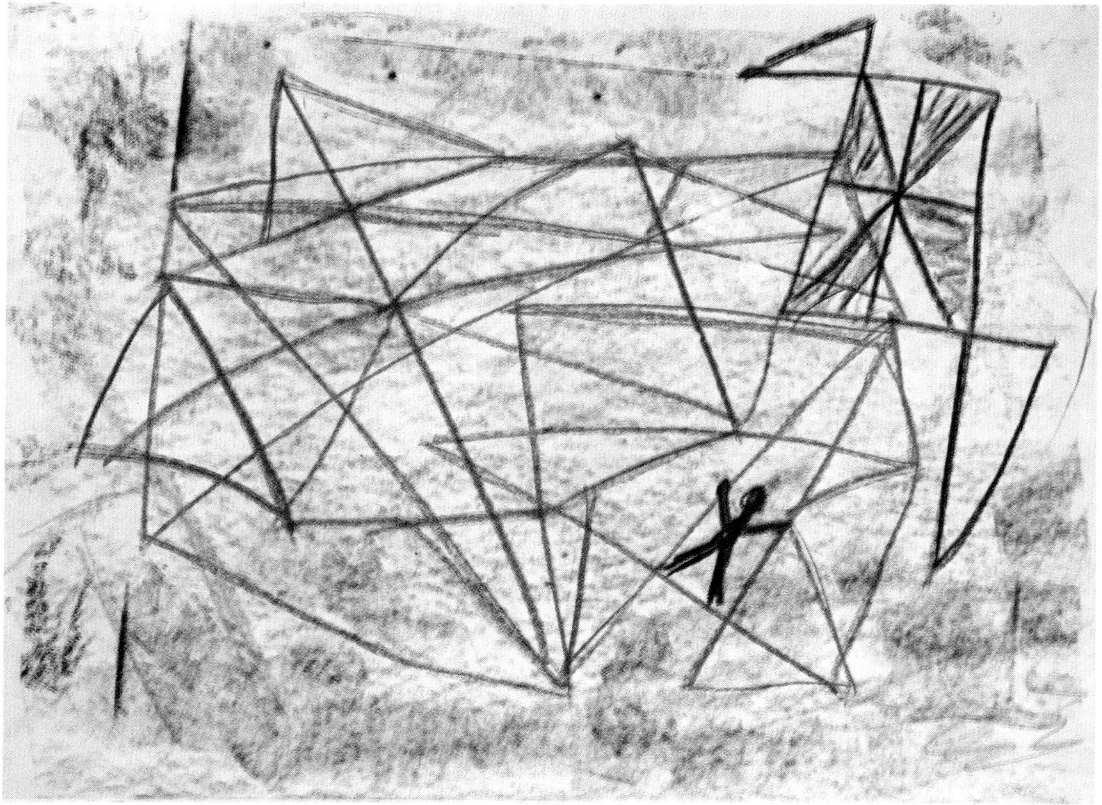

COLOR PLATE XVII

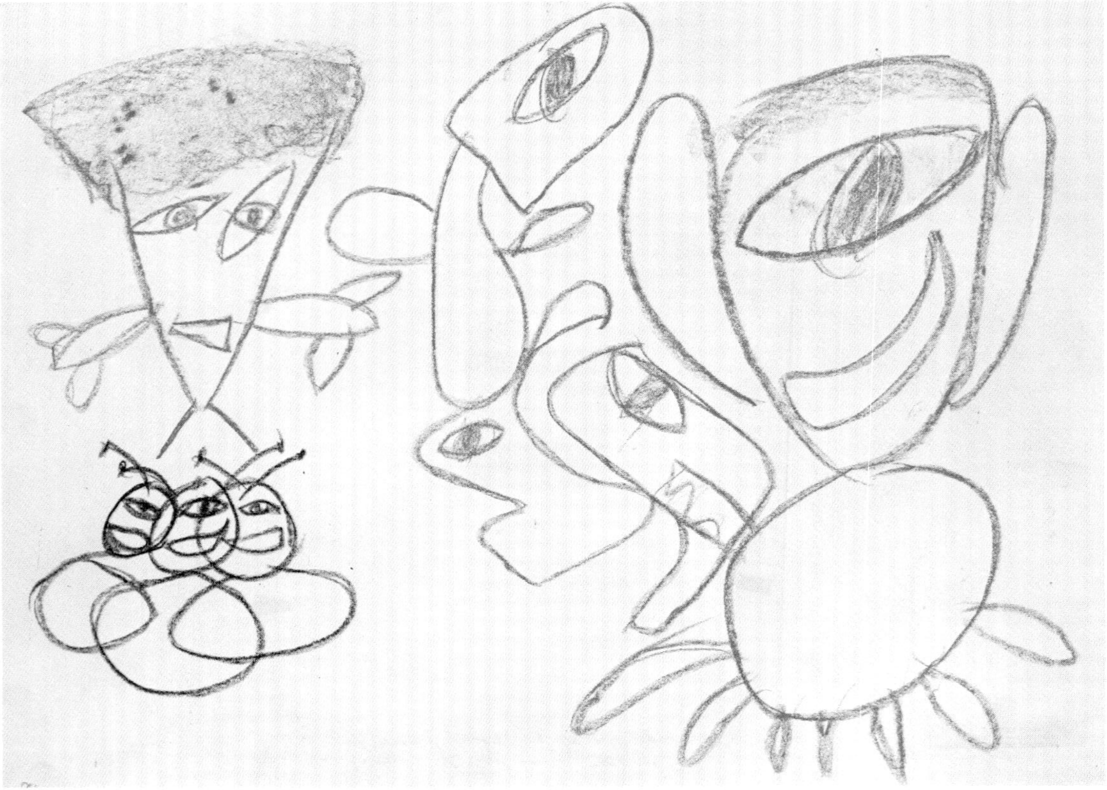

COLOR PLATE XVIII

COLOR PLATE XIX

COLOR PLATE XX

COLOR PLATE XXI

COLOR PLATE XXII

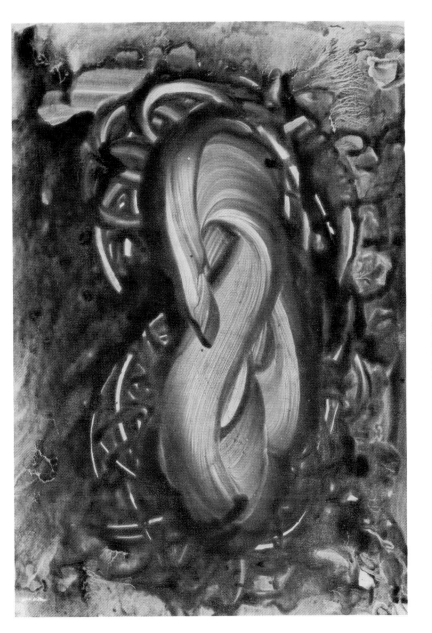

COLOR PLATE XXIII

COLOR PLATE XXIV

COLOR PLATE XXV

COLOR PLATE XXVI

COLOR PLATE XXVII

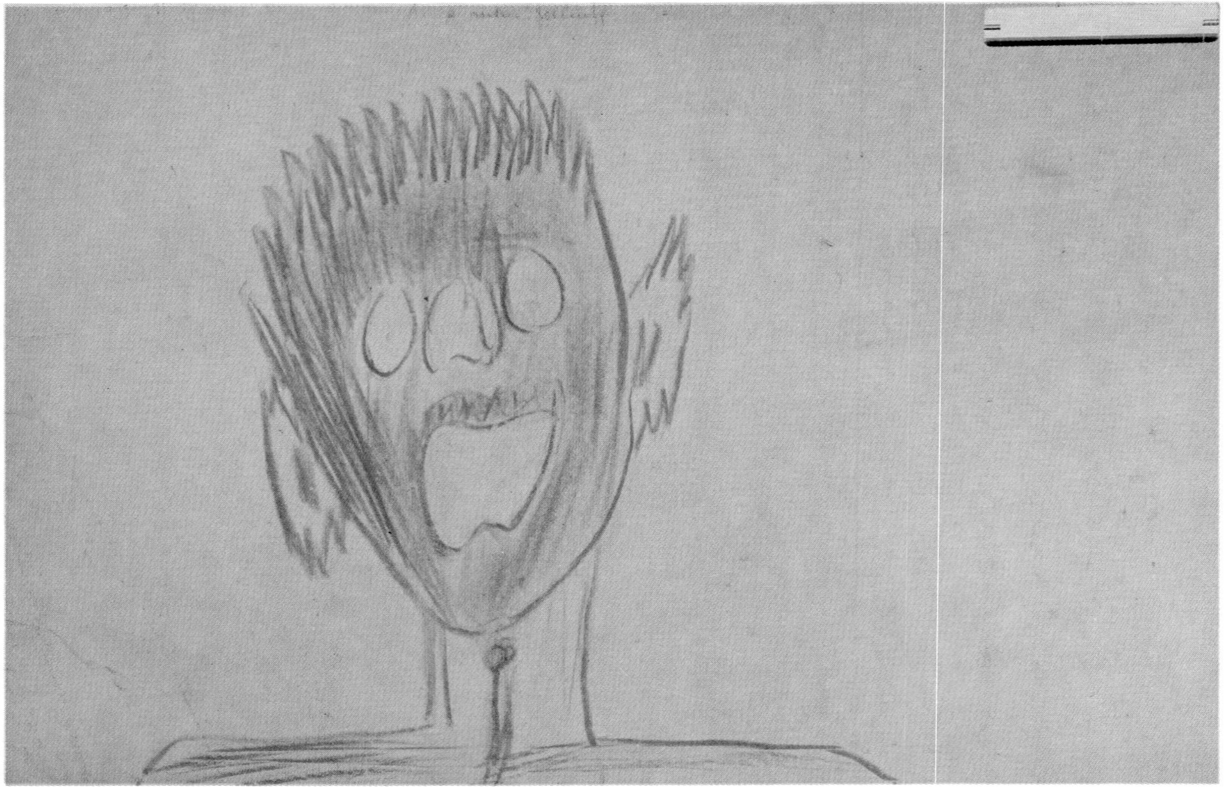

COLOR PLATE XXVIII

COLOR PLATE XXIX

COLOR PLATE XXX

COLOR PLATE XXXI

COLOR PLATE XXXII

Bibliography

Adler, Alfred: *Heilen und Bilden*. München, Bergmann, 1922.

Adler, Alfred: *Social Interest*. New York, Putnam, 1939.

Allen, Grant: *The Colour-Sense*. Boston, Houghton, 1879.

Allport, Gordon: *Becoming: Basic Considerations for a Psychology of Personality*. New Haven, Yale University Press, 1955.

Allport, Gordon: *Personality and Social Encounter*. Boston, Beacon, 1960.

Allport, Gordon: *Pattern and Growth in Personality*. New York, Holt, Reinhart & Winston, 1961.

Allport, Gordon: *The Person in Psychology*. Boston, Beacon, 1968.

Alschuler, R.H., and Hattwick, L.W.: *Painting and Personality*. Chicago, University of Chicago Press, 1947.

Anastasi, A., and Foley, J.P., Jr.: An Analysis of Spontaneous Drawings by Children in Different Cultures. *Journal of Applied Psychology, 20*:689-726, 1936.

Angyal, Andras: *Foundations for a Science of Personality*. Boston, Harvard, 1941.

Arnheim, Rudolf: *Art and Visual Perception*. Berkeley, University of California Press, 1967.

Arnheim, Rudolf: *Visual Thinking*. Berkeley, University of California Press, 1969.

Arsenian, John: Discussion: Notes on Art Therapy. *Bulletin of Art Therapy, 6*:22-25, October, 1966.

Axline, Virginia M.: *Play Therapy*. Boston, Houghton Mifflin, 1947.

Axline, Virginia M.: *Dibs in Search of Self*. Boston, Houghton Mifflin, 1966.

Baker, H., and Kellog, R.: Children's Scribblings. *Pediatrics, 40*:382-390, September, 1967.

Bell, Norman W., and Vogel, Ezra F. (Eds.): *A Modern Introduction to the Family*. Glencoe, Free Press, 1960.

Berkman, Ira P.; Mondshain, B., and Weinberg, L.P.: Awareness Training for Adolescents. *Adolescence, VI*, Winter, 1971.

Bernstein, Lewis, and Burris, B. Cullen: *The Contribution of the Social Sciences to Psychotherapy*. Springfield, Charles C Thomas, 1967.

Biber, B.: *Children's Drawings: From Lines to Pictures*. New York, Bureau of Educational Experiments, 1934.

Birren, Faber: *Functional Color*. New York, Crimson Press, 1937.

Birren, Faber: *Color in Your World*. New York, Collier Books, 1966.

Boenheim, Curt: The Position of Art Therapy Within Contemporary Psychotherapy. *American Journal of Art Therapy*, April, 1970.

385

Bronfenbrenner, Urie: *Two Worlds of Childhood.* New York, Russell Sage Foundation, 1970.

Buber, Martin: *Between Man and Man.* New York, Macmillan, 1965.

Bugental, J.F.T.: *The Search for Authenticity.* New York, Holt, Reinhart & Winston, 1965.

Bugental, J.F.T.: The Challenge That Is Man. *Journal of Humanistic Psychology,* 7:1-9, 1967.

Bugental, J.F.T.: Psychotherapy as a Source of the Therapist's Own Authenticity and Inauthenticity. *Voices,* 4:13-23, 1968. Buhler, Charlotte: *Values in Psychotherapy.* New York, Free Press, 1962.

Buhler, Charlotte: *Psychology for Contemporary Living.* New York, Hawthorn, 1969.

Buhler, Charlotte: Basic Theoretical Concepts of Humanistic Psychology. *American Psychologist,* 26:378-386, April, 1971.

Buhler, C., and Massarik, F. (Eds.): *The Course of Human Life: A Study of Goals in the Humanistic Perspective.* New York, Springer, 1968.

Bühler, K.: *Die Geistige Entwicklung des Kindes.* Ch. V, "Die Entwicklung des Zeichnens," 1918.

Cashdan, Sheldon: Social Participation and Sub-Cultural Influences in the Study of Adolescent Creativity. *Adolescence,* VI:39-52, Spring, 1971.

Cassirer, Ernst: *Essay on Man.* New Haven, Yale University Press, 1944.

Champernowne, H. Irene: Art and Therapy: An Uneasy Partnership. *American Journal of Art Therapy,* 10:130-143, April, 1971.

Clower, Courtney G., Jr., and Metzler, Karl: Finger Painting as an Adjunct to Psychiatric Diagnosis. *Bulletin of Art Therapy,* 5:105-115, April, 1966.

Cohen, John: *Humanistic Psychology.* New York, Macmillan, 1962.

Coleman, J.S.: *Adolescents and the Schools.* New York, Basic Books, 1965.

Coleman, J.S.: *The Adolescent Society.* New York, Free Press, 1961.

Collins, Laurine: *Dreams and Art.* The Forum of The Department of Mental Health Sciences, Hahnemann Medical College and Hospital (Philadelphia), *1,* 1971.

Colm, Hanna: The Role of Affirmation in Analysis. *Psychiatry,* 23:279-285, August, 1960.

Corcoran, Ambrose L.: The Variability of Children's Responses to Color Stimuli. Unpublished Doctoral Dissertation, The Pennsylvania State University, University Park, 1953.

Correnti, Samuel: A Comparison of Behaviorism and Psychoanalysis With Existentialism. *Existentialism,* V:379-388, Summer, 1965.

Crane, Rebecca R.: An Experiment Dealing With Color and Emotion. *Bulletin of Art Therapy,* 1:25-28, Spring, 1962.

Crane, Rebecca R., and Levy, B.I.: Color Scales in Response to Emotionally Laden Situations. *Journal of Consulting Psychology,* 26:515-519, 1962.

Croce, Benedetto: *The Essence of Aesthetic.* London, Henemann, 1921.

Crow, Lester D., and Crow, Alice: *Child Psychology.* New York, Barnes & Noble, 1963.

Dauy Louis: *It Is Still the Morning.* New York, Morrow & Co., 1943.

DeChardin, Pierre Teilhard: *Phenomenon of Man.* New York, Harper, 1959.

Delacroix, Henri: *Psychologie de l'Art.* Paris, Falcan, 1927.

Deregowski, Jan: A Note on the Possible Determinants of "Split Representation" as an Artistic Style. *International Journal of Psychology* (Paris), 5, 1970.

DiLeo, Joseph H.: *Young Children and Their Drawings.* New York, Brunner/Mazel, 1970.

Douvan, Elizabeth, and Adelson, Joseph: *The Adolescent Experience.* New York, John Wiley & Sons, 1966.

Ducasse, Curt John: *The Philosophy of Art.* New York, Dover, 1966.

Dudek, Stephanie Z.: The Artist as Person. Generalizations Based on Rorschach Records of Writers and Painters. *Journal of Nervous and Mental Disease, 150,* March, 1970.

Eckhardt, M.H.: Alienation and the Secret Self: Some Therapeutic Considerations. *American Journal of Psychoanalysis* (Symposium on Alienation and the Search for Identity), *21*:219-226, 1961.

Eng, Hilda: *The Psychology of Children's Drawings.* London, 1931.

Erikson, Erik H.: *Insight and Responsibility.* New York, W.W. Norton, 1964.

Erikson, Erik H.: *Identity: Youth and Crisis.* New York, W.W. Norton, 1968.

Eysenck, H.J.: *Handbook of Abnormal Psychology.* New York, Basic Books, 1961.

Fagan, Joen, and Shepherd, Irma Lee (Eds.): *Gestalt Therapy Now.* New York, Harper & Row, 1970.

Feuer, Lewis S.: *The Conflict of Generations.* New York, Basic Books, 1969.

Fischer, Roland: Art Interpretation and Art Therapy. In I. Jakab (Ed.) *Psychiatry and Art,* Basel, Karger, 1969, p. 33.

Fischer, Roland: A Cartography of the Ecstatic and Meditative States. *Science, 174*:897-904, November 26, 1971.

Fisher, C.; Hull, C., and Holtz, P.: Past Experience and Perception: Memory Color. *American Journal of Psychology, 69*:546-560, 1956.

Foulkes, D.: Theories of Dream Formation and Recent Studies of Sleep Consciousness. *Psychological Bulletin, 62*:236-247, 1964.

French, T.M., and Fromm, E.: *Dream Interpretation.* New York, Basic Books, 1964.

Frank, Jerome D.: *Persuasion and Healing: A Comparative Study of Psychotherapy.* New York, Schocken, 1963.

Frankl, Viktor E.: *The Doctor and the Soul: An Introduction to Logotherapy.* New York, Knopf, 1957.

Frankl, Viktor E.: *Man's Search for Meaning*, rev. ed. Boston, Beacon Press, 1963.

Frankl, Viktor E.: *The Will to Meaning: Foundations and Applications of Logotherapy*. New York, World, 1969.

Freud, S.: *Beyond the Pleasure Principle*. London and Vienna, International Psycho-analytical Press, 1922.

Freud, S.: Infantile Sexuality. In *Three Contributions to the Theory of Sex*, New York, Nervous and Mental Disorders Publishing, 1930.

Freud, S.: *The Interpretations of Dreams*. New York, Basic Books, 1958.

Froebel, Friedrich: *Pedagogics of the Kindergarten*. Translated by Josephine Jarvis. London, Appleton, 1895.

Froebel, Friedrich: *Education of Man*. London, Appleton, 1906.

Froebel, Friedrich: *Chief Writings on Education*. London, Arnold, 1912.

Gardner, Riley W., and Moriarty, Alice: *Personality Development at Preadolescence*. Seattle, University of Washington Press, 1968.

Gatschet, A.S.: Adjectives of Color in Indian Languages. *American Naturalist, 13*:475-485, 1879.

Gatschet, A.S.: Farbenbedeutungen in Nordamerikanischen Sprachen. *Zeitschrift für Ethnologie, 11*:293 ff., 1879.

Gendlin, Eugene T.: *Experiencing and the Creation of Meaning*. New York Free Press, 1962.

Gesell, A.: *Infancy and Human Growth*. New York, Macmillan, 1928.

Gesell, A., and Ames, L.B.: The Development of Directionality in Drawing. *Journal of Genetic Psychology, 68*:45-61, 1946.

Gesell, A., and Ilg, Frances L.: *The Child From Five to Ten*. New York, Harper & Bros., 1946.

Getzels J.W., and Jackson, P.W.: *Creativity and Intelligence*. New York, John Wiley & Sons, 1962.

Gifford, Edward S.: *The Evil Eye: Studies in the Folklore of Vision*. New York, Macmillan, 1958.

Gilson, E.: *Forms and Substances in the Arts*. New York, Charles Scribner's Sons, 1966.

Goethe, Johann Wolfgang: *Color Theory*. Rupprecht Matthaei, Ed. New York, Van Nostrand Reinhold, 1971.

Goldstein, Kurt: *Human Nature in the Light of Psychopathology*. New York, Schocken, 1963.

Gombrich, E.H.: *The Story of Art*. New York, Phaidon, 1957.

Goodenough, F.L.: *Measurement of Intelligence by Drawings*. New York, World Book, 1926.

Goodman, John Stuart: *Malayalam Color Categories*. Bloomington, University of Indiana Press, 1963.

Gotthelf, T.: Continuity of Fantasy; Dreams and Dreaming in the Arts. *Experimental Medicine and Surgery*, 27, 1969.

Groos, Karl: *The Play of Animals*. New York, Appleton, 1898.

Groos, Karl: *The Play of Man.* New York, Appleton, 1901.

Grossberg, J.M.: Behavior Therapy: A Review. *Psychological Bulletin,* 62:73-88, 1964.

Grozinger, W.: *Scribbling, Drawing, Painting.* New York, Praeger, 1955.

Hall, G.S.: *Adolescence: Its Psychology and Its Relation to Physiology, Anthropology, Sociology, Sex, Crime, Religion and Education.* New York, Appleton 1904, vol. 1.

Hall G. S.: *Youth: Its Education, Regimen, and Hygiene.* New York, Appleton, 1904, vol. 2.

Hall, G.S.: The Affiliation of Psychology With Philosophy and With the Natural Sciences. *Science,* 23:297-301, 1906.

Hall, G.S.: Freudian Methods Applied to Anger. *American Journal of Psychology,* 26:439-443, 1915.

Hammer, E.F.: *Creativity: An Exploratory Investigation of the Personalities of Gifted Adolescent Artists.* New York, Random House, 1961. (Available only in Library of Congress.)

Harris, D.B.: *Children's Drawings as Measures of Intellectual Maturity.* New York, Harcourt, Brace & World, 1963.

Horowitz, Mardi J.: Notes on Art Therapy Media and Techniques. *Bulletin of Art Therapy,* 4:71-73, January, 1965.

Huizinga, Johann: *Homo Ludens.* Berlin, 1938.

Hurlock, E.B.: *Child Development,* 4th ed. New York, McGraw-Hill, 1964.

Ichheiser, Gustav: *Appearances and Realities.* San Francisco, Jossey-Bass, 1970.

International Printing Ink Corporation: Three Monographs on Color: *Color Chemistry, Color as Light, Color in Use.* New York, Research Laboratories of the International Printing Ink Corporation, 1935.

James, William: *The Principles of Psychology.* New York, Holt & Company, 1890.

Jones, Richard M.: *The New Psychology of Dreaming.* New York, Grune & Stratton, 1970.

Jung, C.G.: *Memories, Dreams, Reflections.* New York, Pantheon, 1961.

Jung, C.G.: *Man and His Symbols.* New York, Dell, 1968.

Kellog, R.: *The Psychology of Children's Art.* New York, Random House, 1967.

Kessler, Edwin S., and Taboroff, L.H.: The "Exciting Scene" Play Technique. *Quarterly Journal of Child Behavior,* 3:281-301, 1951.

Kiell, Norman: *Psychiatry and Psychology in the Visual Arts and Aesthetics.* Madison, University of Wisconsin Press, 1965.

Klein, Melanie: *The Psychoanalysis of Children.* London, Hogarth Press, 1932.

Klein, M.; Heiman, P., and Money-Kyrle, R.E. (Eds.): *New Directions in Psychoanalysis.* New York, Basic Books, 1957.

Koffka, Kurt: *Principles of Gestalt Psychology.* New York, Harcourt, Brace & World, 1935.

Köhler, Wolfgang: *Gestalt Psychology.* New York, New American Library, 1947.

Köhler, Wolfgang: *The Task of Gestalt Psychology.* Princeton, Princeton University Press, 1969.

Kramer, Edith: *Art Therapy in a Children's Community.* Springfield, Charles C Thomas, 1958.

Kramer, Edith: The Problem of Quality in Art. *Bulletin of Art Therapy,* 3:3-18, October, 1963.

Kramer, Edith: *Art as Therapy With Children.* New York, Schocken, 1971.

Kris, Ernst: *Psychoanalytic Explorations in Art.* New York, Schocken, 1964.

Kugelmass, I. Newton: *The Autistic Child.* Springfield, Charles C Thomas, 1970.

Kwiatkowska, Hanna Yaxa: The Use of Families' Art Productions for Psychiatric Evaluation. *Bulletin of Art Therapy,* 6:52-72, January, 1967.

Langer, Suzanne: *Feeling and Form.* New York, Charles Scribner's Sons, 1953.

Lederman, J.: *Anger and the Rocking Chair: Gestalt Awareness With Children.* New York, McGraw-Hill, 1969.

Lévi-Strauss, Claude: *The Savage Mind.* Chicago, University of Chicago Press, 1966.

Lewin, K.: *Principles of Topological Psychology.* New York, McGraw-Hill, 1936.

Lowenfeld, Margaret: *Play in Childhood.* New York, John Wiley & Sons, 1967.

Löwenfeld, Victor: *The Nature of Creative Activity.* New York, Harcourt & Brace, 1939.

Löwenfeld, Victor, and Brittain, W.L.: *Creative and Mental Growth,* 4th ed., New York, Macmillan, 1964.

Mach, E.: *The Analysis of Sensations and the Relation of the Physical to the Psychical.* London, Open Court Publishing, 1914.

Machover, K.: *Personality Projection in the Drawing of the Human Figure.* Springfield, Charles C Thomas, 1949.

Machover, K.: Human Figure Drawings of Children. *Journal of Projective Techniques,* 17:53-92, 1953.

Magnus, H.: *Histoire de l'Évolution de Sens des Couleurs.* Paris, 1878.

Magnus, H.: *Untersuchungen Über den Farbensinn der Naturvölker.* Jena, Fraher, 1880.

Marshall, Helen: *Children's Plays, Games, and Amusements. A Handbook of Psychology.* London, Oxford University Press, 1931.

Maslow, Abraham: *Toward a Psychology of Being,* 2nd ed. New York, Van Nostrand Reinhold, 1968.

May, Rollo: *Psychology and the Human Dilemma.* New York, Van Nostrand Reinhold, 1966.

May, R.; Angel, E.; and Ellenberger, H.F. (Eds.): *Existence, A New Dimension in Psychiatry and Psychology.* New York, Basic Books, 1958.

Merleau-Ponty, Maurice: *Phenomenology of Perception.* New York, Humanities Press, 1962.

Messer, Alfred A.: *The Individual in His Family.* Springfield, Charles C Thomas, 1970.

Mischel, Walter: *Personality and Assessment.* New York, Wiley, 1968.

Montessori, Maria: *The Montessori Method,* 7th ed. New York, Frederick A. Stokes, 1912.

Montessori, Maria: *La Scoperta del Bambino.* Milan, Garzanti, 1953.

Moustakas, Clark E.: *Creativity and Conformity.* New York, Van Nostrand Reinhold, 1967.

Naumburg, Margaret: *Psychoneurotic Art: Its Function in Psychotherapy.* New York, Grune & Stratton, 1953.

Naumburg, Margaret: Spontaneous Art in Education and Psychotherapy. *Bulletin of Art Therapy,* 4:51-69, January, 1965.

Nell, Renee: Art and Psychotherapy. *Voices,* 4, Winter, 1968.

Parker, Beulah: *My Language Is Me.* New York, Basic Books, 1962.

Pasto, Tarmo A.: Meaning in Art Therapy. *Bulletin of Art Therapy,* 2:73-76, Winter, 1962.

Perls, Frederick; Hefferline, Ralph F., and Goodman, Paul: *Gestalt Therapy.* New York, Dell, 1951.

Perls, F.S.: *Gestalt Therapy Verbatim.* Lafayette, Real People Press, 1969.

Pickford, R.W.: *Psychiatric Art.* Springfield, Charles C Thomas, 1967.

Pickford, R.W.: Etudes Experimentales de Peintures Ecossaises et de Tableaux de Van Gogh. *Sciences de l'Art,* VI:53-63, 1969.

Polanyi, Michael: *The Study of Man.* Chicago, University of Chicago Press, 1959.

Polanyi, Michael: *Personal Knowledge: Towards a Post-Critical Philosophy.* Chicago, University of Chicago Press, 1958.

Prinzhorn, Hans: *Bildnerei der Geisteskranken.* Berlin and New York, Springer-Verlag, 1968.

Rabl-Rückhard, H.J.J.: Zur Historischen Entwicklung des Farbensinnes. *Zeitschrift für Ethnologie,* 12:210, 1880.

Rank, O.: *Art and the Artist.* New York, Knopf, 1932.

Read, Herbert: *The Meaning of Art.* London, Faber & Faber, 1936.

Read, Herbert: *Art and Society.* New York, Schocken, 1966.

Redl, Fritz, and Wineman, David: *The Aggressive Child.* Glencoe, Free Press, 1957.

Rhyne, J.: *The Gestalt Art Experience.* Palo Alto, Science and Behavior Books, 1972.

Ricci, C.: *L'Arte dei Bambini.* Bologne, Zanichelli, 1887.

Riezler, Kurt: *Man: Mutable and Immutable.* Chicago, Regnery, 1951.

Rode, Alex: Perceptions of Parental Behavior Among Alienated Adolescents. *Adolescence, VI:*19-38, Spring, 1971.

Rogers, Carl: *Counseling and Psychotherapy.* Cambridge, Houghton Mifflin, 1942.

Rogers, Carl: The Necessary and Sufficient Conditions of Therapeutic Personality Change. *Journal of Consulting Psychology, 21:*95-103, 1957.

Rogers, Carl: A Process of Conception of Psychotherapy. *American Psychologist, 13:*142-149, 1958.

Rogers, Carl: The Essence of Psychotherapy: A Client-Centered View. *Annals of Psychotherapy, 1:*51-57, 1959.

Rogers, Carl: *On Becoming a Person.* Boston, Houghton Mifflin, 1961.

Rogers, Carl: Toward a Modern Approach to Values: The Valuing Process in the Mature Person. *Journal of Abnormal and Social Psychology,* 68:160-167, 1964.

Rorschach, Hermann: *Psychodiagnostics,* 5th ed. Berne, Verlag Hans Huber, 1951.

Rossi, E.L.: *Self Reflection in Dreams.* Paper presented to the Joint Conference of the Society of Jungian Analysts of Northern and Southern California, Santa Barbara, 1971.

Rossi, E.L.: *Dreams and the Growth of Personality: Expanding Awareness in Psychotherapy.* Long Island City, Pergamon, 1972.

Reusch, Jurgen: *Therapeutic Communication.* New York, W.W. Norton, 1961.

Reusch, Jurgen, and Bateson, Gregory: *Communication.* New York, W.W. Norton, 1951.

Schachtel, E.G.: On Color and Affect. *Psychiatry,* 6:393-409, 1943.

Schachtel, E.G.: *Metamorphosis.* New York, Basic Books, 1959.

Schachtel, E.G.: On Creative Experience. *Journal of Humanistic Psychology, 11:*26-39, Spring, 1971.

Schiller, Friedrich: Über die Ästhetische Erziehung des Menschen (Letters on the Aesthetic Education of Man). In *Schiller's Aesthetic Prose,* New York, Little, Brown, 1845.

Sinrod, Harriet Wadeson, and Bunney, William E.: Manic-Depressive Art. *Journal of Nervous and Mental Disease, 150:*215-231, 1970.

Site, Myer: Art and the Slow Learner. *Bulletin of Art Therapy, 4:*3-19, October, 1964.

Skard, S.: The Use of Color in Literature, A Survey of Research. *Proceedings of the American Philosophical Society, Philadelphia,* 90:3, 1946.

Searl, M.N.: Symposium on Child Analysis. *International Journal of Psychoanalysis,* July, 1924.

Searl, M.N.: Play, Reality and Aggression. *International Journal of Psychoanalysis,* July, 1933.

Small, Leonard: *The Briefer Psychotherapies*. New York, Brunner/Mazel, 1971.

Snyder, F.: Toward an Evolutionary Theory of Dreaming. *American Journal of Psychiatry*, 2:121-136, 1966.

Spencer, H.: The Principles of Psychology. London, 1855, and New York, 1873.

Spiegel, L.A.: The Child's Concept of Beauty: A Study in Concept Formation. *Journal of Genetic Psychology*, 77:11-23, 1950.

Sullivan, Harry S.: *Interpersonal Theory of Psychiatry*. Helen Perry and Mary L. Gawel (Eds.), New York, W.W. Norton, 1968.

Sully, J.: *Studies of Childhood*. London and New York, Appleton, 1896.

Themal, Joachim H.: Children's Work as Art. *Bulletin of Art Therapy*, 2:12-22, Fall, 1962.

Thomas, R.M.: Effects of Frustration on Children's Painting. *Child Development*, 22:131, June, 1951.

Tillich, Paul: *Courage To Be*. New Haven, Yale University Press, 1952.

Tolman, E.C.: *Purposive Behavior in Animals and Men*. New York, Appleton-Century-Crofts, 1932.

Tönnies, F.: *Community and Society*. East Lansing, Michigan State University Press, 1957. (First published 1887.)

Turner, Mary Dilworth: Art as an Adjunct to Psychotherapy. *Voices*, 4, Winter, 1968.

Tyskiewicz, M.: Psychiatric Analysis of Drawings and Paintings of Schizophrenic Children and Adolescents. (In Polish.) *Psychiatria Polska*, 4, July-August, 1970.

Ulman, Elinor: Art Therapy at an Outpatient Clinic. *Psychiatry*, 16, 1953.

Ulman, Elinor: Implications of Art for Psychotherapy and Psychodrama. *Group Psychotherapy*, 12, 1959.

Ulman, Elinor: Psychiatry and the Creative Process: An Exchange of Insights. *Psychiatry*, 23, 1960.

Ulman, Elinor: Art Therapy: Problems of Definition. *Bulletin of Art Therapy*, 1:20, Winter, 1961.

Ulman, Elinor: A New Use of Art in Psychiatric Diagnosis. *Bulletin of Art Therapy*, 4:91-116, April, 1965.

Ulman, Elinor: Editorial: The Professional Development of Art Therapy. *American Journal of Art Therapy*, 10:186 ff., July, 1971.

Ulman, Elinor: Art Education for the Emotionally Disturbed. In *Encyclopedia of Education*, New York, Macmillan, 1971.

Ulman, Elinor: The Power of Art in Therapy. Irene Jakab (Ed.), *Art and Psychiatry*, Basel and New York, Karger, 1971, vol. 3.

Ulman, E., and Levy, Bernard I.: Judging Psychopathology from Paintings. *Journal of Abnormal Psychology*, 72, 1967.

Ulman, E., and Levy, Bernard I.: An Experimental Approach to the Judgment of Psychopathology from Paintings. *Bulletin of Art Therapy*, October, 1968, vol. 8, No. 1.

Vaessen, M.L.J.: Art or Expression. *Bulletin of Art Therapy*, 2:23-30, Fall, 1962.

Valentine, C.W.: *The Psychology of Early Childhood*, 2nd ed. London, Methuen, 1943.

Van Alstyne, Dorothy: *Play Behavior and Choice of Play Material of Preschool Children*. Chicago, University of Chicago Press, 1932.

Wertheimer, Max: *Productive Thinking*, Enlarged ed. New York, Harper & Bros., 1959.

Whitman, R.M.; Kramer, M.; Ornstein, P.H., and Baldridge, B.J.: The Physiology, Psychology and Utilization of Dreams. *American Journal of Psychiatry*, 3:287-302, 1967.

INDEX

A

Adolescence, 85, 257-258, 277, 328-332, 343-344

Adolescents, 211, 275, 290, 328-330
and dreams, 340
and expression, 254, 329, 348
and future, 277

Alschuler, R. H. and L. W. Hattwick, 318-319

Anger, 7-17, 22-23, 36, 42-46, 96-97, 123-124, 131, 157, 160-161, 165-167, 182, 221, 251, 259, 273-275, 285-286
(*see also* Behavior; Hostility)

Anorexia, 207-209, 337

Anxiety, 83, 100-101, 143
parent's, 207
sexual, 20, 52, 55-56, 70, 97, 105, 174-175, 177, 190, 195, 209, 232, 236, 257-259, 279
(*see also* Identity; Self-Image)

Art
distinguished from play, 309, 323-332
(*see also* Materials)

Arnheim, Rudolph, 302, 303, 317
(*see also* Gestalt Psychology of Art)

Art Expression
agent of change, 327-328
awareness, 334-336
pace of, 348
interaction with play, 326-327
limitations of, 347-349
(*see also* Awareness; Change; Transference)

Art Therapy, Group, 164, 218

Awareness, ix-xi, 24, 58, 66, 85-86, 99-101, 161, 179, 217-218, 221-222, 229-231, 248-249, 281-282, 333-338, 340-341, 347-348

B

Behavior
aggressive, 16, 17, 27, 29, 42-43, 47-48, 63, 87-88, 124-125, 130-131, 171, 246, 259
bizarre, 13, 20-21, 98, 120, 208
compulsive, 7, 50, 80, 123-124, 142-143, 171-172, 318, 327
defensive, 9, 39, 42, 51, 160, 271, 286
destructive (*see* Productions)
infantile, 33, 80, 81, 106, 109, 122, 130, 253-254
manipulative, 27, 32, 106, 189, 226
regressive, 16-17, 33, 71, 91, 105-106, 109, 122, 135-136, 142, 183-184, 194, 231-234, 285
(*see also* Productions; Violence)

C

Change, xi, 16, 47-48, 58, 73-74, 90-91, 106-108, 112-118, 120, 125, 129-130, 133-136, 154, 157, 207, 226-239, 256-257, 291, 340
(*see also* Art Expression; Behavior; Family; Psychological Occurrences)

Cephalopod Theory
suggested revision of, 139-140

Clinical Observations, 12-13, 27, 50-51, 62, 79-80, 124, 156, 170, 205, 210-211, 245, 265-266

Clover, C. G., 311

Cognitive Process, 338-340, 345

Color
appropriateness of, 321
interpretations of, 316, 320-321
use by small children, 318-319

395